API Recipes with
MuleSoft®
Anypoint Platform™

WHISHWORKS™
www.whishworks.com

www.whitefalconpublishing.com

API Recipes with MuleSoft® Anypoint Platform™
WHISHWORKS™
www.whishworks.com

www.whitefalconpublishing.com

ISBN - 978-93-86210-90-6

WHISHWORKS Limited,
47 - 50 Peascod Street,
Windsor,
SL4 1DE,
United Kingdom
Phone: +44 20 3475 7980

WHISHWORKS IT Consulting Private Limited,
Cyber Gateway,
C-Block, 2nd Floor, Wing-2,
Madhapur, Hyderabad,
Telangana, India - 500081
Phone: +91 40 4265 6565

Contents

WHISHWORKS™

WHISHWORKS™

WHISHWORKS™

Preface

The idea behind bringing out this book is to communicate some basic concepts of implementing APIs with MuleSoft Anypoint Platform. Handcrafted by Mule specialists at WHISHWORKS, the book talks about the how-to-do's in MuleSoft Anypoint Platform with easy to digest API recipes.

This book primarily targets developers, architects and IT managers to help them start and finish MuleSoft Anypoint Platform implementations, with a practical approach, without any dependencies. Each recipe in this book will help readers build solutions from scratch. The book clearly explains concepts with real time examples and code snippets to run. Therefore, even if you are new to Mule, but carry sound knowledge of Java, you should be able to understand this book and master on MuleSoft Anypoint Platform.

Introduction

MuleSoft Anypoint Platform allows enterprises to truly achieve digital transformation with API-led connectivity for application integration and APIs through a single platform. This allows developers to connect applications together quickly and easily, enabling them to efficiently exchange data. MuleSoft Anypoint Platform allows different applications to communicate with each other via a transit system, without making any changes or modifications in the original applications.

This book presents a practical approach towards implementing APIs with MuleSoft Anypoint Platform. All the recipes have been tried and tested by experts; and are precisely put in the book to help readers take a step-by-step approach towards areas such as - implementing simple APIs, deploying APIs in CloudHub, applying governing policies on APIs, security of each API through 3rd party vendors, getting streams of data from 3rd party, API Queue Management and Traffic Management, and much more.

This book is for all those technology geeks out there who would like to start scaling their technical knowledge on MuleSoft Anypoint Platform with some real hands-on short bullets on how-to-do's. It is also dedicated to architects who can benefit from and put together proven design patterns based on some of the recipes elaborated here.

Once you finish reading this book, you will be confident enough to use the MuleSoft Anypoint Platform. You should be able to create transit systems that can carry data between applications within your enterprise or across the Internet. You will be able to migrate data with perfection across platforms or on cloud.

Acknowledgements

This book is an effort of all our WHISHians who brought-in their immense experience of working on different sized real-time project implementations based on MuleSoft Anypoint Platform. Therefore, all the recipes documented here are based on real-time implementations. We thank the entire team of resources at WHISHWORKS who have contributed, directly or indirectly, to this book.

Deepest Gratitude to the Management Team for
continuous motivation to publish this book

Sri Arardhi, CEO & Founder, WHISHWORKS
Pankaj Kankatti, CIO & Co-founder, WHISHWORKS
Kranthi Kumar Vempati, CTO & Co-founder, WHISHWORKS
Suman Konkumalla, CSO & Co-founder, WHISHWORKS
Murthy Aradhi, COO & Co-founder, WHISHWORKS

Principal Authors from WHISHWORKS

Rakesh Gudur
Kishan Kumar Soni
Sanjay Swarnkar
Sunita Panghal
Pavan Dubba
Suriyanarayanan Jeyapal

Special thanks to

Ashish Agnihotri
Archana Dadhich
Suneeta Jasthi
Srikanth Abdullapur
Sravanthi Baskara
Prashant Kamojwala
Koteswararao Sunkavalli
Ramakrishna Narkedamilli
Meghna Karampuri
Arvind Kumar Trivaluroo

RECIPE 1

Setting up CloudHub environment

The administrator of the IT systems of an organization has many crucial rights including creation of 'n' number of business groups and assignment of users to these business groups. The administrator has the right to invite users to join the organization and also to delete users from the organization. The admininstrator has the right to assign different roles to different users, and can also set up different environments like development, QA and production environment.

This API recipe flashes a light on how to manage organization's administrator access. This API explains about the variety of rights an organization's administrator owns and how they impact the organization.

Pre-requisites
1. MuleSoft CloudHub Account with admin privileges (https://anypoint.mulesoft.com)

Process

High Level Steps:
A. Creating an Organization
B. Adding Users
C. Assigning Roles
D. Setting up Development, QA and Production environments

A. Creating an Organization
1. Open a browser and login to Anypoint Platform https://anypoint.mulesoft.com/. On the right side, (highlighted in the below image) the organization name can be seen.

Figure 1.1: Login to Anypoint Platform

2. Click on **Business Groups** icon highlighted in the below image:

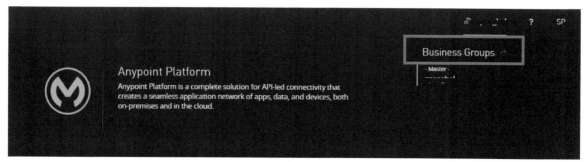

Figure 1.2: Business Group Icon

3. Now click on **Add Business Group** to add a business group.

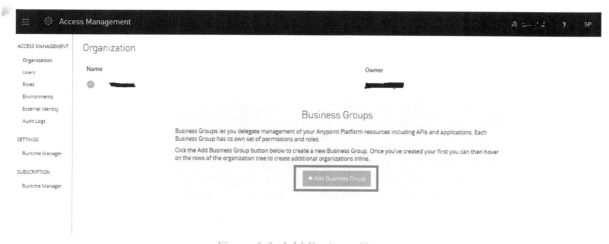

Figure 1.3: Add Business Group

4. Business group can be added by completing the following form:

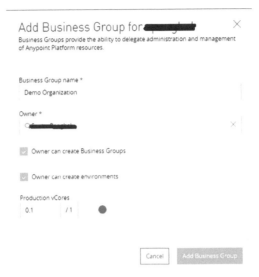

Figure 1.4: Business Group Form

5. Business groups can be created up to any hierarchy level as per the requirement, by clicking the plus sign. Only the owner of the organization can delete a business group.

Figure 1.5: Business Groups Hierarchy of Organization

6. Once the user has created multiple business groups, user can navigate between the business groups through the menu on the top right corner.

Figure 1.6: Business Groups

7. By clicking on the **organization** tab, user can see his organization name and this name can be edited. The organization's portal domain is the organization's original name.

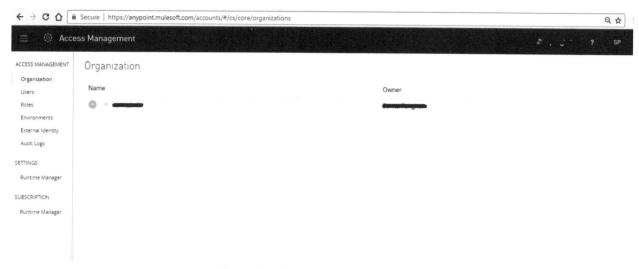

Figure 1.7: Access Management Page

8. The administrator (owner) of the organization can change the default session timings and organization's domain.

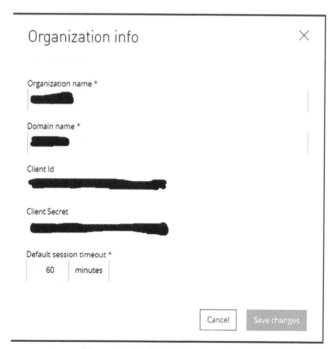

Figure 1.8: Organization Form

B. Adding Users
1. Select the desired business group and then click on **Users** as shown in the below image:

Figure 1.9: Users

Select a user by clicking the round checkbox against it. With administrative rights a user could be enabled, disabled or deleted by clicking the respective buttons on top. In newer version of Anypoint Platform **Delete** is replaced by **Remove all permissions**. Disabling a user means the user will not be able to login through this organization.

Figure 1.10: Select User

2. When the admin deletes or removes all permissions of a user from the organization then all permissions/roles assigned to the user and user itself are removed. But when the user is deleted from a specific business group then only the permissions and roles assigned to the user are removed for that specific business group.

Figure 1.11: Delete User

3. Invite a user by clicking on the **Invite user** button.

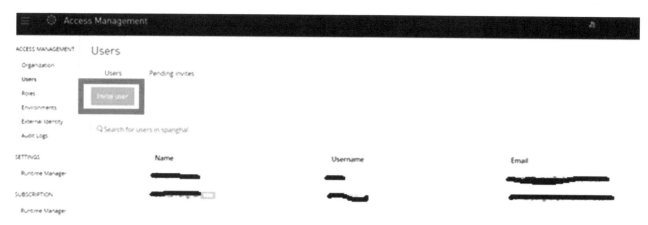

Figure 1.12: Invite User

4. A form will appear after the **Invite user** button is clicked. Fill the mandatory fields in the form. The **email id** is the only mandatory field. Admin can enter multiple email ids with a comma separator. **Add a role by name** field is an optional field.

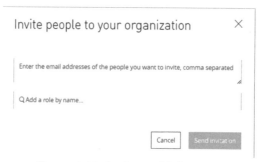

Figure 1.13: Invite multiple users

5. Admin can check the list of pending invitations by clicking on **Pending invites** tab.

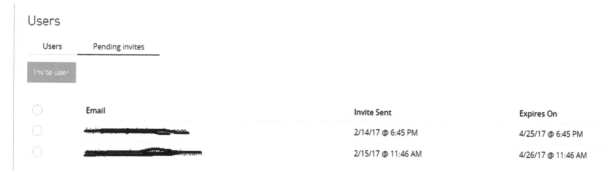

Figure 1.14: Pending invitations

C. Assigning Roles

1. Select the desired business group and then click on **Roles** as shown in the below image:

Figure 1.15: Roles

2. Admin user can see that a number of roles have already been defined in the business group. More roles can also be added by clicking on **Add role** tab as shown below:

Figure 1.16: Add Role

3. Click on the button **Add role** and fill the required information (Role name and Role description).

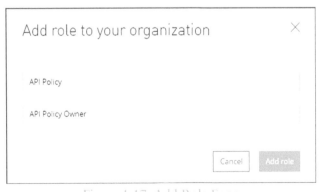

Figure 1.17: Add Role Form

WHISHWORKS™

4. User can see that the role has been added.

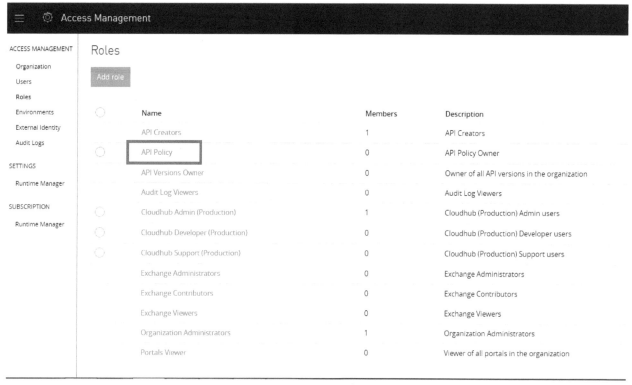

Figure 1.18: Roles

5. By clicking on **API Policy** role, admin user can change the permissions of APIs, Runtime Manager, and Data Gateway. To assign the permissions of APIs, select the **API** first -> select the **version** -> select the **permission** to assign.

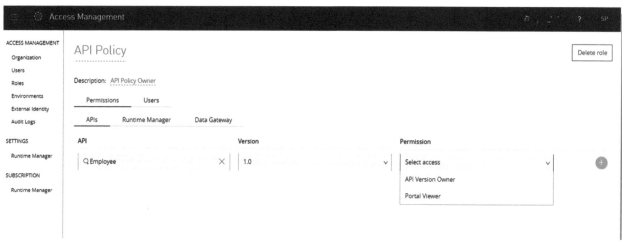

Figure 1.19: API Policy

6. To assign the permissions of Runtime Manager, click on the **Runtime Manager** tab and select the **Environment** then select the **Permission**(s) to assign.

Figure 1.20: Runtime Manager Role

7. To assign the permissions of Data Gateway, click on the **Data Gateway** tab and select the **Environment** then select the **Permission**(s) to assign.

Figure 1.21: Data Gateway Role

8. Click on the **+ plus sign** on the right side to save those permissions to that role.

Figure 1.22: Adding Permissions to Role

D. Setting up Environment

1. Select the desired business group and then click on **Environments** as shown in the below image:

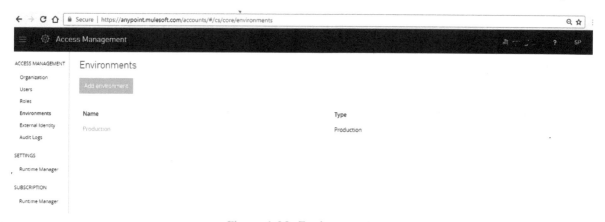

Figure 1.23: Environments

2. Click on **Add environment** tab to add a new environment. A form appears after the click, fill the **name of the environment** and choose the type **Production/Sandbox.**

Figure 1.24: Add Environment

3. The newly added eronments.

Figure 1.25: Added Environments

4. User can edit the environment by clicking on **Environment**. User can either **Delete** the environment or **Update** the name of the environment.

Figure 1.26: Edit environment

Anticipated Issues

1. Allocating Production vCores to the newly created business group will make sure that these vCores are available to this business group only. Therefore, making them unavailable to the organization.

References

1. https://docs.mulesoft.com/access-management/organization

RECIPE 2

RAML Editor for API Implementation

API is the acronym for Application Programming Interface, which is a software intermediary that allows two applications to talk to each other.

One of the most popular types of APIs is RAML (RESTful API Modeling Language) which can be used over nearly any protocol, when used for web APIs. RAML is powerful and provides a toolbox of patterns that help solve a lot of reliability, scalability and integration challenges you might face.

RAML is recommended as a good spec building tool as it offers the most support for Spec-Driven Development, and it also allows you to incorporate design best practices, enables you to reuse code, and lets you take advantage of design patterns to ensure consistency in your API.

Pre requisites
1. MuleSoft Anypoint Studio 6.1 or above (https://www.mulesoft.com/lp/dl/studio) installed
2. MuleSoft CloudHub Account (https://anypoint.mulesoft.com)

Process

High Level Steps:
A. API-First Design Approach Using RAML - how RAML is used to bring APIs to life

A. Implementation of API
1. First, review the requirements of the API.
2. Sign in to Anypoint Pplatform.

Figure 2.1: Anypoint Platform Login

3. Anypoint Platform home screen appears. Click on **API Manager.**

Figure 2.2: Anypoint Platform Home

4. Anypoint Platform **API Administration** page appears. Click on **Add new API.**

Figure 2.3: API Manager – Add API

5. **Add API** dialogue opens:
a. Fill the **API name** as Book Catalogue.
b. Set **Version name** as 1.0.
c. Add a **Description** as 'To create, get and delete book from catalogue'.
d. Retain the rest of the fields as populated by default.
e. Click on **Add** button.

Figure 2.4: ADD API

6. The **Book Catalogue API** home page appears. Click on **Define API in API designer** as shown below. The RAML document is shown with the information previously entered.

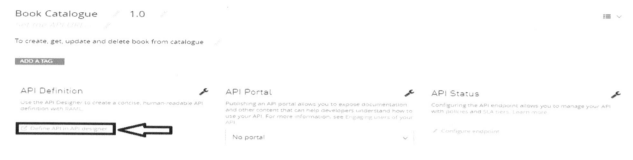

Figure 2.5: Book Catalogue API

7. **API Designer** page appears. The API Designer will provide an empty API definition to start with.
   a. RAML Explorer: work with different RAML definitions at the same time
   b. RAML Editor: Define API
   c. Shelf: Suggested command available to use depends on the position of cursor
   d. API Console: Live preview of API

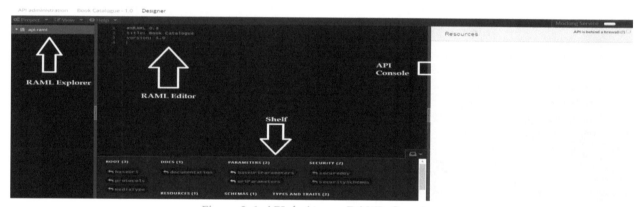

Figure 2.6: API designer - RAML Creation

8. As per the requirements, RAML file is written as below:

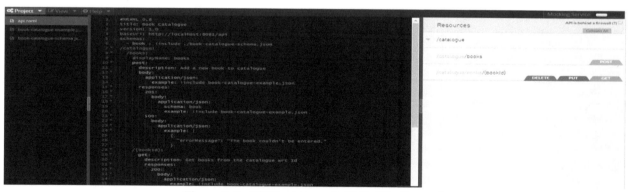

Figure 2.7: API Designer - RAML File Created

```
#%RAML 0.8
title: Book Catalogue
version: 1.0
baseUri: http://localhost:8081/api
schemas:
  - book : !include ./book-catalogue-schema.json
/catalogue:
  /books:
    displayName: books
    post:
      description: Add a new book to catalogue
      body:
        application/json:
          example: !include book-catalogue-example.json
      responses:
        201:
          body:
            application/json:
              schema: book
              example: !include book-catalogue-example.json
        500:
          body:
            application/json:
              example: |
                {
                  "errorMessage": "The book couldn't be entered."
                }
    /{bookId}:
      get:
        description: Get books from the catalogue wrt Id
        responses:
          200:
            body:
              application/json:
                example: !include book-catalogue-example.json
      put:
        description: Modify a book Price
        body:
          application/json:
            example: !include book-catalogue-example.json
        responses:
          200:
            body:
              application/json:
                schema: book
                example: !include book-catalogue-example.json
      delete:
        description: delete the book record
        responses:
          204:
            body:
              application/json:
                example: |
                  {
                    "Status": "Successfully Deleted"
                  }
```

Two files are included in the above RAML file. These are:

I.   book-catalogue-example.json

```json
{
  "Id": "24",
  "Title": "Matilda",
  "Author": "Rohald Dahl",
  "Price": "$5.21"
}
```

II.   book-catalogue-schema.json

```json
{
  "properties": {
    "Id": {
      "description": "BookId to which order is to be assigned",
      "type": "string",
      "required":true
    },
    "Title": {
      "description": "Book Title to which order is to be assigned",
      "type": "string",
      "required":true
    },
    "Author": {
      "description": "Book Author to which order is to be assigned",
      "type": "string",
      "required":true
    },
    "Price": {
      "description": "Book Price to which order is to be assigned",
      "type": "string",
      "required":true
    }
  }
}
```

9.   It is easy to check all the methods in API console as shown below:

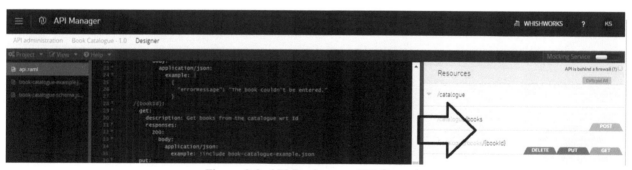

Figure 2.8: API Designer – API Console

Figure 2.9: API Console – Zoomed Version

10. Click on **Save** button. Next, click on **Book Catalogue – 1.0** to proceed to Book Catalogue API home page.

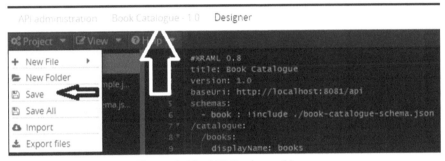

Figure 2.10: API Designer Home

11. Click on **Download as a .zip file** to export these files.

Figure 2.11: API Administration– API Definition

Anticipated Issue
NA

References
1. https://sites.google.com/a/mulesoft.com/api-led-connectivity-workshop

RECIPE 3

Designing your API with Swagger in Anypoint API Designer

Open API Specification (OAS) 2.0, widely known as Swagger is a powerful tool to define the structure of REST APIs. One can easily design, describe and document the API in Swagger editor. The API Designer in MuleSoft CloudHub account supports the below mentioned specifications:

- RAML 0.8 and 1.0
- Open API Specification (OAS) 2.0, widely known as Swagger

Whenever a user imports an Open API Specification in API Designer, the API Designer converts OAS code to RAML. Once the user completes the designing of the API in the Anypoint API Designer (in RAML specification), the user can implement the API in Anypoint Studio. This recipe explains how one can design an API with Swagger Editor in API Designer and use the file in Anypoint API Designer.

GitHub location of this recipe: https://github.com/WHISHWORKS/mule-api-recipes/tree/publish_v1.0/design-api-with-swagger

Pre requisites
1. MuleSoft Anypoint Studio 6.1 or above (https://www.mulesoft.com/lp/dl/studio) installed
2. MuleSoft CloudHub Account (https://anypoint.mulesoft.com)
3. Swagger Editor (http://editor.swagger.io/#!/)

Process

High Level Steps:
A. Design the API in Swagger Editor
B. Import the Swagger

A. Design API in Swagger Editor
1. Open the browser and go to http://swagger.io/.

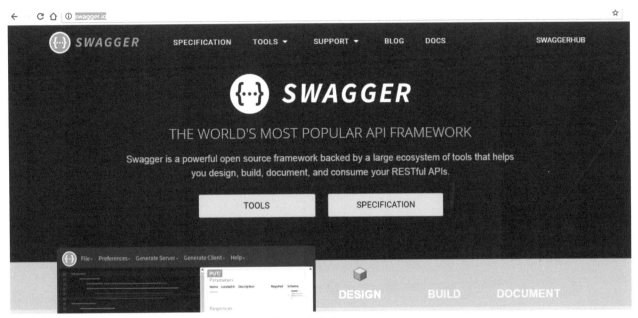

Figure 3.1: Swagger

2. Click on Tools -> Swagger Editor as shown in the image below:

Figure 3.2: Open Swagger Editor

3. Click on the Online Editor if you don't have Swagger installed in your system.

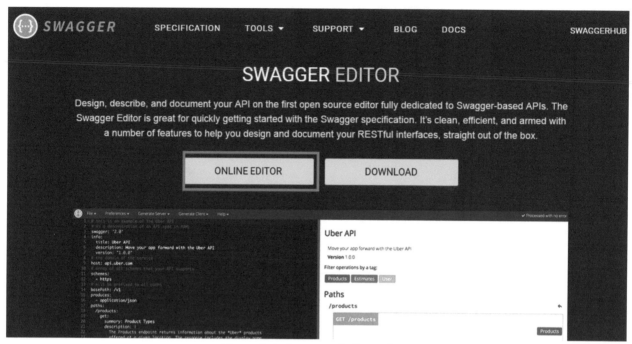

Figure 3.3: Swagger Online editor

4. You will find a pre-written YAML example on the page with basic functionality. The user can use this example to design the API or can remove it and write YAML from scratch.

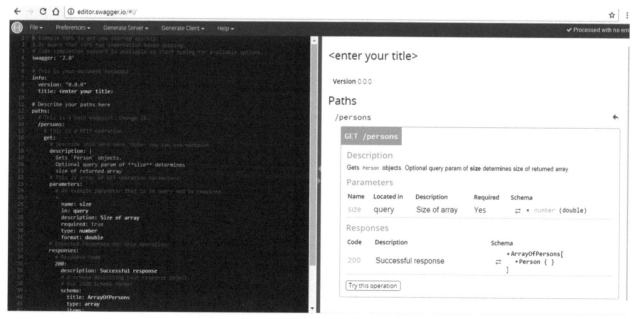

Figure 3.4: Swagger Editor

5. For instance, a user writes code for Basic Authentication API.

Figure 3.5: API in swagger

Figure 3.6: API Code

6. YAML code in text format is as below:

```
---
swagger: '2.0'
info:
  version: "1.0.0"
  title: Basic Auth Example
  description: |
    An example for how to use Basic Auth with Swagger.
    Server code is available [here](https://github.com/mohsen1/basic-auth-server).
It's running on Heroku.

    **User Name and Password**
    * User Name: `user`
    * Password: `pass`
host: basic-auth-server.herokuapp.com
schemes:
  - http
  - https
securityDefinitions:
  basicAuth:
    type: basic
    description: HTTP Basic Authentication. Works over `HTTP` and `HTTPS`
paths:
  /:
    get:
      security:
        - basicAuth: []
      responses:
        200:
        description:  Will send `Authenticated` if authentication is succesful,
otherwise it will send `Unauthorized`
```

7. Click on **File -> Download YAML**. A file with the name **swagger.yaml** is downloaded in user's PC.

Figure 3.7: Download YAML

B. Testing

1. Open the browser and go to https://anypoint.mulesoft.com/. Sign in to Anypoint Platform (Signup, in case user doesn't have Anypoint Platform account) and create a new API.

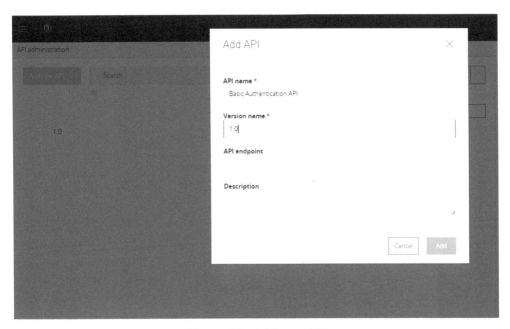

Figure 3.8: Add new API

2. Click on the newly-created API and then click on **Edit** in API designer.

Figure 3.9: Edit in API designer

3. After clicking on **Edit in API designer,** an editor comes up where one can design the API with RAML. But if one wants to design the API in OAS then click on **Project** in the left corner and then click on **Import** as shown in the figure below:

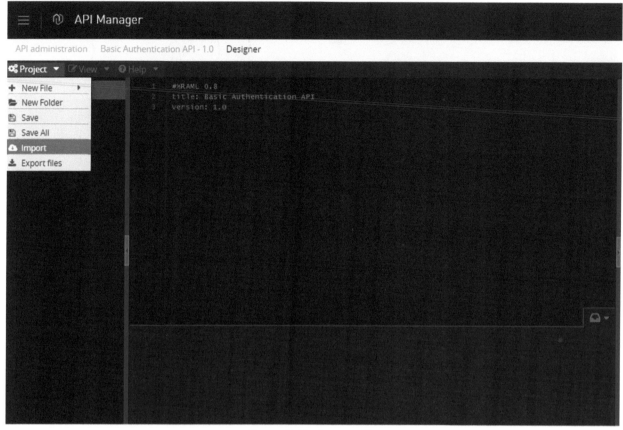

Figure 3.10: Import file

4. Import file form will appear next. Choose **OAS file** from the dropdown.

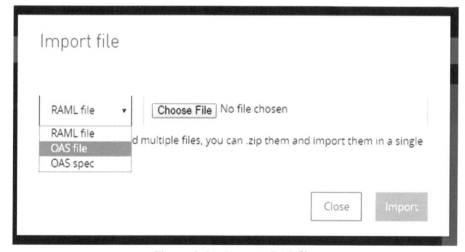

Figure 3.11: Import OAS file

5. Click on **Choose File** and choose the file **swagger.yaml.**

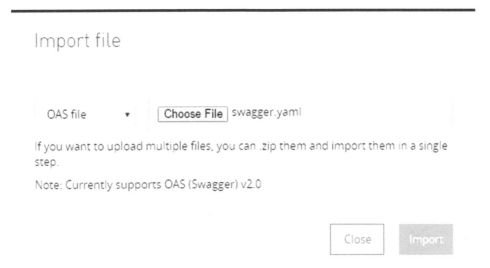

Figure 3.12: Choose desired file

6. The file is added to the editor thereby completing the design. The API is ready for use now.

Figure 3.13: Imported file is added

Improvisations

1.   One can download Swagger in their system and then design their APIs in OAS.

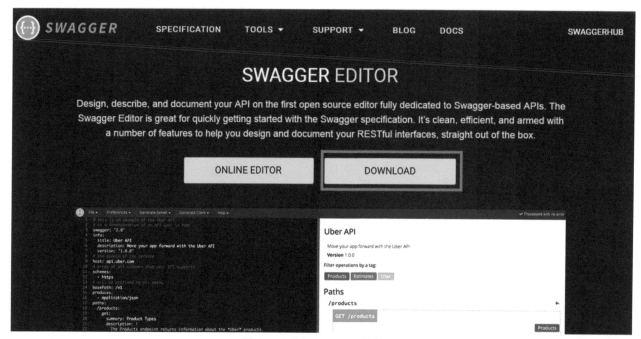

Figure 3.14: Swagger Editor

References

1. http://editor.swagger.io/#!/
2. https://docs.mulesoft.com/api-manager/designing-your-api

RECIPE 4

Implementing a Simple API and Deploying to CloudHub

PI, Application Programming Interface, traditionally has been a programmable interface to an application. It has now evolved in to a more powerful interfacing mechanism than merely exposing an application. In today's Internet of Things (IoT) world, an API is a programming interface to a vast variety of systems ranging from applications to devices. With an API, a device can talk to another device and the two can become connected devices. The term IoT is exactly what this API enables the devices (things) to form a network of devices talking to each other.

There are numerous providers of API platform in the market, but the one that stands out of the lot is MuleSoft's Anypoint Platform for APIs. It is a robust, flexible and scalable platform to manage the APIs. MuleSoft calls IoT as 'API-led connectivity'. This book basically deals with few of the basic and most important to-do's on this platform.

This recipe would boost your confidence level on MuleSoft Anypoint Platform for how easy and quick it is to implement a simple API and deploy to MuleSoft's cloud platform, CloudHub. The API to be implemented here is assumed to be of a Book Catalogue.

GitHub location of this recipe:
https://github.com/WHISHWORKS/mule-api-recipes/tree/publish_v1.0/book-catalogue

Pre-requisites

1. RAML file with Book Catalogue operations, designed in MuleSoft API Designer (<GitHub location of this recipe>/src/main/api/book-catalogue.raml)
2. MuleSoft Anypoint Studio 6.1 or above (**https://www.mulesoft.com/lp/dl/studio**) installed
3. MySQL Database accessible from cloud with Admin rights to create database and users
4. MySQL Connector/J connector JAR (mysql-connector-java-5.1.18) to connect database available from **https://dev.mysql.com/downloads/connector/j/**
5. MuleSoft CloudHub Account with admin privileges (**https://anypoint.mulesoft.com**)

Process
High Level Steps:

A. Implementation of the API – demonstrate POST method implementation. In this process, a book catalogue is sent as a request and the data is persisted to MySQL Database.

B. Deployment to CloudHub
C. Testing

A. Implementation of the API

1. Download the MySQL DDL script from <GitHub location of this recipe>/src/main/sql/book-catalogue.sql
2. From the command line on the MySQL server system execute
   mysql –u[admin_user] –p[admin_password] < [/path/to/]book-catalogue.sql

```
# book-catalogue.sql

CREATE USER 'bc_user'@'%' IDENTIFIED BY 'password';
CREATE DATABASE book_catalogue CHARACTER SET utf8;
GRANT ALL PRIVILEGES ON book_catalogue.* TO 'bc_user'@'%' IDENTIFIED BY 'password';
USE book_catalogue;
CREATE TABLE books (Id int, Title varchar (255), Author varchar (255), Price varchar (255));
```

NOTE: This MySQL database should be accessible over the public internet.

3. Download mysql-connector-java-5.X.XX.zip from https://dev.mysql.com/downloads/connector/j/ as mentioned in pre-requisites.
4. Download the RAML file from GitHub location as mentioned in pre-requisites above.
5. Launch Mule Anypoint Studio and create a new Mule Project as shown below:
   File > New > Mule Project

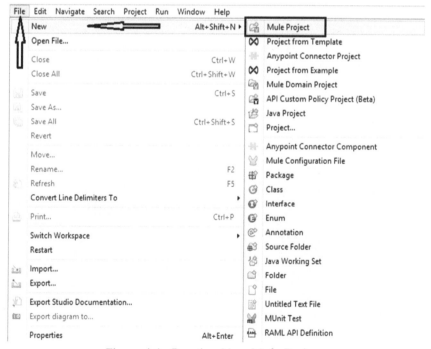

Figure 4.1: Creating New Mule Project

6. In the New Mule Project dialogue that comes up, provide the Project Name as 'book-catalogue'. Select the checkbox Add APIkit components and provide the path of the book-catalogue.raml file downloaded above. Click Finish.

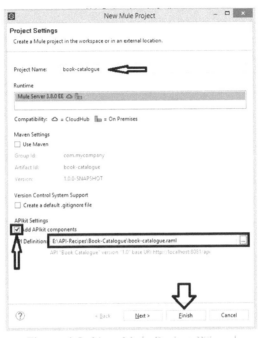

Figure 4.2: New Mule Project Wizard

7. This will create a skeleton project and skeleton Mule Flows for each of the HTTP operations PUT, GET, POST and DELETE along with a main APIkit Router flow and APIkit Console flow based on the RAML definition.

Figure 4.3: Generated Mule Flows from RAML

8. Create and configure the Global Component for MySQL Database as shown below:
a. Click on **Global Elements** as shown above.
b. Click on **Create** button.

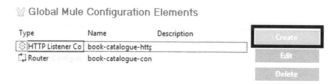

Figure 4.5: Choose Global Type

c. Choose Global Type dialogue appears. Search for MySQL in Filter field for MySQL Database Connector.

d. Select **MySQL Configuration** that appears under Connector Configuration as shown below and click OK.

Figure 4.6: Global Element - Connector Configuration

e. **Global Element Properties** dialogue would be displayed.
f. Fill **Host** [mysql_server_IP or DNS], **Port** [default 3336], **User** [bc_user], **Password** [password] and **Database** [book_catalogue] details in MySQL configuration as shown below:

NOTE: The User, Password and Database should match as given in MySQL DDL script file A.2 above.

g. Click **Add File** to add MySQL connector driver to connect to the MySQL Database. Select the zip/jar file downloaded in step A.3 above.
h. Click **Test Connection** to check that database connector is configured correctly and is able to successfully connect to MySQL.

Figure 4.7: Global Element - MySQL Configuration

i. Successful connection message should be shown as below. Click **OK** on the Test connection dialogue.

Figure 4.8: Test Connection

j. Click **OK** button in the Global Element Properties dialogue.

k. The configured MySQL element should appear in Global Element tab as shown below:

Figure 4.9: Global Element

9. Navigate to the **Message Flow** tab.

a. The skeleton Mule Flow for POST will look as below:

Figure 4.10: POST Method Skeleton

b. Click on the **Configuration XML** tab and search with the flow name i.e. post: /catalogue/books: book-catalogue-config. The corresponding POST Mule Flow XML content should look like:

```
<flow name="post:/catalogue/books:book-catalogue-config">
<set-property propertyName="Content-Type"
value="application/json" doc:name="Property"/>
<set-payload value="{&#xA; &quot;Id&quot;: &quot;24&quot;,&#xA;
&quot;Title&quot;: &quot;Matilda&quot;,&#xA; &quot;Author&quot;:
&quot;Rohald Dahl&quot;,&#xA; &quot;Price&quot;:
&quot;$5.21&quot;&#xA;}" doc:name="Set Payload"/>
</flow>
```

10. Implement the HTTP POST method in post:/catalogue/books:book-catalogue-config flow.

a. In this POST Mule Flow replace the XML with the following XML content:

```
<flow name="post:/catalogue/books:book-catalogue-config">
    <set-payload value="#[payload]" doc:name="Set Payload"/>
    <dw:transform-message doc:name="Transform Message">
        <dw:set-payload><![CDATA[%dw 1.0
%output application/java
---
{
    Id: payload.Id,
    Title: payload.Title,
    Author: payload.Author,
    Price: payload.Price
}]]></dw:set-payload>
    </dw:transform-message>
    <db:insert config-ref="MySQL_Configuration" doc:name="Add record to database">
        <db:parameterized-query><![CDATA[Insert into books (Id, Title, Author,
Price) Values (#[payload.Id], #[payload.Title], #[payload.Author], #[payload.
Price]);]]></db:parameterized-query>
    </db:insert>
    <set-payload value="{STATUS: Successfully Created}" doc:name="Set Payload"/>
</flow>
```

In the code above, the request JSON is received and transformed to database object type. The database then inserts the data using the statement 'Insert into books (Id, Title, Author, Price) Values (#[payload.Id], #[payload.Title], #[payload.Author], #[payload.Price])'.

   b.   Save the file and click on **Mule Flow** tab. The corresponding POST Mule Flow should now look like:

post:/catalogue/books:book-catalogue-config

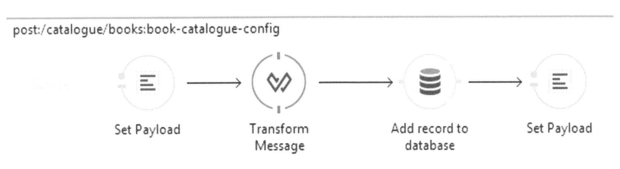

Set Payload   Transform Message   Add record to database   Set Payload

▶ Error handling

Figure 4.11: POST Mule Flow

11.   Similarly, the GET, PUT and DELETE methods can be implemented. The complete implementation can be found at GitHub location of this recipe provided above.
12.   Now that all the flows are completed, it's time to build and deploy the application to CloudHub.

B. Deployment to CloudHub

1. Right click on the **'book-catalogue'** project and Export the zip file of the project as shown below:

Figure 4.12: Export Option

2. Select **Mule** > Anypoint Studio Project to Mule Deployable Archive (includes Studio metadata) and click **Next.**

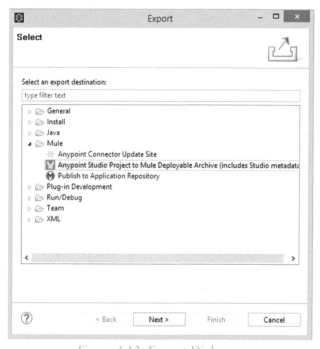

Figure 4.13: Export Dialogue

3. Select the path on the computer where the archive should be saved. Uncheck **Attach project source** checkbox as shown below. Click **Finish.**

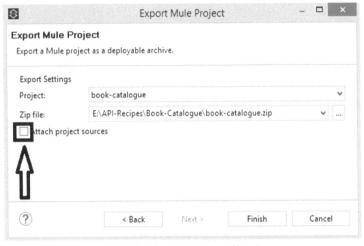

Figure 4.14: Export Application

4. Open a browser and login to Anypoint platform https://anypoint.mulesoft.com/.
5. Select **Runtime Manager.**

Figure 4.15: Anypoint Platform Home

6. **Runtime Manager** Page appears. Click on **Deploy Application.**

Figure 4.16: Runtime Manager – Deploy Application

7. The Deploy Application page opens:
a. Fill a unique name in **Application Name** i.e. book-catalogue-api.
b. Click on **Choose file** to select archive (.zip) file which is exported from Anypoint Studio in step B.3 above.
c. Change **Worker size** to 0.1 vCores.
d. Retain the rest of the fields as populated by default.
e. Click on **Deploy Application.**

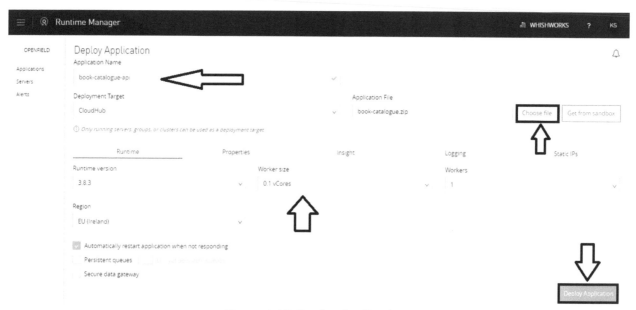

Figure 4.17: Deploy Application

8. Now the application deployment will start as shown below with the status **Deploying.**

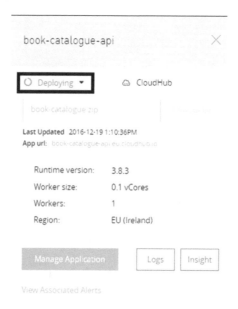

Figure 4.18: Deploy In-Progress Status

9. After some time, status should change to green icon with the status **Started** as shown below:

Figure 4.19: Application Deployed Status

10. Once the project is deployed, copy the **App url:** as shown above (*book-catalogue-api.eu.cloudhub.io*). NOTE: This URL may vary depending on the cloud instance.

C. Testing

1. Open the browser and access deployed API http://book-catalogue-api.eu.cloudhub.io/console/.

Book Catalogue

Figure 4.20: Book Catalogue Console

The test console is launched with all the methods and resources available for the book-catalogue API.

2. Test **POST** method for resource **/catalogue/books**:

a. Click on **POST** button as shown above. Use the **default data** (sample as shown below) that is populated in the body.

```
{
  "Id": "24",
  "Title": "Matilda",
  "Author": "Rohald Dahl",
  "Price": "$5.21"
}
```

Figure 4.21: POST Method Request

b. Click **POST** button to invoke the API. This should return JSON response.

```
{STATUS: Successfully Created}
```

Figure 4.22: POST Method Response

c. A new row will be created in the database table **books.**
3. Test GET method for resource **/catalogue/books** with URI parameter **bookId.**
a. Click on **GET** in the same screen as shown below:

Figure 4.23: Book Catalogue Console - GET

b. Provide **bookId** '24' as shown below:

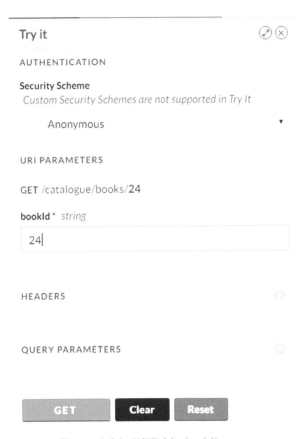

Figure 4.24: GET Method Request

c. Click **GET** to invoke the API. Book details would be returned as shown below:

Response ▲

Status

200

Headers

connection:
  keep-alive

content-length:
  68

content-type:
  application/json;charset=UTF-8

date:
  Fri, 16 Dec 2016 09:27:10 GMT

server:
  nginx

Body

```
1  [
2    {
3      "Title": "Matilda",
4      "Price": "$5.21",
5      "Author": "Rohald Dahl",
6      "Id": 24
7    }
8  ]
```

Figure 4.25: GET Method Response

d. This should return JSON as shown below:

```
{
"Id": "24",
"Title": "Matilda",
"Author": "Rohald Dahl",
"Price": "$5.21"
}
```

The response is the book detail for book ID 24. Note that this is the catalogue created in **POST** method in step C.2.b.

4. Similarly, the PUT and DELETE methods can be tested.

Anticipated Issues

1. MySQL Database connection not established: Ensure that the database is accessible from CloudHub.

Improvisations

1. The MySQL Driver can also be added using pom.xml if the project is mavenised. The Maven dependency is as below:

```xml
<dependency>
      <groupId>org.mule.modules</groupId>
      <artifactId>mule-module-db</artifactId>
      <version>${mule.version}</version>
      <scope>provided</scope>
</dependency>

<dependency>
      <groupId>mysql</groupId>
      <artifactId>mysql-connector-java</artifactId>
      <version>5.1.6</version>
</dependency>
```

References

1. https://www.mulesoft.com/resources/api-management
2. https://sites.google.com/a/mulesoft.com/api-led-connectivity-workshop

RECIPE 5

Deploy a Proxy on CloudHub

The Anypoint Platform offers API-driven approach to build integration solutions. The platform has three-layered API approach.
   a) User Experience API
   b) Process API
   c) System API

The process and system API components are developed and deployed to CloudHub **Runtime Manager**. Such applications are responsible to hold the business logic and backend system.

The benefits of applying a proxy are to:
a)   secure the runtime application
b)   expose the services without providing internal details
c)   enforce policies so that any violation need not be addressed by the runtime application
d)   control traffic and access to runtime application

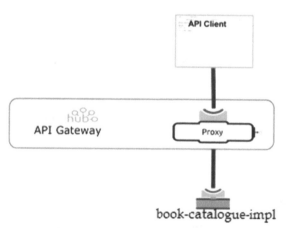

Figure 5.1: Proxy Flow Diagram

This recipe would boost your confidence level on MuleSoft Anypoint Platform for how easy and quick it is to create a proxy application that serves to stop attacks aimed at the actual application and deploy to MuleSoft's cloud platform CloudHub. The API to be implemented here is assumed to be of a Book Catalogue.

GitHub location of this recipe:
https://github.com/WHISHWORKS/mule-api-recipes/tree/publish_v1.0/deploy-api-proxy

Pre-requisites
1. MuleSoft CloudHub account(https://anypoint.mulesoft.com)
2. Administrative Access to API Manager and Runtime Manager
3. MuleSoft Anypoint Studio 6.1 or above (https://www.mulesoft.com/lp/dl/studio) installed
4. Source folder of application **book-catalogue** is available at
   https://github.com/WHISHWORKS/mule-api-recipes/tree/publish_v1.0/book-catalogue
5. MySQL Database accessible from cloud with Admin rights to create database and users (Refer to Recipe **'WHISHWORKS_APIRecipes_Implementing_a_New_API'** for more information)
6. Postman plugin for Chrome is installed from https://www.getpostman.com/docs/introduction

Process
High Level Steps:

A. Deployment of existing application **book-catalogue** to CloudHub
B. Create a Proxy API
C. Configure an API proxy & Deploy to CloudHub
D. Test the API Proxy
A. **Deploment of existing application book-catalogue to CloudHub**

1. Download deployable zip file from the GitHub location of this recipe provided above or, export **book-catalogue** application (which is mentioned in pre-requisites) as a deployable archive zip file(Refer to recipe **'WHISHWORKS_APIRecipes_Implementing_a_New_API'**) and save it to computer.
2. Login to Anypoint Platform https://anypoint.mulesoft.com/ select **Runtime Manager.**

Figure 5.2: Anypoint Home - Runtime Manager

3. Runtime Manager page appears. Click on **Deploy Application.**

Figure 5.3: Runtime Manager – Deploy Application

4. The Deploy Application page opens:
a. Write a unique name in the Application Name i.e. **book-catalogue-impl.**
b. Click on **Choose file** to select archive (.zip) file which is saved to computer as mentioned in step A.1.
c. Change **Worker size** to 0.1 vCores.
d. Retain the rest of the fields as populated by default.
e. Click on **Deploy Application.**

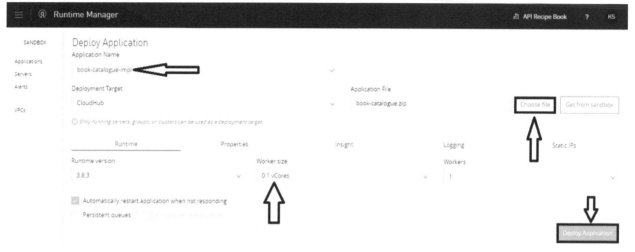

Figure 5.4: Deploy Application

5. Now the application deployment will start as shown below with the status **Deploying.**

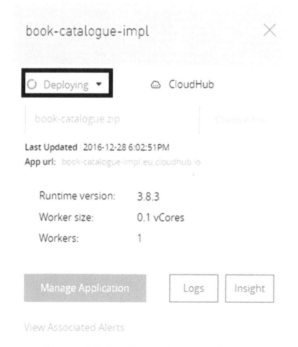

Figure 5.5: Deploy In-Progress Status

6. After some time, the status will change to **green icon** with **Started** as shown below:

Figure 5.6: Deploy Started Status

7. Once the project is deployed, copy the following URL which is shown in the above image (*book-catalogue-impl.eu.cloudhub.io*).
   NOTE: This URL may vary depending on the cloud instance.

B. **Create a Proxy API**

1. Click on the icon shown below:

Figure 5.7: Runtime Manager

2. Select **API Manager.**

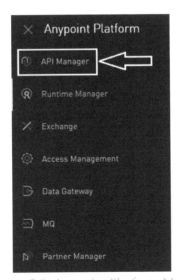

Figure 5.8: Anypoint Platform Menu

3. **API Manager** page appears. Click **Add new API.**

Figure 5.9: API Manager

1. The **Add API** page will be displayed. Fill the fields as follows:
a. Enter the API name as **Book Catalogue UX.**
b. Enter the Version name as **1.0.**
c. Leave the API Endpoint blank for now.
d. Enter the description as **User Experience API to access book catalogue Application.**
e. Click **Add.**

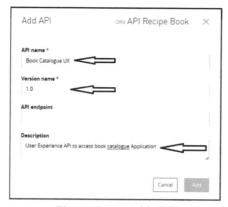

Figure 5.10: Add API

2. The **API administration** page for newly created API appears.

Figure 5.11: Book Catalogue UX API

3. It's time to configure an API Proxy with this API.

C. **Configure an API proxy & Deploy to CloudHub**

1. Back in the API Administration page, click on **Configure endpoint** under API Status as shown below:

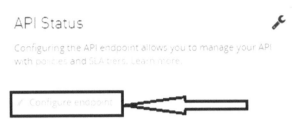

Figure 5.12: API Status

2. Fill the information as follows:

a. Select **Endpoint with a proxy.**

b. Leave the Type to the default HTTP URL.

c. Set the **Implementation URL** ({copied URL from step A.7}/api) to: **http://book-catalogue-impl.eu.cloudhub.io/api**. This is the URL where the implementation service API is available.

d. Check the **checkbox Configure proxy for CloudHub,** since we will deploy it to Anypoint Platform CloudHub service.

e. Retain the rest of the fields as populated by default.

f. Click **Save** & **Deploy.**

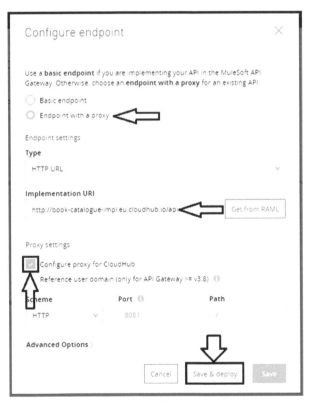

Figure 5.13: Configure Endpoint

3. **Deploy Proxy** dialogue would be displayed. Click on **Deploy Proxy** as shown below:

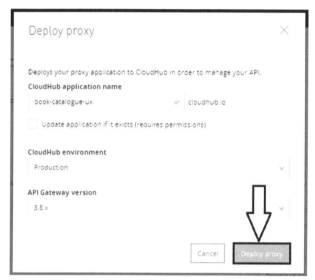

Figure 5.14: Deploy Proxy

4. Proxy API deployment will start. The deploy status will indicate **Starting Application.**

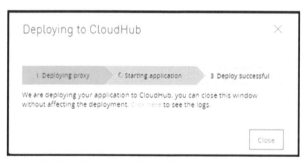

Figure 5.15: Deploying to CloudHub – Starting Application

5. After some time, the status should change to **Deploy successful** as shown below:

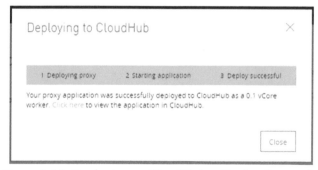

Figure 5.16: Deploying to CloudHub – Deploy Successful

6.   Click on **Close** button.
7.   Once the API is deployed, API Status content will be shown as below. Copy the **API URL** under **API Status** (*book-catalogue-ux.eu.cloudhub.io*).

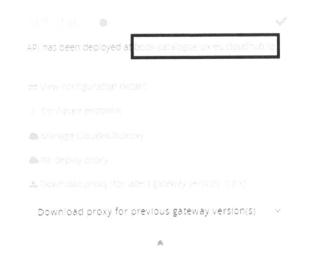

Figure 5.17: API Status – After Proxy API Deployment

D. Test the API Proxy

1.   Launch **Postman** Chrome Application as mentioned in pre-requisites.

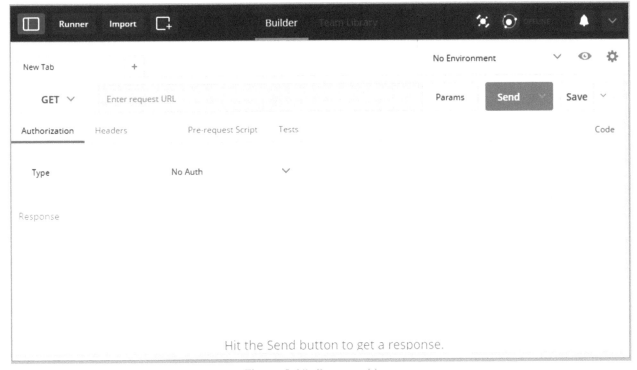

Figure 5.18: Postman Home

2. Test **POST** Method.
3. Select **POST** Method which has to be tested from dropdown.
4. Provide the URL (Copied URL + /catalogue/books)
   http://book-catalogue-ux.eu.cloudhub.io/catalogue/books to post the book details in book catalogue as shown below:

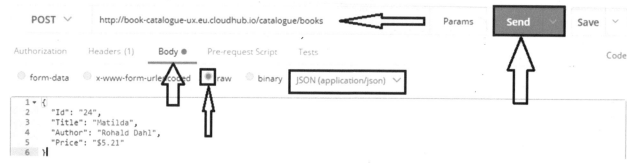

Figure 5.19: POST Request in Postman

5. Click **Body**. Select **raw** and then select **JSON (application/json)** from the dropdown.
6. Provide book details sample data as shown below:

```
{
  "Id":  "24",
  "Title":  "Matilda",
  "Author":  "Rohald Dahl",
  "Price":  "$5.21"
}
```

7. Click **Send** to invoke the API.
8. Click **Raw** and the response will be as shown below:

```
{STATUS: Successfully Created}
```

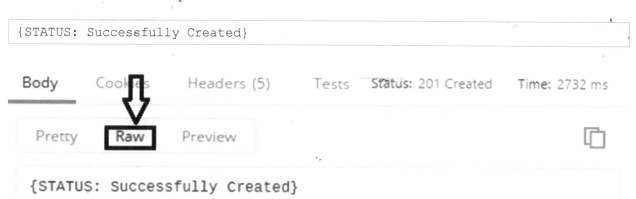

Figure 5.20: POST Response in Postman

9. Test **GET** Method.
10. Select **GET** Method which has to be tested from the dropdown.
11. Provide the URL (Copied URL + /catalogue/books/{bookId})
    http://book-catalogue-ux.eu.cloudhub.io/catalogue/books/{24} to get books details in book catalogue with respect to the **ID** as shown below:

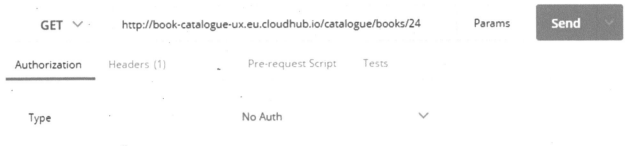

GET ∨ ·   http://book-catalogue-ux.eu.cloudhub.io/catalogue/books/24   Params   **Send** ∨

Authorization   Headers (1)   Pre-request Script   Tests

Type   No Auth   ∨

Figure 5.21: GET Request in Postman

12. Click **Send** to invoke the API.
13. Response will be shown as below. Select **Pretty** to show the response in JSON format.

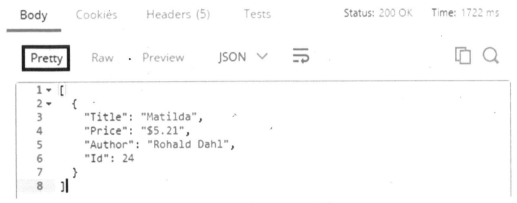

Body   Cookies   Headers (5)   Tests   Status: 200 OK   Time: 1722 ms

Pretty   Raw · Preview   JSON ∨ ⇉   ⧉ Q

```
1 ▾ [
2 ▾   {
3         "Title": "Matilda",
4         "Price": "$5.21",
5         "Author": "Rohald Dahl",
6         "Id": 24
7       }
8     ]
```

Figure 5.22: GET Response in Postman

14. The response is the book details for book ID 24.
    Note: This is the catalogue created in POST method in step d.2.e.
15. Similarly, the PUT and DELETE methods can be tested.

References

1. https://docs.mulesoft.com/api-manager/setting-up-an-api-proxy
2. https://sites.google.com/a/mulesoft.com/api-led-connectivity-workshop

RECIPE 6

Implementation of a new API through API-led Connectivity

PI, Application Programming Interface, is the way to connect applications, data, and devices that will give the organization greater agility and flexibility. With an API, a device can talk to another device and the two can become connected devices. But the problem lends itself to a service-oriented approach in which application logic is broken into individual services and then reused across multiple channels. MuleSoft's API-led connectivity approach provides a framework to allow businesses to tackle new problems presented by mobility, ensuring security, connecting data between departments, on-premises systems and the cloud. This methodology allows organizations to easily **add more and more devices and solutions into the mix, while maintaining high performance of the whole system.** This comes in the form of a multi-tier architecture with three distinct API layers: **System, Process,** and **Experience.**

System APIs are those APIs which extract sensitive information from your systems.

Process APIs allow defining a common process which the organization can share, and these APIs orchestrate invocation across multiple system APIs. The orchestrations may perform data aggregation, conditional routing, filtering and more.

Experience APIs are the means by which data can be reconfigured in an appropriate format according to how the information is displayed on any particular device.

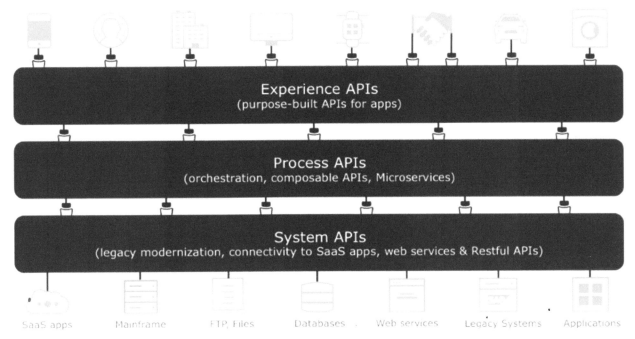

This recipe would boost your confidence level on MuleSoft Anypoint Platform for how easy and quick it is to implement a simple API with API-led approach. The API to be implemented here is assumed to be of a Book Catalogue.

GitHub location of this recipe:
https://github.com/WHISHWORKS/mule-api-recipes/tree/publish_v1.0/api-led-connectivity

Pre-requisites

1. RAML file with Book Catalogue operations, designed in MuleSoft API Designer (**<GitHub location of this recipe>**/x-book-catalogue/src/main/api/book-catalogue.raml)
2. MuleSoft Anypoint Studio 6.1 or above (https://www.mulesoft.com/lp/dl/studio) installed
3. MySQL Database accessible from cloud with admin rights to create database and users
4. MySQL Connector/J connector JAR (mysql-connector-java-5.1.18) to connect database available from https://dev.mysql.com/downloads/connector/j/

Process

High Level Steps:

A. Implementation of the API – demonstrate POST method implementation. In this process, a book catalogue is sent as a request and the data is persisted to MySQL Database and CSV file through API-led three layered approach.
B. Testing

A. Implementation of the API
This implementation includes three layers namely Experience Layer, Process Layer & System Layer.

Experience layer
1. Download the RAML file from GitHub location as mentioned in pre-requisites above.
2. Launch **Mule Anypoint Studio** and create a new **Mule Project** as shown below:
   File > New > Mule Project

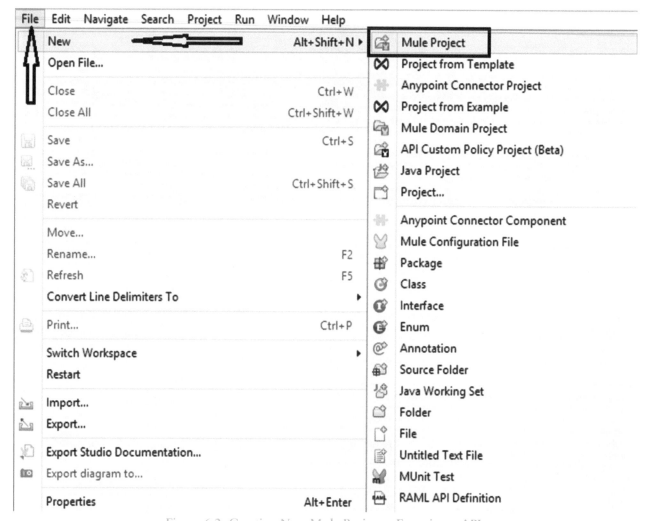

Figure 6.2: Creating New Mule Project – Experience API

3. In the **New Mule Project** dialogue that comes up, provide the **Project Name** as 'x-book-catalogue'. Select the checkbox **Add APIkit components** and provide the path of the **x-book-catalogue.raml** file downloaded above. Click **Finish**.

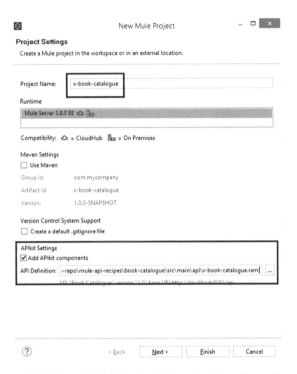

Figure 6.3: New Mule Project Wizard – Experience Layer

4. This will create a skeleton project and skeleton Mule Flows for each of the HTTP POST operations along with a main APIkit Router flow and APIkit Console flow based on the RAML definition.

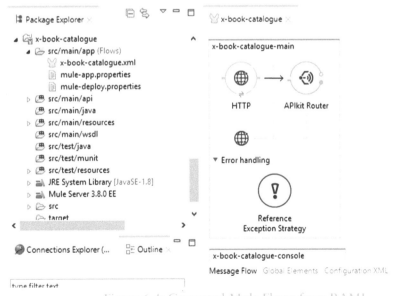

Figure 6.4: Generated Mule Flows from RAML

5. Remove the **Property** component from **booklist** flow and drag and drop a **HTTP** component in the process section of the flow as shown below:

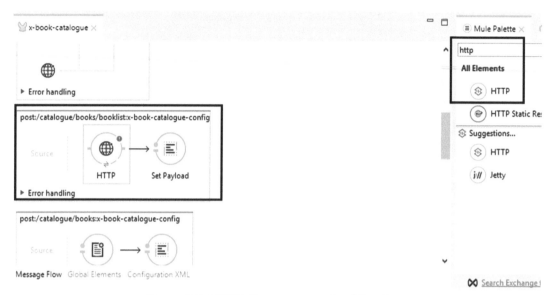

Figure 6.5: HTTP Component – Booklist Flow

6. Click on **HTTP component** and in the Connector Configuration, click on **add icon** to add a **HTTP Request Configuration**. Following window opens up:
    Provide **Host:** localhost; **Port:** 8082 and click **Ok.**

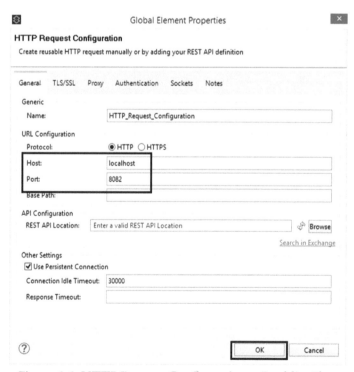

Figure 6.6: HTTP Request Configuration – Booklist Flow

7. Further in URL settings, give **Path:** p-book-file & **Method:** POST as shown below:

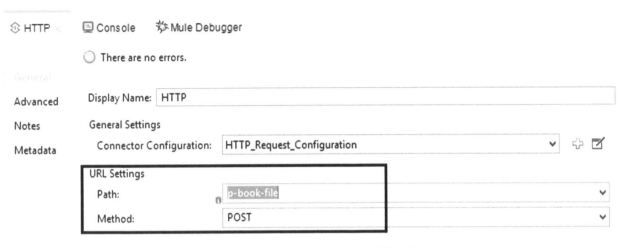

Figure 6.7: URL Settings – Booklist Flow

8. Now delete **Property** and **Set Payload** component from the **books** flow and drag and drop **HTTP component** in to the process section of the flow as shown below:

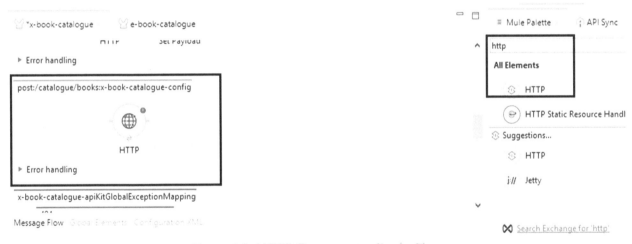

Figure 6.8: HTTP Component – Books Flow

9. Click on **HTTP Component** and in the **Connector Configuration**, click on **add icon** to add a **HTTP Request Configuration.** Provide the following details
Provide **Host:** localhost; **Port:** 8083

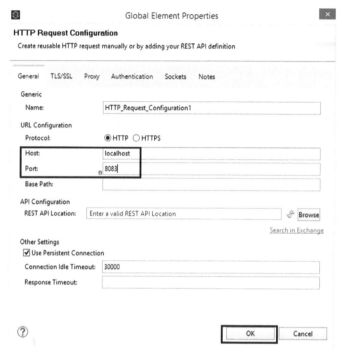

Figure 6.9: HTTP Request Configuration – Books Flow

10. Click on **HTTP component** and give URL Settings as following
Path: **p-book-post** Method: **POST.**

Figure 6.10: URL Settings – Books Flow

11. The Experience API development is complete.

Process Layer

1. Launch Anypoint Studio and create a **New Mule Project:**
   File > New > Mule Project; and Provide **Project Name: p-book-catalogue** and click **Finish** as shown below:

Figure 6.11: New Mule Project – Process API

2. Drag and drop an **HTTP component** and In Basic Settings, click on add icon to **add Connector Configuration** with the following details:
   Host: All Interfaces [0.0.0.0] (Default); **Port:** 8082

Figure 6.12: HTTP Configuration – Process API

3. In the Basic Settings, give **Path:** /p-book-file.

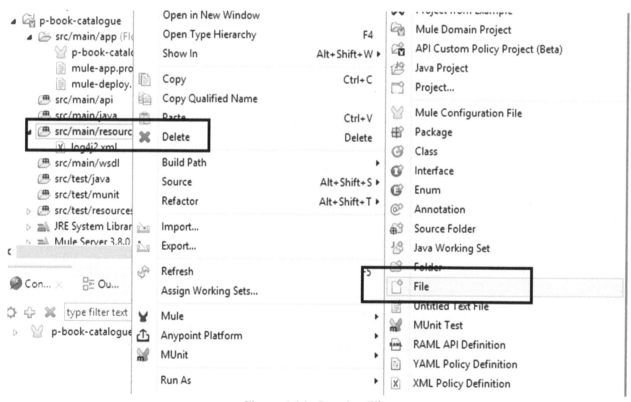

Figure 6.13: HTTP Basic Settings – Process API

4. Right click on **src/main/resources** and create a new file as shown below:

Figure 6.14: Creating File

5. Give File Name as: **example.json** and click **Finish.**

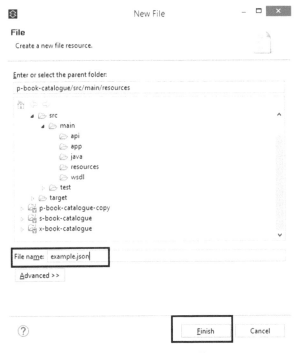

6. Copy the following content in the file in Studio as shown below:

```
{
        "Id": "24",
        "Title": "Matilda",
        "Author": "Rohald Dahl",
        "Price": "$5.21"
}
```

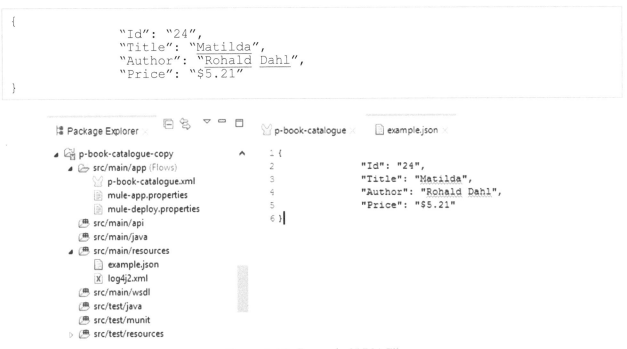

7. Drag and drop **Transform Message** Component from **Mule Palette** as shown below:

Figure 6.17: Transform Message Component

8. Click on **Transform Message** and then click on **Define Metadata** as shown below:

Figure 6.18: Define Input Metadata

9. In the **Select metadata type** window, click on **Add** and give **Type id:** JSON and click **Create type** as shown below:

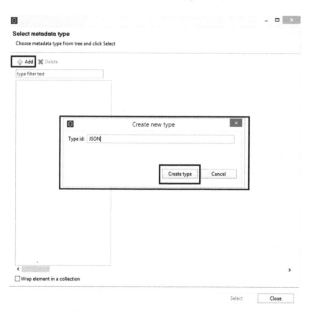

Figure 6.19: Create New Type

10. In the next window select type as **JSON** and from the dropdown select **Example** and give path to the example.json created above as shown below:

Figure 6.20: Metadata Type

11. In the output section of Transform Message element, click on **Define metadata** as shown below:

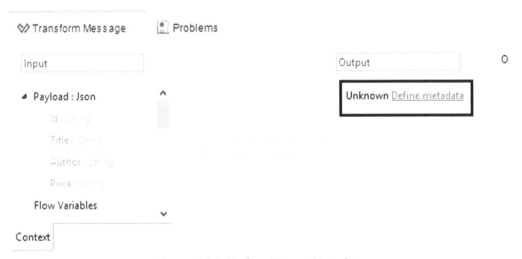

Figure 6.21: Define Output Metadata

12. In the **Select metadata type** window, click on **Add** and give Type id: **CSV** as shown below:

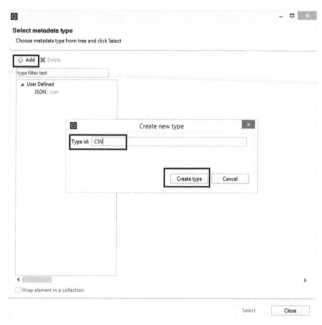

Figure 6.22: Create New Type - CSV

13. In the next window, select type as **CSV** and add 4 columns. Also make sure that **CSV includes header row** is checked as shown below:

Figure 6.23: Metadata Type - CSV

14. Rename above 4 columns as Id, Title, Author, Price respectively and click **Select** as shown below:

Figure 6.24: Metadata Type – CSV Update

15. Next, do one to one mapping between same elements of Transform Message as shown below:

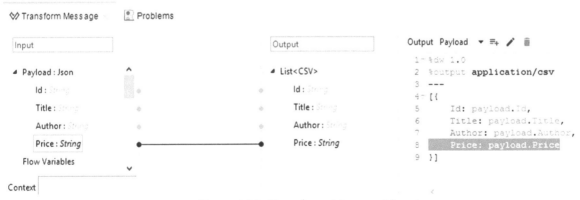

Figure 6.25: Transform Message Mapping

16. Now drag and drop an **HTTP component** after Transform message as shown below:

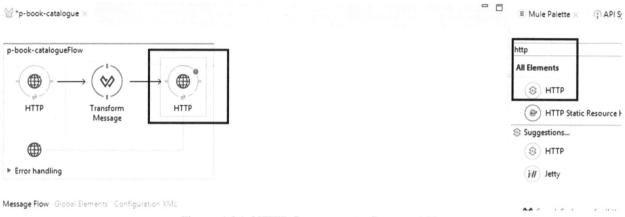

Figure 6.26: HTTP Component – Process API

17. Click on **HTTP component** and click on add icon to add a **Connector Configuration** and give the following details in the configuration window:
    Host: localhost; **Port:** 8083 and click **OK.**

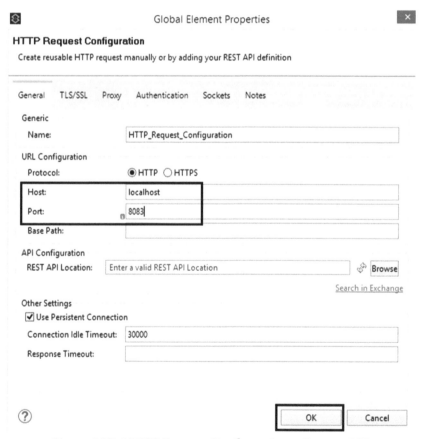

Figure 6.27: HTTP Request Configuration – Process API

18. In the URL settings of HTTP component, provide the following details:
Path: s-book-file; **Method**: POST as shown below:

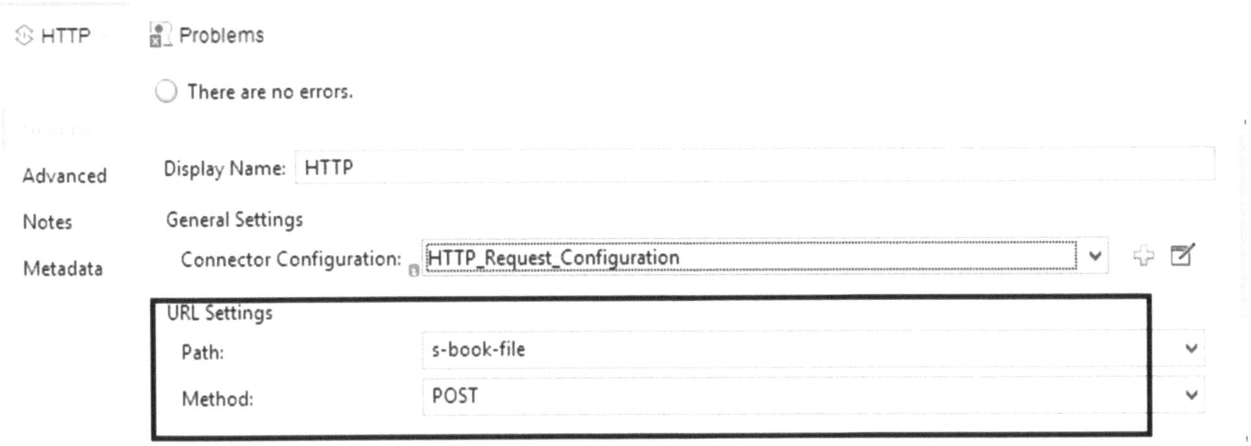

Figure 6.28: URL Settings – Process API

19. Now, Process API development is complete.

System layer

1. Download the MySQL DDL script from <GitHub location of this recipe>/s-book-catalogue/src/main/sql/book-catalogue.sql.

2. From the command line on the MySQL server system execute
mysql –u[admin _user] –p[admin_password] < [/path/to/]book-catalogue.sql.

```
# book-catalogue.sql

CREATE USER 'bc_user'@'%' IDENTIFIED BY 'password';
CREATE DATABASE book_catalogue CHARACTER SET utf8;
GRANT ALL PRIVILEGES ON book_catalogue.* TO 'bc_user'@'%' IDENTIFIED BY 'password';
USE book_catalogue;
CREATE TABLE books (Id int, Title varchar (255), Author varchar (255), Price varchar (255));
```

NOTE: This MySQL database should be accessible from cloud.

3. Download mysql-connector-java-5.X.XX.zip from https://dev.mysql.com/downloads/connector/j/ as mentioned in pre-requisites.

4. Launch **Mule Anypoint Studio** and create a new **Mule Project** as shown below:
File > New > Mule Project

5. In the **New Mule Project** dialogue that comes up, provide the **Project Name** as 's-book-catalogue'. Click **Finish.**

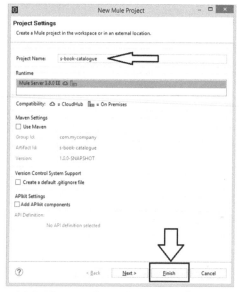

Figure 6.29: New Mule Project Wizard – System API

6. This will create an empty project as shown below:

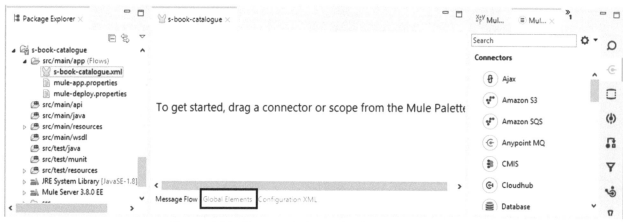

Figure 6.30: Generated Empty Project – System API

7. Click on **Global Elements** as shown above.
8. HTTP Connector should be added as a Global element.
   a.   Click on **Create** button.

Figure 6.31: Global Mule Configuration Elements - Create

b. **Choose Global Type** dialogue appears. Search for HTTP in **Filter** field for HTTP Listener Configuration connector.

Figure 6.32: Choose Global Type

c. Select **HTTP Listener Configuration** that appears under **Connector Configuration** as shown below and click **OK.**

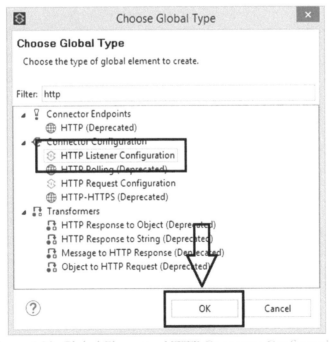

Figure 6.33: Global Element – HTTP Connector Configuration

d. **Global Element Properties** dialogue would be displayed. Click **OK.**

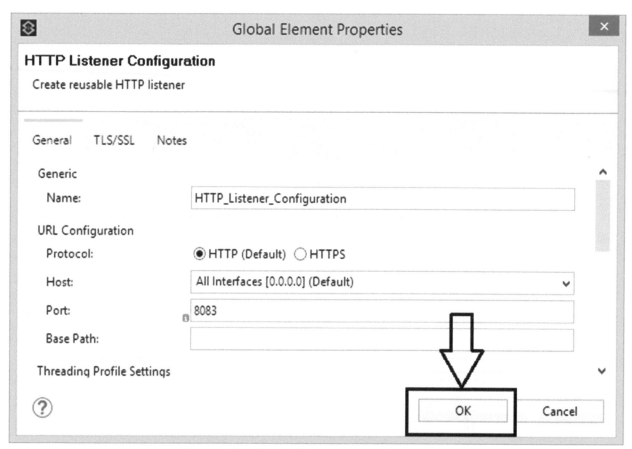

Figure 6.34: Global Element Properties - HTTP

e. The Global element will be updated in **Global Elements** tab as shown below:

Figure 6.35: Global Element – HTTP Update

9. Add **Database connection** details in **mule-app.properties** file as given in the GitHub repository.

10. Create and configure the Global Component for MySQL Database as shown below:

    a.   Click on **Create** button as shown above.

    b.   **Choose Global Type** dialogue appears. Search for **MySQL** in **Filter** field for MySQL Database Connector.

Figure 6.36: Choose Global Type

    c.   Select **MySQL Configuration** that appears under **Connector Configuration** as shown below and click **OK**.

Figure 6.37: Global Element - MySQL Connector Configuration

d. **Global Element Properties** dialogue would be displayed.
e. Fill **Host** ${db.host}, **Port** ${db.port}, **User** ${db.user}, **Password** ${db.password} and **Database** ${db.database} details in MySQL configuration as shown in the below figure.

   NOTE: The User, Password and Database should match as given in MySQL DDL script file step 2 above.

f. Click **Add File** to add MySQL connector driver to connect to the MySQL Database. Select the zip/jar file downloaded in step 3 above.
g. Click **Test Connection** to check that the database connector is configured correctly and is able to successfully connect to MySQL.

Figure 6.38: Global Element - MySQL Configuration

h. Successful connection message should be shown as below. Click **OK** on the **Test connection** dialogue.

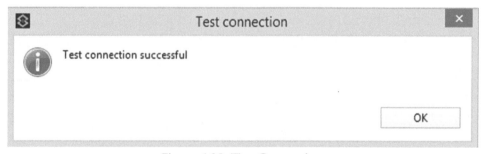

Figure 6.39: Test Connection

i. Click **OK** button in the **Global Element Properties** dialogue.
j. The configured MySQL element should appear in **Global Element** tab as shown below:

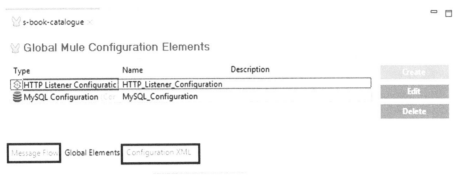

11. Navigate to **Message Flow** tab.
   I. POST Flow to push books records in **books** table
   a. Drag **Flow element** from **Mule Palette** and drop it in the Message Flow tab as shown below:

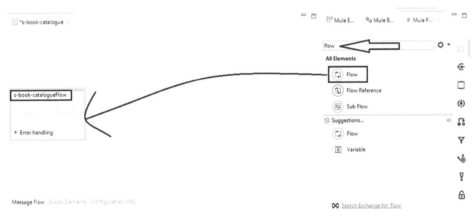

Figure 6.41: Flow Skeleton

   b. Click on Flow name to rename it to **s-book-catalogue-db-flow.**
   c. Search HTTP connector and drag it to a source inside the flow as shown below:

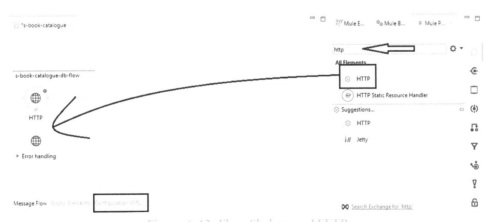

Figure 6.42: Flow Skeleton – HTTP

d. Double click on **HTTP connector**, provide the **Path** as '**/s-book-post**'in under Basic setting and save it.

e. Click on the **Configuration XML** tab and search with the flow name i.e. s-book-catalogue-db-flow. The corresponding **POST** Mule Flow XML content should look like:

```
<flow name="s-book-catalogue-db-flow">
  <http:listener config-ref="HTTP_Listener_Configuration" path="/" doc:name="HTTP"/>
</flow>
```

f. In this **POST** Mule Flow replace the XML with the following XML content:

```
<flow name="s-book-catalogue-db-flow">
  <http:listener  config-ref="HTTP_Listener_Configuration"  path="/s-book-post"
doc:name="HTTP"/>
  <json:json-to-object-transformer returnClass="java.util.HashMap" doc:name="JSON
to Object"/>
  <logger message="Before DB*****************#[payload] " level="INFO" doc:name="Data
before pushing in DB"/>
  <db:insert config-ref="MySQL_Configuration" doc:name="Add record to database">
     <db:parameterized-query><![CDATA[Insert into books (Id, Title, Author,
Price) Values (#[payload.Id], #[payload.Title], #[payload.Author], #[payload.
Price]);]]></db:parameterized-query>
  </db:insert>
  <set-payload value="{STATUS: Successfully Created}" doc:name="Status"/>
</flow>
```

In the code above, the request JSON is received and transformed to database object type. The database then inserts the data using the statement 'Insert into books (Id, Title, Author, Price) Values (#[payload.Id], #[payload.Title], #[payload.Author], #[payload.Price])'.

g. **Save** the file and click on **Mule Flow** tab. The corresponding **POST** Mule Flow should now look like:

Figure 6.43: 1ˢᵗ Mule Flow

II. POST Flow to write books records in **CSV file**
a. Again, drag **Flow element** from **Mule Palette** and drop it in the Message Flow tab as shown below:

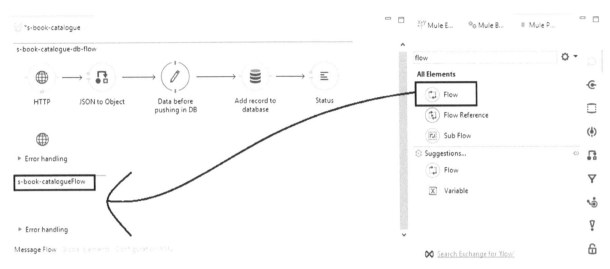

Figure 6.44: 2nd Flow Skeleton

b. Click on **flow name** to rename it to **s-book-catalogue-file-flow.**
c. Search HTTP connector and drag it to a source inside the flow as shown below:

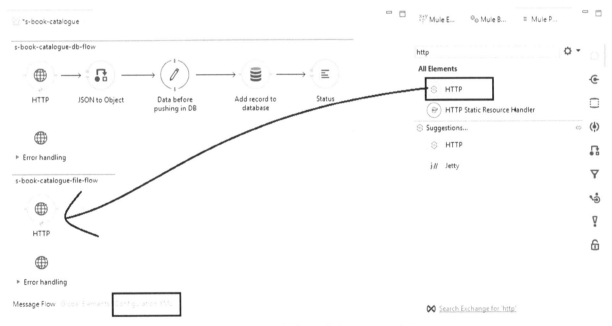

Figure 6.45: 2nd Flow Skeleton – HTTP

d. Double click on **HTTP connector,** provide the **Path** as **'/s-book-file'** in under Basic setting and save it.
e. Drag **Logger** component from the Palette and double click on it to open its configuration. Provide the details as shown below:

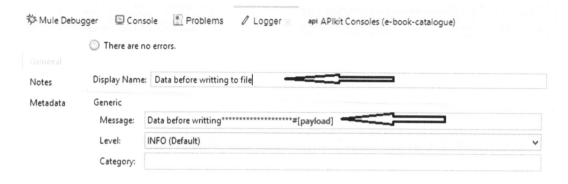

Figure 6.46: Logger Configuration

f.   Drag **File endpoint** from the **Palette** as shown below:

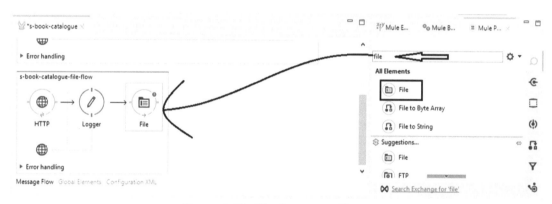

Figure 6.47: File Connector Drag

g.   Double click on **File** to open its configuration as shown below:
   i.   Provide path as per the OS
   ii. Provide File name as books.csv
   iii. Click add icon to open its connector properties and click **OK.**

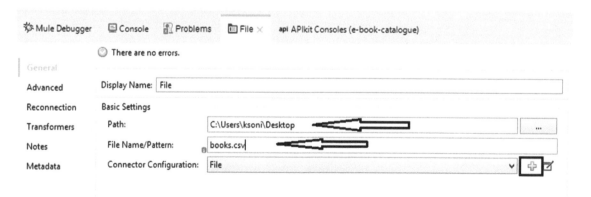

Figure 6.48: File Connector Configuration

h.   Drag **Set Payload** from the **Palette** and double click on it to open its configuration. Provide the details as shown below:

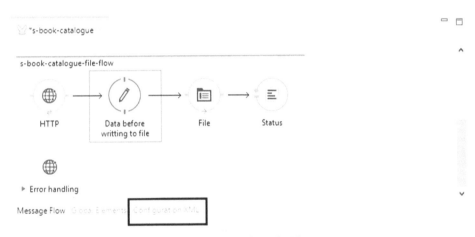

Figure 6.49: Set Payload Configuration

i.   **Save** the file and the corresponding **POST** Mule Flow should now look like:

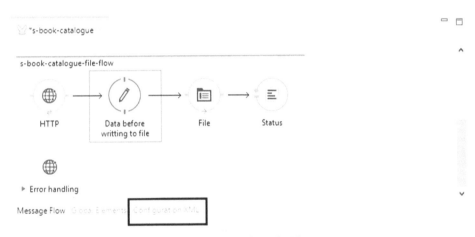

Figure 6.50: 2ⁿᵈ Mule Flow

j.   Click on **Configuration XML** tab and search with the flow name i.e. `s-book-catalogue-file-flow`. The corresponding **POST** Mule Flow XML content should look like:

```
<flow name="s-book-catalogue-file-flow">
     <http:listener   config-ref="HTTP_Listener_Configuration"   path="/s-book-
file" doc:name="HTTP"/>
   <logger    message="Data    before    writting********************#[payload]"
level="INFO" doc:name="Data before writting to file"/>
   <file:outbound-endpoint path="C:\Users\ksoni\Desktop" outputPattern="books.
csv" connector-ref="File" responseTimeout="10000" doc:name="File"/>
   <set-payload value="{Message written successfully}" doc:name="Status"/>
</flow>
```

12. Now, System API development is complete.

B. Testing

1. Launch Anypoint Studio and Open all the 3 projects namely x-book-catalogue, p-book-catalogue & s-book-catalogue. Also open **Run** -> **Run Configurations** as shown below:

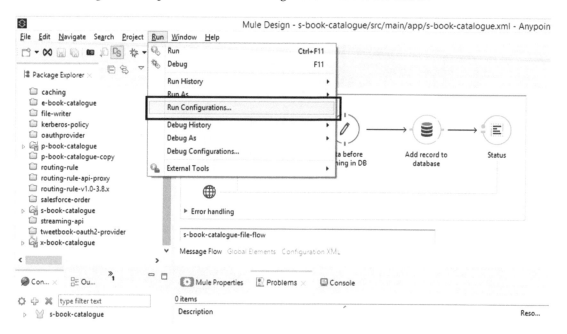

Figure 6.51: Run Configurations

2. Following window opens up, Click on **New Launch Configuration**, give Name: **api-led-connectivity.**

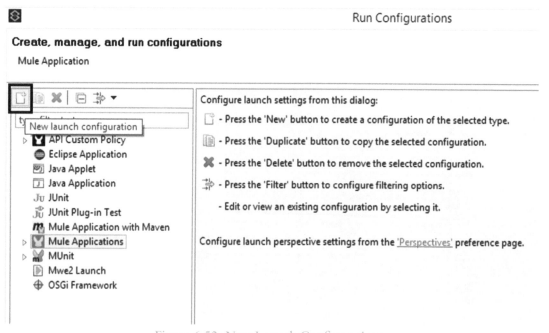

Figure 6.52: New Launch Configurations

3. Select all the 3 projects(API layer) to run simultaneously and click **Run** as shown below:

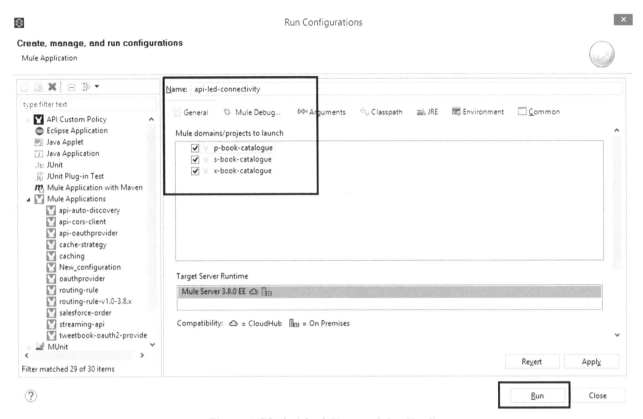

Figure 6.53: Api-Led-Connectivity Config

4. Console should show following for successful running of all 3 APIs:

Figure 6.54: Console

5. Open the browser and go to http://localhost:8081/console/.

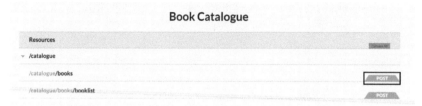

Figure 6.55: Book Catalogue Console

The test console is launched with all the methods and resources available for the book-catalogue API.

6. Test **POST** method for resource **/catalogue/books:**
   a.   Click on **POST** button. Use the **default data** (sample as shown below) that is populated in the body.

```
{
  "Id": "24",
  "Title": "Matilda",
  "Author": "Rohald Dahl",
  "Price": "$5.21"
}
```

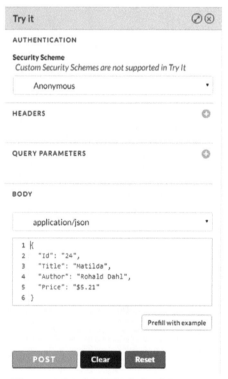

Figure 6.56: POST Method Request

   b.   Click **POST** button to invoke the API. This should return JSON response.

```
{STATUS: Successfully Created}
```

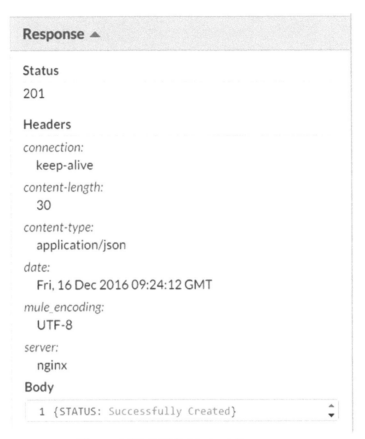

Figure 6.57: POST Method Response

   c.   A new row will be created in the database table **books.**

7. Test **POST** method for resource **/catalogue/books/booklist:**
   a.   Click on **POST** button. Use the **default data** (sample as shown below) that is populated in the body.

```
{
  "Id": "24",
  "Title": "Matilda",
  "Author": "Rohald Dahl",
  "Price": "$5.21"
}
```

Figure 6.58: POST Method Request

b. Click **POST** button to invoke the API. This should return response as:

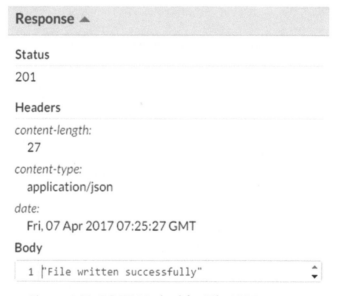

Figure 6.59: POST Method for File API Response

c. A new file will be created in the location provided and data inserted looks as shown below:

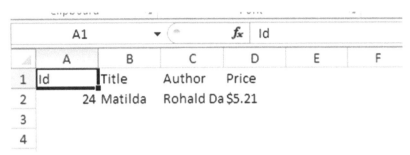

Figure 6.60: File Output

Anticipated Issues
1. MySQL Database connection not established: Ensure that the database is accessible from CloudHub.

Improvisations
1. The MySQL Driver can also be added using pom.xml if the project is mavenised. The Maven dependency is as below:

```xml
<dependency>
        <groupId>org.mule.modules</groupId>
        <artifactId>mule-module-db</artifactId>
        <version>${mule.version}</version>
        <scope>provided</scope>
</dependency>

<dependency>
        <groupId>mysql</groupId>
        <artifactId>mysql-connector-java</artifactId>
        <version>5.1.6</version>
</dependency>
```

References
1. https://blogs.mulesoft.com/dev/api-dev/apis-great-architecture/
2. https://sites.google.com/a/mulesoft.com/api-led-connectivity-workshop

RECIPE 7

API Auto-Discovery

API auto-discovery helps developers to automatically deploy APIs to CloudHub while creating or editing an API project in Anypoint Studio. Auto-discovery eliminates the need to manually export the API to CloudHub. When an application that incorporates auto-discovery is run, the auto-discovery process registers and starts the application in API Manager. Registration and start up occurs without user intervention. Auto-discovery can be configured for each flow that is to be managed using a global element although in this recipe, it is applied at the application level.

GitHub Location of this recipe:
https://github.com/WHISHWORKS/mule-api-recipes/tree/publish_v1.0/api-auto-discovery/

Pre requisites
1. **MuleSoft Anypoint Platform** Account with admin privileges https://anypoint.mulesoft.com/
2. Anypoint Studio installed https://www.mulesoft.com/lp/dl/studio/

Process
High Level Steps:
A. Anypoint Studio Configuration
B. Enable Auto-Discovery on an API
C. Verifying API Deployment

A. Anypoint Studio Configuration
1. Open the browser. Login to CloudHub account with URL https://anypoint.mulesoft.com/.

Figure 7.1: CloudHub Login

2.   After login, click **Access Management -> Open.**

Figure 7.2: Access Management

3.   The Access Management page opens. Click **Organization** on the left hand side under Access Management. Select the Organization from the list to which this API is to be deployed.
NOTE: There could be multiple organizations available.

Figure 7.3: Organization Option

4.   The **Business Group info** dialogue will appear. This dialogue has the 'Business Group name', 'Owner', 'Client Id' and 'Client Secret' for the Organization.

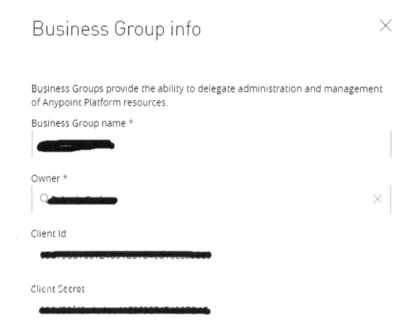

Figure 7.4: Client ID & Client Secret

5. Copy the Client ID and Client Secret to a notepad. They will be used for auto-discovering the API.
6. Now, launch Anypoint Studio. Once the Studio is launched, navigate to **Window** -> **Preferences** as shown below:

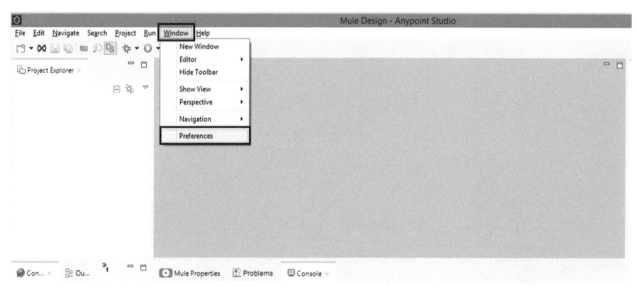

Figure 7.5: Anypoint Studio

7. It opens up a Preferences dialogue box. On the left hand side, click **Anypoint Studio** -> **Anypoint Platform for APIs**. Provide **Client Id** and **Client Secret** generated in step 5 in the boxes provided (as shown below). Retain the rest of the text fields as is.

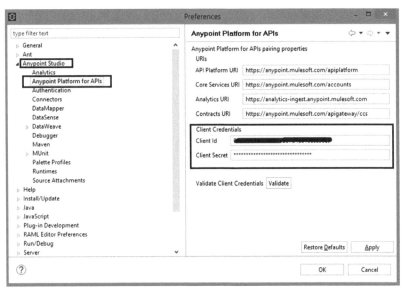

Figure 7.6: Preferences

8.   Click on **Validate**.

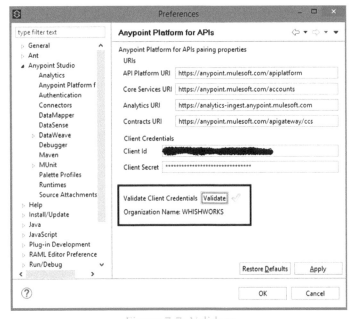

Figure 7.7: Validate

9.   Once the validation is successful, an icon indicating success will appear. Click on **OK** in the Preferences dialogue.

B. Enable Auto Discovery on API
  1.   Download the project from GitHub location mentioned in prerequisites section.
  2.   Create a new project in Anypoint Studio.

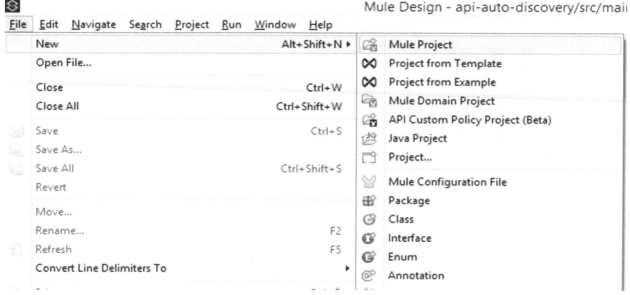

Figure 7.8: New Project

3.   Give the name of the project as **api-auto-discovery** and click **Finish** as shown below:

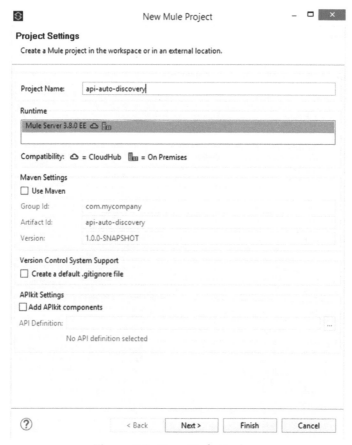

Figure 7.9: New Mule Project

4. Create a new RAML file in src/main/api as shown below:

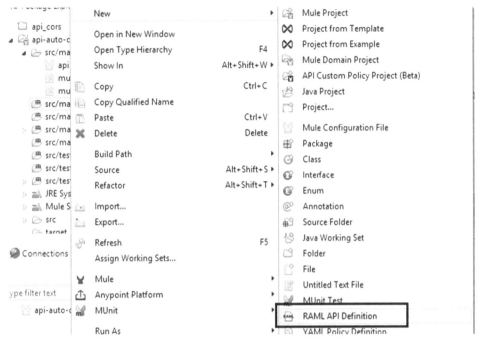

Figure 7.10: New RAML

5. Give File name as **api-auto-discovery.raml** and click **Finish** as shown below:

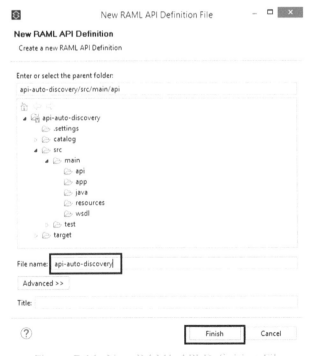

Figure 7.11: New RAML API Definition File

6. Copy the content of RAML from GitHub location <GitHub Location of this recipe>/src/main/api/api-auto-discovery.raml and put it in api-auto-discovery.raml just created as shown below:

```
 api-auto-discovery ×        api-auto-discovery.raml ×
9          application/json:
10     responses:
11      201:
12       body:
13        application/json:
14         example: |
15          {"message" : "Testing API Auto Discovery" }
16
17      400:
18       body:
19        application/json:
20         example: |
21          {"message" : "something went wrong"}
```

Figure 7.12: api-auto-discovery.raml

7. Generate flows from RAML as shown below:

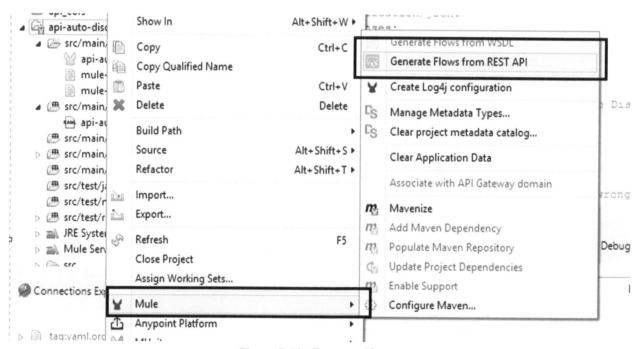

Figure 7.13: Generate Flows

8. Generated flows look as shown below:

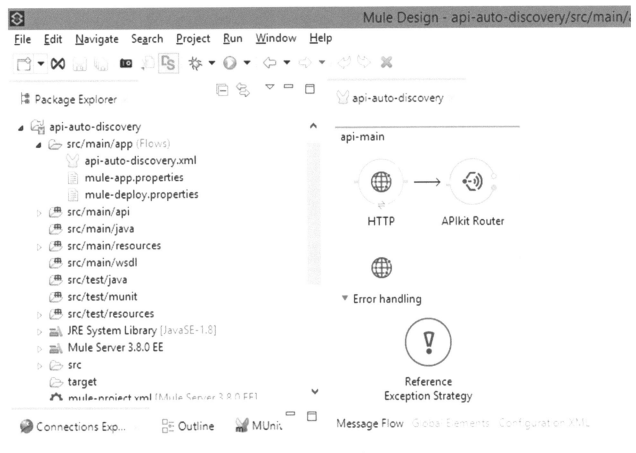

Figure 7.14: api-auto-discovery

9. Navigate to the **Global Elements** tab of the Mule Config file **api-auto-discovery.xml** and click on **Create** button.

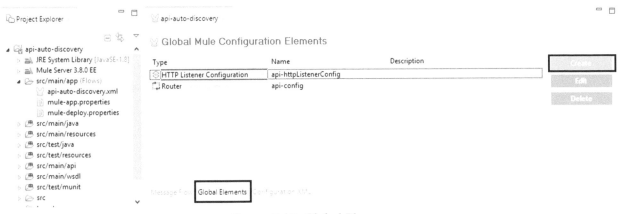

Figure 7.15: Global Elements

10. From the list of **Global Type,** click on **Component configurations.**

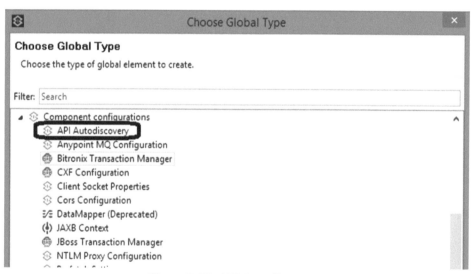

Figure 7.16: Choose Global Type

11. Select **API Autodiscovery** under **Component configurations** as below:

Figure 7.17: API Autodiscovery

12. Fill the following details in Auto-discovery settings:

   a. API Name: api-auto-discovered
   b. API Version: 1.0
   c. Flow Name: api-main (Flow containing APIKitRouter component in Mule Config file api-auto-discovery.xml)
   d. Check "Automatically create an API if it doesn't exist"
   e. APIKit Router configurations: Select 'api-config' from the dropdown menu

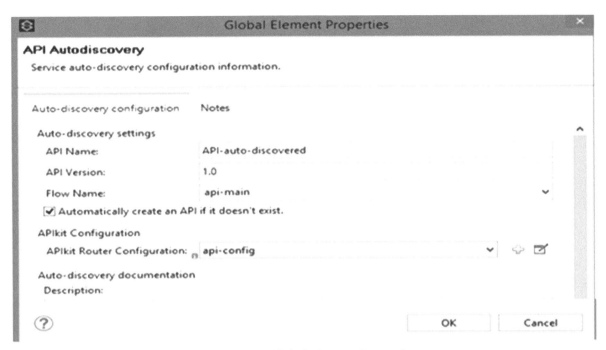

Figure 7.18: Global Element Properties

13. In the Studio as shown below, right click on the **api-auto-discovery project** and run as **Mule Application**:

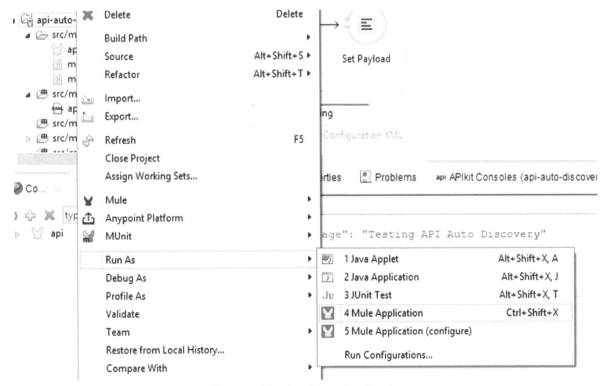

Figure 7.19: Run Mule Application

14. Once the application is deployed successfully, the following message is displayed in the Studio Console:

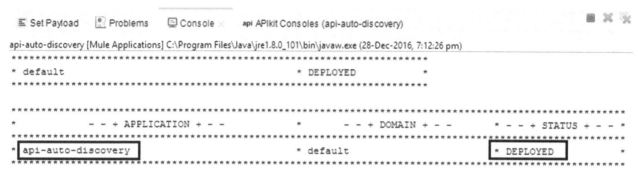

Figure 7.20: Studio Console

C. Verifying API Deployment

1. Now go to browser. Login to CloudHub account with URL https://anypoint.mulesoft.com/.

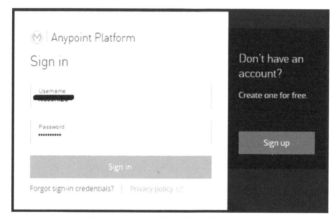

Figure 7.21: CloudHub Login

2. Click on **API Manager -> Open.**

Figure 7.22: API Manager

3. In the list of APIs, api-auto-discovered with version 1.0 as given in A.5, will be seen as shown in the figure below:

Figure 7.23: api-auto-discovered

4. The API with RAML definition is now created in CloudHub and ready to be used.

Anticipated Issues

1. The user should have administrative access to API Manager, else it's not possible to retrieve Client ID and Client Secret.
2. API will not be created or updated in CloudHub if the project is not deployed locally after being created or updated in Studio.
3. Provide the correct Client ID and Client Secret for the selected Organization. Else the Validation in step A.8 will fail.

References

1. https://docs.mulesoft.com/api-manager/api-auto-discovery

RECIPE 8

Managing API through API console

 nypoint Platform allows the API Administrator to manage an API through the service lifecycle. Some of the functions include editing the name of an API, updating the version, setting the URL and deleting an API. API Console also helps us manage different versions of an API.

This recipe shows how a user can manage an API.

GitHub location of this recipe: https://github.com/WHISHWORKS/mule-api-recipes/tree/publish_v1.0/manage-api

Pre-requisites
1. MuleSoft CloudHub Account (https://anypoint.mulesoft.com)
2. An existing API deployed and running.
3. Basic knowledge of API creation.

Process

High level Steps:
A. Managing an API - delete version or export version, edit the name, URL, description of the API.
B. API Versioning - adding another version of an API and keeping the older version at the same time.

A. Managing an API
1. Sign in to Anypoint Platform and go to API Manager Page and select the API which has to monitor.

☰   ⋒   **API Manager**

Mythical Mobile Experience API   Add Version ⌄

    1.0   ⊙ Active   Public portal ↗

Figure 8.1: Select the API

2. Click on the dropdown icon as shown below and four options will be displayed as below:
  ➢ Depreciate Version
  ➢ Delete Version
  ➢ Export Version
  ➢ Request API access terms & conditions

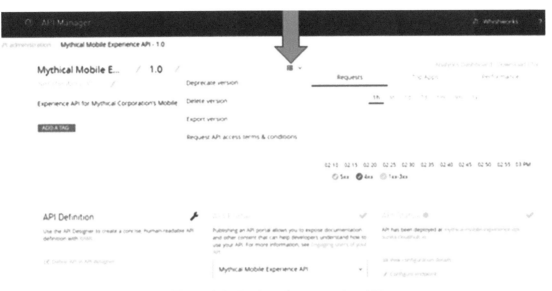

Figure 8.2: Options for managing API

By clicking on **Export version,** user can download the current version of the API in zip form. Once the code is downloaded, it can be opened in the Anypoint IDE to add custom logic to the API. Similarly, the API can be deprecated or deleted by using this option.

3. Modifying the different aspects of API like name, URL, description, version as explained below:
  ➢ Edit the name of the API as shown below:

Figure 8.3: Edit the name of the API

➢ Modify the version of the API as shown in the image below:

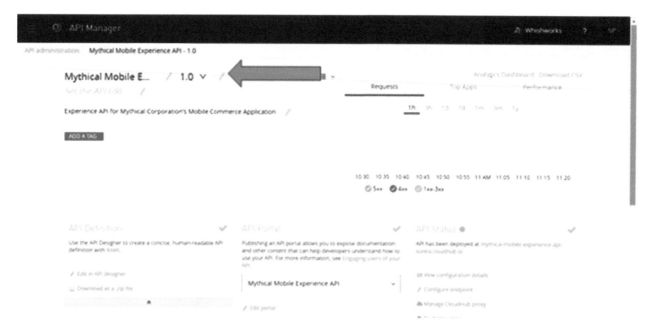

Figure 8.4: Edit the version of the API

➢ User can set the URL of the API as shown below:

Figure 8.5: Edit the URL of the API

➢ User can also edit the description as shown below:

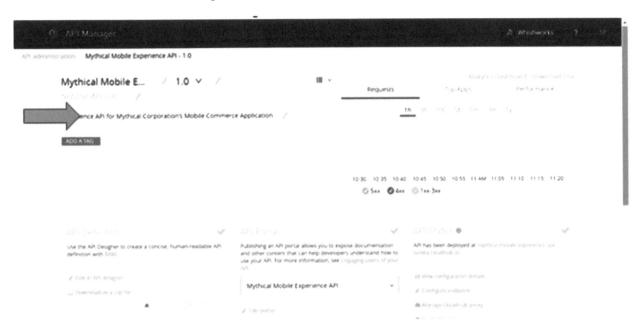

Figure 8.6: Edit the description of the API

B. API Versioning

Often, a new version of an API has to be deployed due to change in the API definition. For example, the input payload of the API may change due to change in business requirement or a policy may have to be applied to the API. But we may also need to maintain the existing API at the same time. Thus, versioning an API helps us in maintaining the original API along with the new updated API in different unique versions.

In Anypoint Platform, it is very easy to create a new version of the API, by following the given steps as below:

1. Go to '**API Manager**' Page in Anypoint Platform. Notice the '**Add Version**' tab against each API.

Figure 8.7: Add Version tab of the API

2. Click on **Add version** tab and a new form will appear as shown below, asking about the new version where name of the API is auto-filled.

Figure 8.8: Detailed Add API Version Tab

3. After adding the newest version, check the updated versions of the API as shown below:

Figure 8.9: Multiple versions of the API

4. Click on **Version 2.0 of Mythical Mobile Experience API** then we can find three options in the API portal
- No Portal
- Create new Portal
- Mythical Mobile Experience API

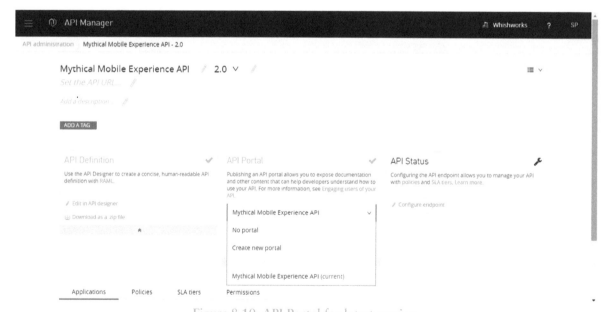

Figure 8.10: API Portal for latest version

5. If a user creates a new portal then the process is self-explanatory, but if a user chooses the same API portal as used in version 1.0 (Mythical Mobile Experience API) then the user can notice that the API Portal URL and API Portal Console are always unique as API version is appended at the end in them (as shown in the images below).

Uniqueness of API Portal URL makes sure that user is accessing the correct portal for the API version which has to consume.

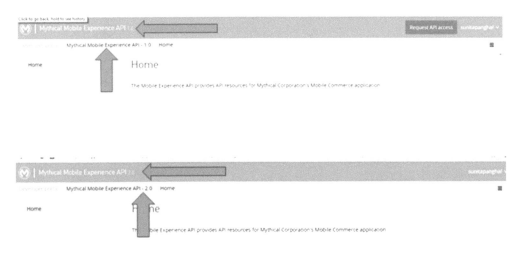

Figure 8.11: Uniqueness of API Portal

Anticipated Issues

1. User should be the owner of the API or has super user permission to add a new version of the API.
2. As shown in the below image, a user can see the 'Add Version' option only for those APIs which have been created by the user.

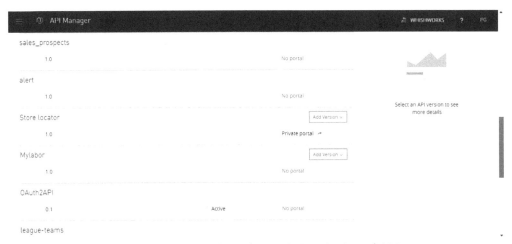

Figure 8.12: Anticipated Issue in Versioning of API

References

1. https://docs.mulesoft.com/api-manager/

RECIPE 9

Sharing APIs with Developers and Partners

APIs should be shared with developers and partners so that they can be consumed for composite application development. Traditionally, the service information is documented in Wiki pages or internal company portals. The downside of this approach is extra effort to document and manage the service specification and inability to share with partners outside the firewall.

With MuleSoft Anypoint Platform, it is easy to share the API definitions without compromising security. Moreover, a developer portal can be created in few minutes. There is no need of external Wiki pages or portals.

This recipe demonstrates how to share an API with other developers by creating a portal from the API Manager.

Figure 9.1: Anypoint API Portal

GitHub location of this recipe:
https://github.com/WHISHWORKS/mule-api-recipes/tree/publish_v1.0/leagues

1. RAML file and its JSON files with Leagues operations, designed in MuleSoft API Designer (<GitHub location of this recipe>/leagues-v1.0.zip)
2. MuleSoft CloudHub Account with admin privileges (https://anypoint.mulesoft.com)

Process
High Level Steps:
    A.   Create an API
    B.   Create New Portal
    C.   Sharing API with developers/partners

A. **Create an API**
1. Download the .zip file from '**<GitHub location of this recipe >/leagues-v1.0.zip**' as mentioned in pre-requisites.
2. Open a browser and login to Anypoint Platform https://anypoint.mulesoft.com/.
3. Select **API Manager**.

Figure 9.2: Anypoint Home - API Manager

4. API Manager Page appears. Click **Add new API.**

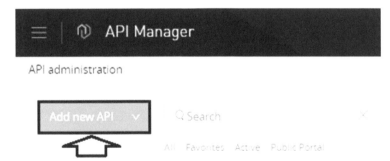

Figure 9.3: API Manager

5. The Add API page will be displayed. Fill the fields as follows:
    a.   Enter the API name as **Leagues UX.**
    b.   Enter the Version name as **1.0.**

c. Leave the the API Endpoint blank for now.
d. Enter a description of User Experience API as **League Application.**
e. Click **Add.**

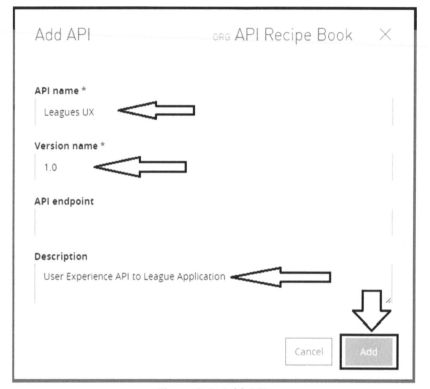

Figure 9.4: Add API

6.   The API administration page for newly created API appears.

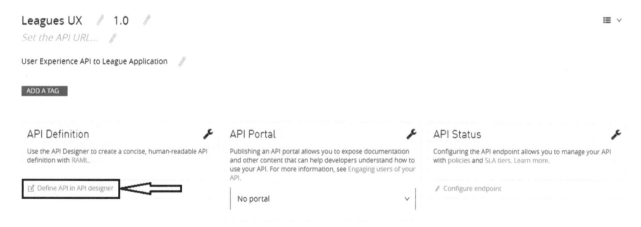

Figure 9.5: Leagues UX dashboard

7.   Click on **Define API** in API designer as shown above.

8. **API Designer** page appears. The API Designer will provide an empty API definition to start as shown below:

Figure 9.6: Leagues UX API Designer

9. Click on **Project** dropdown and select **Import** as shown below:

Figure 9.7: Import Option

10. **Import File** dialogue opens.
11. Choose the **leagues-v1.0.zip** file from the desktop which is downloaded in step A.1. Click on **Import** as shown below:

Figure 9.8: Import File

12. **Path already exists** dialogue appears. Click on **Replace** as shown below:

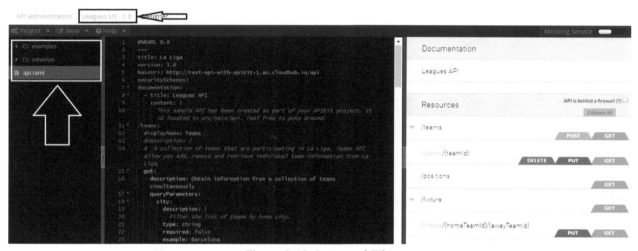

Figure 9.9: Replace existing File

13. RAML file with the example and schema JSON files will be imported as shown below:

Figure 9.10: Imported File

14. Click on <u>Leagues UX - 1.0</u> as shown above. Leagues UX administration page opens.

Figure 9.11: Leagues UX dashboard - Portal

B. **Create New Portal**
   1. Click **Create new portal** under API Portal as shown above.

2. A blank portal will be launched which has placeholders for Web UI objects, API reference, themes, etc., to create and edit the developer portal as shown below:

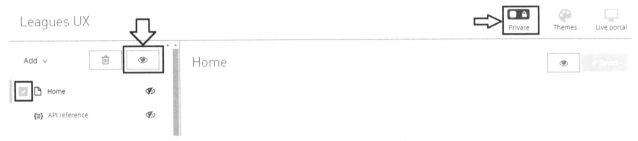

Figure 9.12: Portal Dashboard

3. Select the checkbox next to the Home page. Make the page visible by clicking the 👁 (visible) icon.

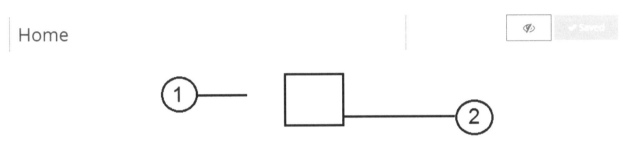

Figure 9.13: Home Default Portal

4. Add text to describe the API by clicking on **Mark '1'** as shown above.
5. Add an image and select a theme of choice by clicking on **Mark '2'** as shown above. Choose image file (**<GitHub location of this recipe>**/image/football.jpeg and **<GitHub location of this recipe>**/image / fixures.jpeg) as shown below:

Figure 9.14: Home Portal

6. Click on **Save** to save the image for this portal.
7. Now, click on **API reference**. It will automatically load the API definitions, resources and other references based on the RAML.

Figure 9.15: API Reference

C Sharing API with developers/partners

1. Make the portal public by clicking on  to toggle to to make this API shareable to external developers and partners as shown below:

Figure 9.16: API Access

2. Launch the view by clicking '**Live portal**' as shown below:

Figure 9.17: Live Portal

3. A new window is launched which can be shared across developers and partners by sharing the URL as shown below:

Figure 9.18: Developer Portal

4. If it is public then this API will be accessible with external partners by sharing the URL.
5. If it is private then this API can be accessed with internal same environment developers but not with external partners.

Anticipated Issues

1. The pages are blank. When the 'Live Portal' is launched, ensure that the pages are 'set to visible' using the eye button.

References

1. https://docs.mulesoft.com/api-manager/engaging-users-of-your-api
2. https://docs.mulesoft.com/api-manager/tutorial-create-an-api-portal

RECIPE 10

Adding JSON Schema as Reference in RAML

With MuleSoft Anypoint Platform, APIs are defined using RAML specification and the supported editor. The APIs can contain schemas to allow API consumers understand the input and output message structure supported by the API definition. Similarly, an example can be provided.

When the API specification contains more resources, the specification can become complex if all the code artefacts are included in a single file. Hence, to make the definition easy to read and manage, it is recommended to define certain artefacts separately and import into the RAML.

RAML supports "!include" to reference JSON schema and example files. This recipe demonstrates how "!include" can be used to make the RAML readable.

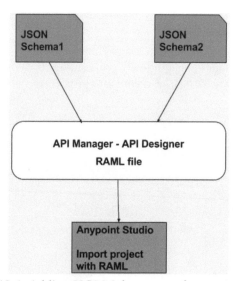

Figure 10.1: Adding JSON Schema as reference in RAML

GitHub location of this recipe:
https://github.com/WHISHWORKS/mule-api-recipes/tree/publish_v1.0/json-schema-in-raml/

1. **MuleSoft Anypoint Platform** Account: https://anypoint.mulesoft.com/
2. **Access** to API **league-teams** in **CloudHub**

A. Review RAML with inline schema
B. Create separate schema files
C. Reference schema in RAML

A. Review RAML with inline schema
1. The RAML below has the inline schema defined. (Refer to league-teams-inline-schema.raml available in the GitHub location of this recipe provided above)

```
get:
    description: Obtain information from a collection of teams simultaneously
    queryParameters:
      city:
        description: |
          Filter the list of teams by home city.
        type: string
required: false
        example: Barcelona
    responses:
      200:
        body:
          application/json:
            schema: |
              {
                    "type": "object",
                    "$schema": "http://json-schema.org/draft-03/schema",
                    "items": {
                        "description": "The team is the basic unit for keeping
track of a roster of players. With the Team APIs, you can obtain team-related
information, like the team name, stats, points, and more.",
                        "name": "Team",
                        "properties": {
                            "homeCity": {
                                "description": "Name of the city to which this
team belongs",
                                "type": "string",
                                "required": true
                            },
                            "id": {
                                "description": "A three-letter code that identifies
the team id",
                                "maxLength": 3,
                                "minLength": 3,
                                "type": "string",
                                "required": true
                            },
                            "name": {
                                "description": "Name of the team",
                                "type": "string",
                                "required": true
                            },
```

```
                                "stadium": {
                                        "description": "Name of the stadium",
                                        "type": "string"
                                }
                        },
                        "type": "object"
                },
                "name": "Teams",
                "required": true,
                "type": "array"
        }
```

2. As it is apparent above, the API definition is difficult to understand. The other disadvantage is the complexity to add more resources and maintain the API.

B. Create separate schema files

1. The schema files can be divided into independent files so that the lines of code reduce.
2. Identify the schema files in the section A above.
3. Create a schema file **teams-schema-response.json** with the following data and save to your computer.

```
{
  "$schema": "http://json-schema.org/draft-03/schema",
  "items": {
        "description": "The team is the basic unit for keeping track of a roster
of players. With the Team APIs, you can obtain team-related information, like
the team name, stats, points, and more.",
        "name": "Team",
        "properties": {
                "homeCity": {
                        "description": "Name of the city to which this team belongs",
                        "type": "string",
                        "required": true
                },
                "id": {
                        "description": "A three-letter code that identifies the team id",
                        "maxLength": 3,
                        "minLength": 3,
                        "type": "string",
                        "required": true
                },
                "name": {
                        "description": "Name of the team",
                        "type": "string",
                        "required": true
                },
                "stadium": {
                        "description": "Name of the stadium",
                        "type": "string"
                }
        },
        "type": "object"
  },
  "name": "Teams",
  "required": true,
  "type": "array"
}
```

4. Similarly, an example file can also be defined, **teams-example.json** is defined in this case. Content of this file can be found at <GitHub location of this recipe>/schema/teams-example.json/.

C. **Reference Schema in RAML**
1. Sign in to CloudHub account https://anypoint.mulesoft.com/

Figure 10.2: CloudHub Login

2. After login click API Manager -> Open.

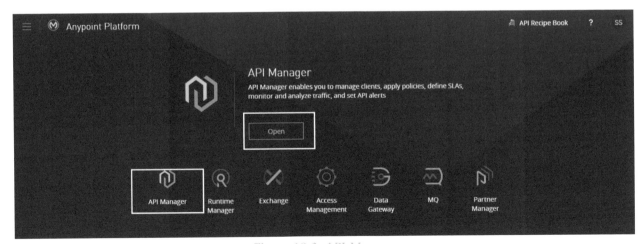

Figure 10.3: API Manager

3. In the API administration page search for **league-teams** API as shown below:

Figure 10.4: API Manager league-teams

4. Click on **version 0.1** which will open **API administration page** of league-teams then click on **Edit** in API designer in API Definition section as shown below:

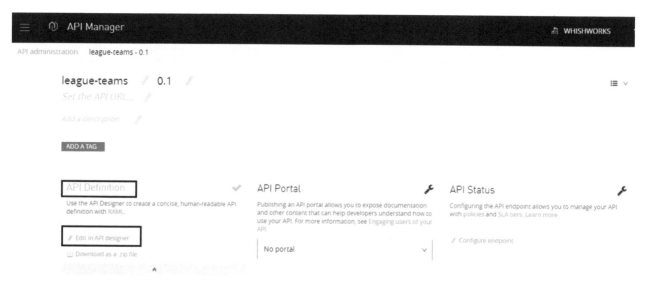

Figure 10.5: API Definition

5. Following window opens:

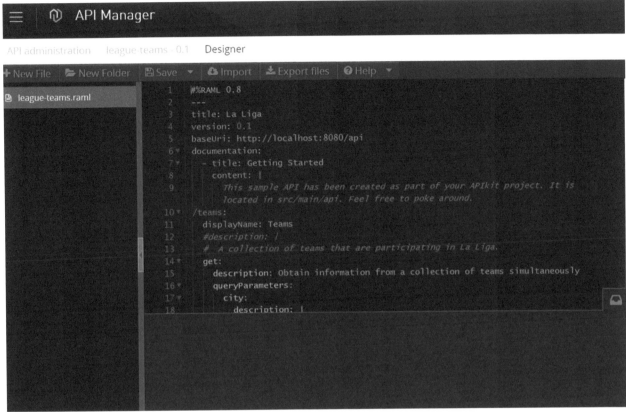

Figure 10.6: API Designer

6. For the **GET** resource, a schema and example are required.
7. The RAML editor on CloudHub allows developers to create folders and add reference-able files.
8. In the RAML editor, click on **New Folder. Add a new folder** dialogue appears.

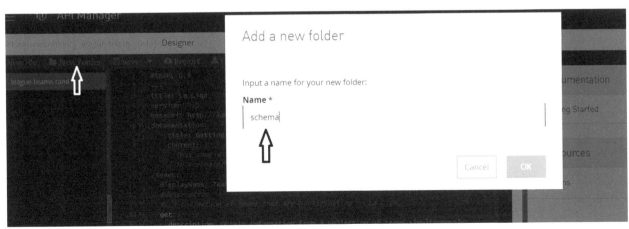

Figure 10.7: Add New Folder

9. Provide a name (schema in this example), and click **OK.**
10. Use the **import** link to launch the screen below:

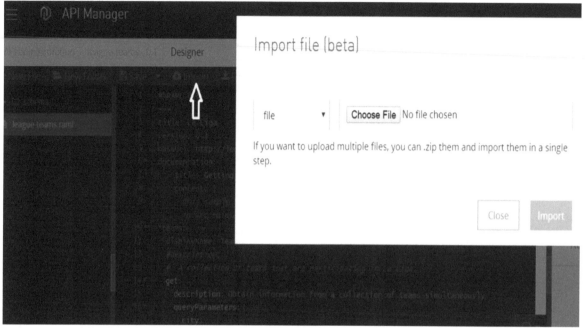

Figure 10.8: Import File

11. Select the **teams-schema-response.json** from your computer. The file will be loaded into the editor. Click **Save.**

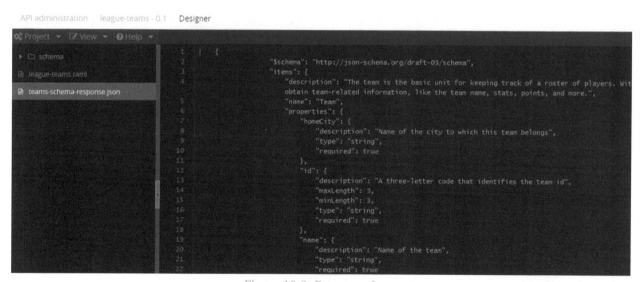

Figure 10.9: Response Json

12. Repeat the above steps 10 & 11 to import **teams-example.json.** Notice that a new file appears. Click **Save** on the RAML editor bar.

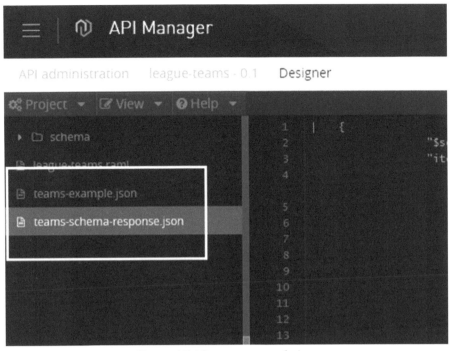

Figure 10.10: team-example.json

13. Using the drag & drop capability on the editor, move the JSON files to schema folder.

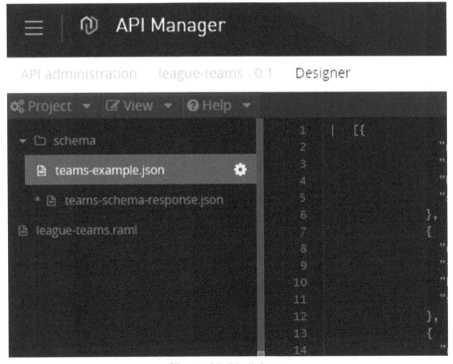

Figure 10.11: Schema

14. The schema and example JSON files can be referenced as:

```
schema: !include schemas/teams-schema-response.json
example: !include schema/teams-example.json
```

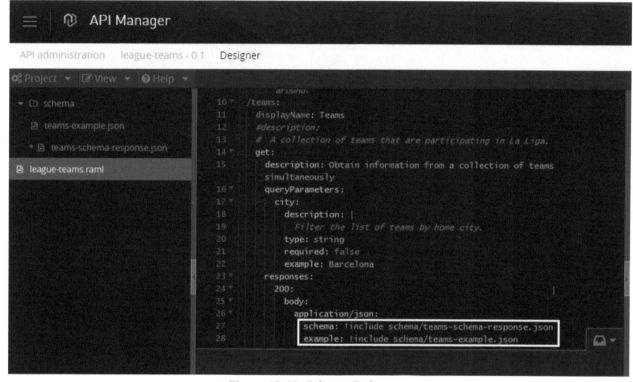

Figure 10.12: Schema Reference

15. Notice that the RAML file looks cleaner and easy to maintain. Similarly, other RAML files can be imported so that the APIs are grouped according to the file types.
16. Resultant definition file is in league-teams.raml can be found at GitHub location of this recipe provided above.

Anticipated Issues

1. NA

References

1. https://docs.mulesoft.com/anypoint-platform-for-apis/apikit-tutorial
2. http://raml.org/

RECIPE 11

Importing RAML into another RAML Definition

The idea of importing one RAML into another RAML definition is to encourage re-use of the definitions as much as possible. A part of RAML which needs to be re-used or extended in different use cases should be separated. This would make the code modular as well.

As shown in the figure below, a PAYMENT RAML can be re-used by importing it in different RAMLs like History, Science, and Literature.

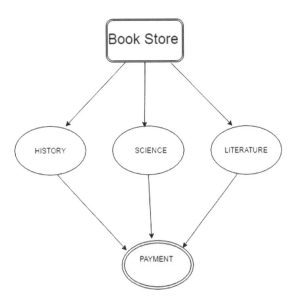

Figure 11.1: Import RAML

This recipe shows how to import one RAML into another RAML.
GitHub location of this recipe: https://github.com/WHISHWORKS/mule-api-recipes/tree/publish_v1.0/import-raml

WHISHWORKS™

1.   Anypoint Platform API Designer
2.   Basic knowledge of RAML and APIs

Process

High Level Steps:
A.   Creating an API with multiple RAML files and then importing one RAML to another.
B.   Testing the API.

A. Creating an API with multiple RAMLs
1.   Login to Anypoint Platform and create a new API. Edit the API in the Designer by creating book-catalogue.raml as shown below :

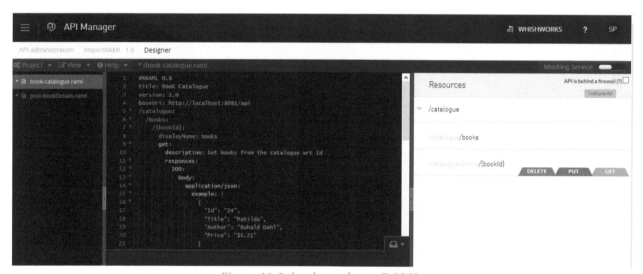

Figure 11.2: book-catalogue RAML

2.   Magnified image of book-catalogue API is :

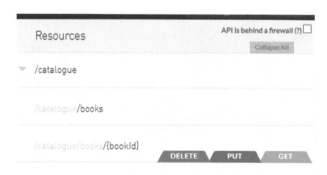

Figure 11.3: book-catalogue API Resources

3. Sample RAML code of book-catalogue.raml is as below :

```
#%RAML 0.8
title: Book Catalogue
version: 1.0
baseUri: http://localhost:8081/api
/catalogue:
  /books:
    /{bookId}:
      displayName: books
      get:
        description: Get books from the catalogue wrt Id
        responses:
          200:
            body:
              application/json:
                example: |
                  {
                    "Id": "24",
                    "Title": "Matilda",
                    "Author": "Rohald Dahl",
                    "Price": "$5.21"
                  }
      put:
        description: Modify a book Price
        body:
          application/json:
            example: |
              {
                "Id": "24",
                "Title": "Matilda",
                "Author": "Rohald Dahl",
                "Price": "$5.21"
              }
        responses:
          200:
            body:
              application/json:
                example: |
                  {
                    "Id": "24",
                    "Title": "Matilda",
                    "Author": "Rohald Dahl",
                    "Price": "$5.21"
                  }
      delete:
        description: delete the book record
        responses:
          204:
            body:
              application/json:
                example: |
                  {
                    "Status": "Successfully Deleted"
                  }
```

4. Now go to **Project -> New File -> Raml 1.0 -> API spec** and add file with the name **"post-bookDetails. raml"** and write the POST method for book details in the same.

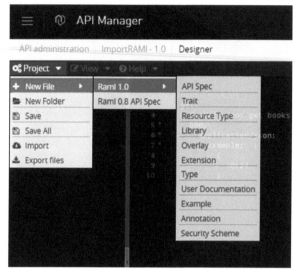

Figure 11.4: Create new RAML

5. RAML of book-catalogue.raml is as below :

```
post:
      description: Add a new book to catalogue
      body:
        application/json:
          example: |
            {
              "Id": "24",
              "Title": "Matilda",
              "Author": "Rohald Dahl",
              "Price": "$5.21"
            }
      responses:
        201:
          body:
            application/json:
              example: |
                {
                  "Id": "24",
                  "Title": "Matilda",
                  "Author": "Rohald Dahl",
                  "Price": "$5.21"
                }
        500:
          body:
            application/json:
              example: |
                {
                  "errorMessage": "The book couldn't be entered."
                }
```

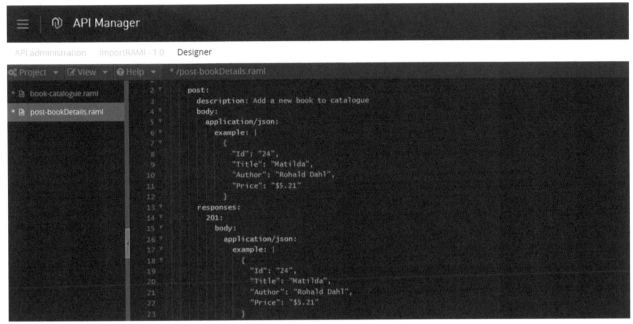

Figure 11.5: book-catalogue RAML

6. Now add the line **"/PostBookDetails: !include post-bookDetails.raml"** in the book-catalogue.raml as shown in the image.
7. The line **/PostBookDetails: !include post-bookDetails.raml** will import the post-bookDetails RAML into the book-catalogue RAML.

```
1    #%RAML 0.8
2    title: Book Catalogue
3    version: 1.0
4    baseUri: http://localhost:8081/api
5    /catalogue:
6      /books:
7        /PostBookDetails: !include post-bookDetails.raml
8      /{bookId}:
9        displayName: books
10       get:
11         description: Get books from the catalogue wrt Id
12         responses:
13           200:
14             body:
15               application/json:
```

Figure 11.6: Include book-catalogue RAML into book-catalogue RAML

B. Testing

After importing the post-bookDetails RAML in the book-catalogue RAML, one can clearly see that the POST method originates from the post-bookDetails RAML while the PUT, GET, and DELETE methods originate from book-catalogue RAML.

Figure 11.7: Book-catalogue raml after inclusion of post-bookDetails raml

Magnified version of the above image is:

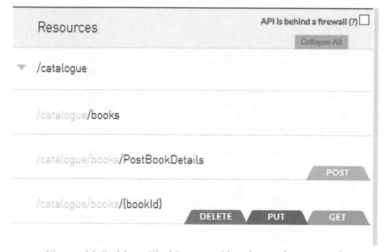

Figure 11.8: Magnified image of book-catalogue raml

Use Case

The example above is simple to depict RAML import. Consider that we have a travel domain site with business units as Air, Hotel and Train bookings.

The main components of each product are its search, booking and payment flow. Since these are different products, inventory, search and other behaviors will be different but the payment part will be the same for each product.

Hence, we can keep the payment part in one RAML so that it can be used by each product as shown in the diagram below. By modeling payment as a separate file, we can also offer Air division to extend the definition and customize as required by the Airlines business process.

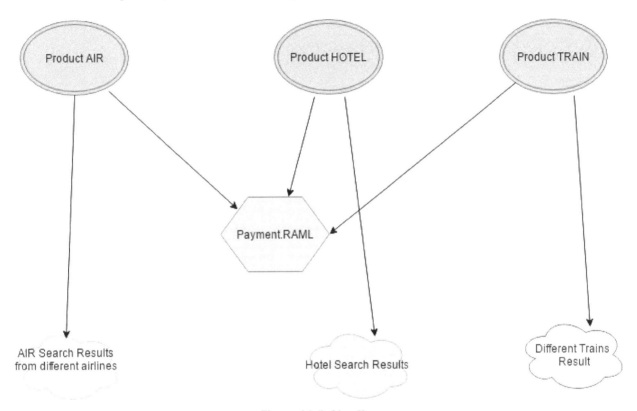

Figure 11.9: Use Case

References
1. http://raml.org/developers/raml-200-tutorial

RECIPE 12

Set up email alerts in applications in CloudHub

A lerts give visibility to events that might need attention and notify administrators about necessary actions. With MuleSoft Anypoint Platform, it is easy to set up alerts that trigger an email whenever certain events related to an application or servers occur. This mechanism works in the same way for applications deployed on CloudHub or on premise servers.

Runtime Manager provides several out-of-the-box standard alert types like -

- Exceed a certain number of events processed in a certain time period
- A deployment completes with success or failure
- CloudHub encounters a problem with the worker on an application via the worker monitoring system

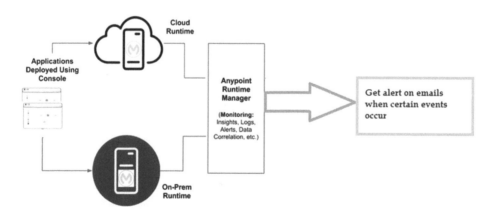

Figure 12.1: Alerts Flow Diagram

The objective of this recipe is to explain the procedure to create alerts and manage them.
GitHub location of this recipe:
https://github.com/WHISHWORKS/mule-api-recipes/tree/publish_v1.0/salesforce-contracts

1. Access to MuleSoft Anypoint Platform
2. MuleSoft Anypoint Studio 6.1 or above (https://www.mulesoft.com/lp/dl/studio) installed
3. MuleSoft CloudHub Account with admin privileges (https://anypoint.mulesoft.com)
4. Application **salesforce-contracts** is available at GitHub location of this recipe provided above.
5. This application is available on CloudHub with the name **salesforce-contracts-api.**
6. The application is in **Undeployed** state.

A. Create an Alert
B. Testing
C. Managing Alerts

A. Create an Alert

1. Open the browser and login to MuleSoft Anypoint Platform https://anypoint.mulesoft.com/login/.
2. Click on **Runtime Manager** as shown below:

Figure 12.2: Anypoint Home

3. The **Runtime Manager** page is displayed, listing all deployed applications and APIs as shown below:

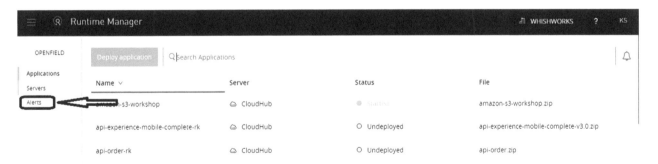

Figure 12.3: Runtime Manager

4. Click **Alerts** from the left menu as shown above.
5. The **Alerts** page appears, click on **plus icon**.

Figure 12.4: Alerts Home

6. The **Create an Alert** page appears. It's time to create an alert.
7. Create a Deployment success alert.
a. Fill a unique name in **Name** of the alert i.e. **salesforce-contracts-api-deployment-alert**.
b. Select an **Application type** from the dropdown i.e. **CloudHub Applications**.
c. Select an **Application** from the dropdown i.e. **salesforce-contracts-api**.
d. Select the condition **Deployment success** from the list of conditions under the dropdown.
e. The **Subject** will be auto filled after selecting the condition for the alert. It can be modified as per your needs.
f. The **Message** will be auto filled. It can be modified as per your needs.
g. Select **Users** to get alerts. Also freely write email addresses of people who aren't in the list of users under the dropdown.
h. Retain the rest of the fields as populated by default.

Figure 12.5: Create an Alert

i.   Click **Create Alert**.

j.   After **Alert** creation, updated alert list will be displayed as shown below. The content of the Alert can be seen on the right part of the screen as shown below:

Figure 12.6: Alerts

k.   Now, successful deployment of the Alert has been created for the API. It's time to deploy the application to CloudHub.

B. Testing

1.   Click on **Applications** as shown below:

Figure 12.7: Alerts - Applications

2.   The **Runtime Manager** page will be displayed listing all applications. Search for the API for which alert has been created.

Figure 12.8: Runtime Applications

3. Select the API. The content of the API can be seen as shown below:

Figure 12.9: Runtime Applications Un-deployed Status

4. It can be seen that the API is **undeployed** in CloudHub. Click on the dropdown to select **Start** option to deploy this API on CloudHub.

Figure 12.10: Applications - deployed options

5. Select **Start.** Now, the application deployment will start as shown below:

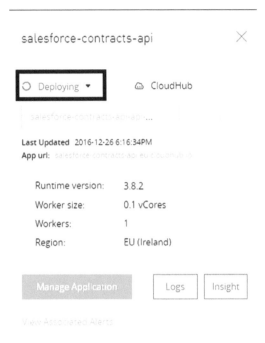

Figure 12.11: Deployment in-progress State

6. Wait for successful deployment. After some time, the status should change to green icon with a status **Started** as shown below:

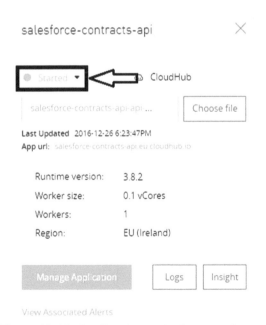

Figure 12.12: Applications - deployment Started

7. Once the API is deployed successfully, the Anypoint Platform will send an email alert as per the configuration done in step A.7 with following content as shown below:

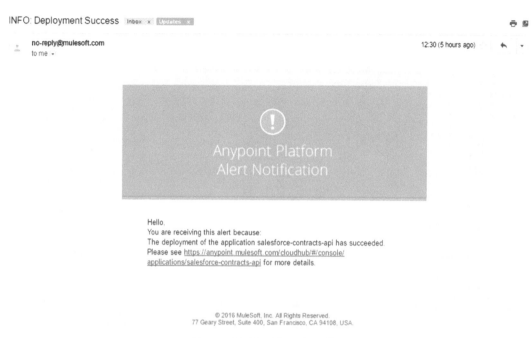

Figure 12.13: Alert Email

C. Manage Alerts

1. The Anypoint Platform provides capability to manage alerts. The section below details various alert management features.

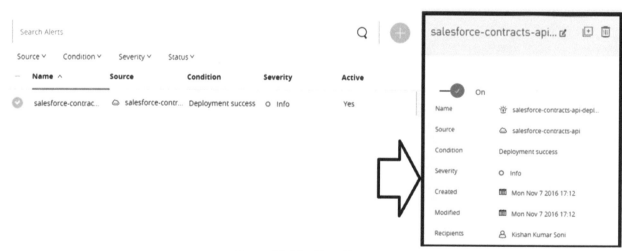

Figure 12.14: Alert Content

2. The Zoomed version of the selected part of the previous image is shown below:

Figure 12.15: Alert Content – Zoomed Version

a. Editing an existing alert can be done by clicking on the icon marked as '1' in the above image.
b. Select one or more alerts and then, from the alert panel, click the duplicate icon, marked as '2' in the above image.
c. To delete an alert, select an alert from the alert panel, click the delete icon as marked '3' in the above image.
d. Complete history of the time whenever the alert was triggered, can be seen as shown in the above image marked as '4'.
e. Select one or more alerts in the alert menu and click the switch from 'ON' to 'OFF' or vice versa which is shown in the above image marked as '5'.

Anticipated Issues

1. Check spam folder for alerts in case the alert is not available in the inbox folder.

Improvisations

There are more existing alerts available such as Deployment Failed alert, Event Traffic Threshold alert, etc.

• Create Deployment Failed alert
a. Fill a unique name in **Name** of the alert i.e. **salesforce-contracts-api-failed.**
b. Select an **Application type** from the dropdown i.e. **CloudHub Applications.**
c. Select an **Application** from the dropdown i.e. **salesforce-contracts-api.**
d. Select the condition **Deployment failed** from the list of conditions under dropdown.
e. The **Subject** will be auto filled after selecting the condition for the alert. It can be modified as per your needs.
f. The **Message** will be auto filled. It can be modified as per your needs.

g. Select **Users** to get alerts. Also freely write email addresses of people who aren't in the list of users under the dropdown.

h. Retain the rest of the fields as populated by default.

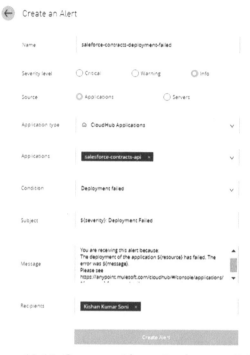

Figure 12.16: Create an Alert – Deployment Failed

i. The configured alert should be created and listed in the alerts screen. On the right side of the alert, the content of the alert can be seen.

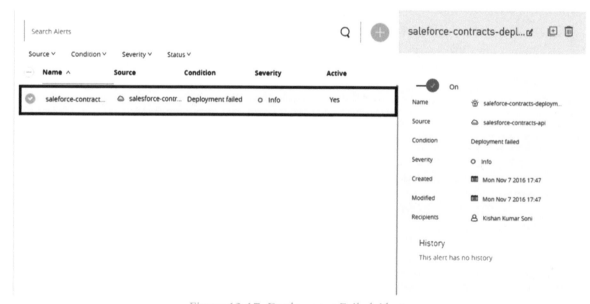

Figure 12.17: Deployment Failed Alert

j. Deploy existing API on CloudHub, and then wait for deployment failure.

k. Once the deployment has failed, an email will be sent automatically to the email ids which were mentioned at the time of alert creation with the following content as shown below:

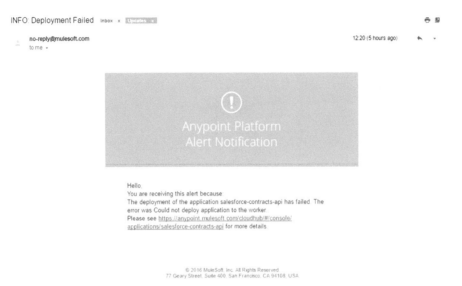

Figure 12.18: Deployment Failed Alert Email

- Event Traffic Threshold alert

a. To create an alert for this event, select condition 'Exceeds event traffic threshold'.

Figure 12.19: Exceeds event traffic threshold condition

b. Fill a unique name in **Name** of the alert i.e. **salesforce-contracts-events-exceeded.**

c. Select an **Application type** from the dropdown i.e. **CloudHub Applications.**

d. Select an **Application** from the dropdown i.e. **salesforce-contracts-api.**

e. Select the condition **Exceed events traffic threshold** from the list of conditions under dropdown.

f. Fill both **Threshold exceeds** and **frequency** parameters i.e. 3 events in a minute as the event threshold.

g. The **Subject** will be auto filled after selecting the condition for the alert. It can be modified as per your needs.

h. The **Message** will be auto filled. It can be modified as per your needs.

i. Select **Users** to get alerts. Also freely write email addresses of people who aren't in the list of users under the dropdown.

j. Retain the rest of the fields as populated by default.

Figure 12.20: Exceeds alerts Creation

k.   An alert should be created and listed. On the right of the below screen, the content of the alert can be seen.

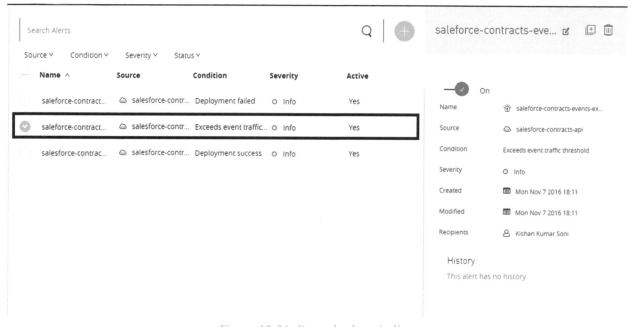

Figure 12.21: Exceeds alerts in list

l. Deploy existing API on CloudHub.

m. Once deployment is successful, hit the URL more than the threshold limit for the configured duration. If number of hits cross the threshold limit, an email will be triggered with following content:

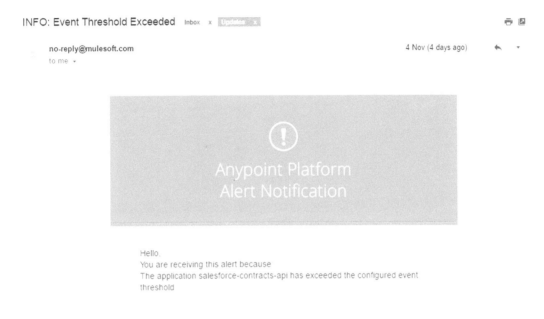

INFO: Event Threshold Exceeded Inbox x Updates x

no-reply@mulesoft.com   4 Nov (4 days ago)
to me ▾

Anypoint Platform
Alert Notification

Hello,
You are receiving this alert because
The application salesforce-contracts-api has exceeded the configured event threshold

Figure 12.22: Exceeds alerts Alert Email

References

1. https://docs.mulesoft.com/runtime-manager/alerts-on-runtime-manager

RECIPE 13

Implementing Cross Origin Resource Sharing (CORS) on an API

Under the Same Origin policy, a web browser permits scripts contained in the first web page to access data in the second web page, but only if both web pages have the same origin. However, if a script from one domain tries to access restricted content of another domain, browser will show Cross Origin Resource Sharing (CORS) error.

CORS defines a way in which a browser and server can interact to determine whether or not it is safe to allow the cross-origin request.

The objective of this recipe is to apply CORS policy to an API whereby the API will have a list of trusted domains so that a request originated from any of these domains is not blocked by the browser since an exception has been added to the API (server) side.

Figure 13.1: CORS flow

CORS Flow:
1. The client application sends the request with requested method specified & the origin.
2. The server sends the response back to the client, if the origin is allowed to access that resource.

GitHub location of this Recipe:
https://github.com/WHISHWORKS/mule-api-recipes/tree/publish_v1.0/api-cors-policy

Pre requisites
- A. MuleSoft Anypoint Studio installed https://www.mulesoft.com/lp/dl/studio/
- B. Access to an App api-cors-policy-app for extracting Order information from Salesforce is already deployed on CloudHub http://api-cors-policy-app.eu.cloudhub.io/console/
- C. GitHub link for api-cors-policy-app <GitHub location of this recipe>/api_cors/
- D. Access to a client application api-cors-client
- E. GitHub link for api-cors-client <GitHub location of this recipe>/api-cors-client/

Process
High Level Steps:
- A. Enabling CORS on an API
- B. Testing CORS Secured API

A. Enabling CORS on an API
1. Sign in to CloudHub account https://anypoint.mulesoft.com/.

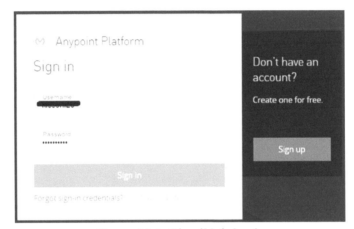

Figure 13.2: CloudHub Login

2. After login, click **API Manager -> Open.**

Figure 13.3: API Manager

3. The API administration page lists all active APIs. Search for salesforce_order API to which the policy needs to be applied as shown below:

Figure 13.4: salesforce_order API

4. Click on **Version 1.0.**
5. API administration screen for the salesforce-order API shall be presented.
6. Click on **Policies** tab as highlighted below:

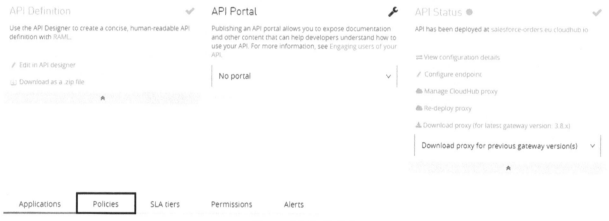

Figure 13.5: Policies

7. Select **"Cross-Origin resource sharing"** from the list of available policies and click on **Apply.**

Figure 13.6: CORS Policy

8. A dialog opens; uncheck **Public resource.**

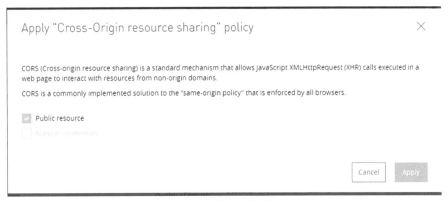

Figure 13.7: CORS

9. If **Public resource** is unchecked, the following options show up:

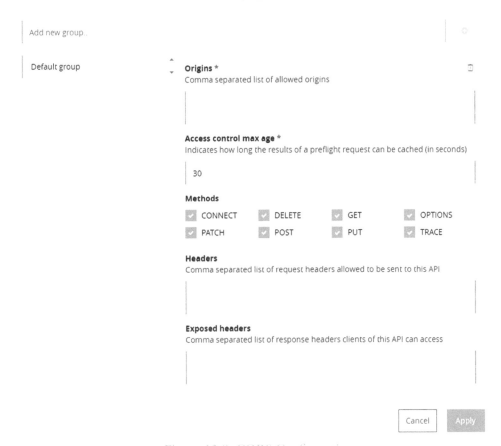

Figure 13.8: CORS Configuration

10. Notice that here all the HTTP Methods are enabled. That means this API can accept any method over CORS.

11. For the Default group, specify domain name http://localhost:8081 and click on **Apply** as shown below:

Figure 13.9: CORS Configuration

12. This policy will appear in the list of applied policies.

Figure 13.10: CORS Policy Applied

B. Testing the CORS Secured API

1. The application used to test involves making a GET call to the salesforce_order API deployed in CloudHub. Since this application will run on localhost, the browser has to make a GET request call to a different domain to access the API which normally is not allowed. But after applying CORS policy in the API the request will be allowed.
2. Download api-cors-client project from the as mention in pre-requisite at step E. .
3. Import api-cors-client project (downloaded in last step) in Anypoint Studio.

Figure 13.11: Anypoint Studio

4. Import dialogue opens, click **Anypoint Studio generated Deployable Archive(.zip)** and click **Next**

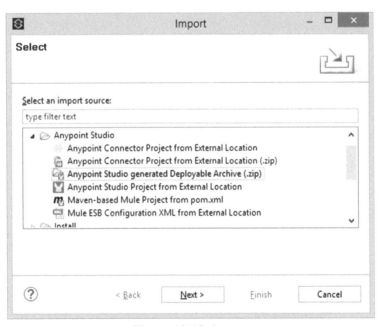

Figure 13.12: Import

5. Browse zip file which is downloaded in step B.2. click **Finish** as shown below.
6. After importing, flow should look as shown below:

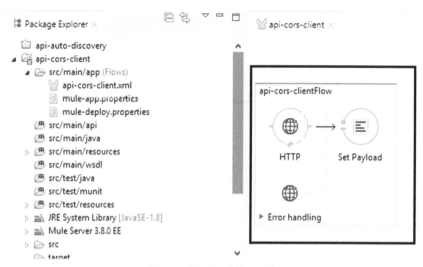

Figure 13.13: Client Flow

7. Make sure in the flow set Payload component has the following HTML code:

```html
<!DOCTYPE html>
<html>
<head>
<title>Demo</title>
</head>
<body>
Calling an API
<p id="demo"></p>
<script  src="http://ajax.googleapis.com/ajax/libs/jquery/1.7.1/jquery.min.js"
type="text/javascript">
</script>
<script>
        function UserAction() {
      var data_json;
      $.ajax({
              headers: { "Accept": "application/json"},
              type: 'GET',
          url: 'http://salesforce-orders.eu.cloudhub.io/order/80128000000y1O1,
              crossDomain: true,
              success: function(data, textStatus, request){
                        data_json = JSON.stringify(data);

                        document.getElementById("demo").innerHTML = data_json;
              }

              });

      }
UserAction();

</script>

</body>
</html>
```

8. Run the client application in Anypoint Studio.

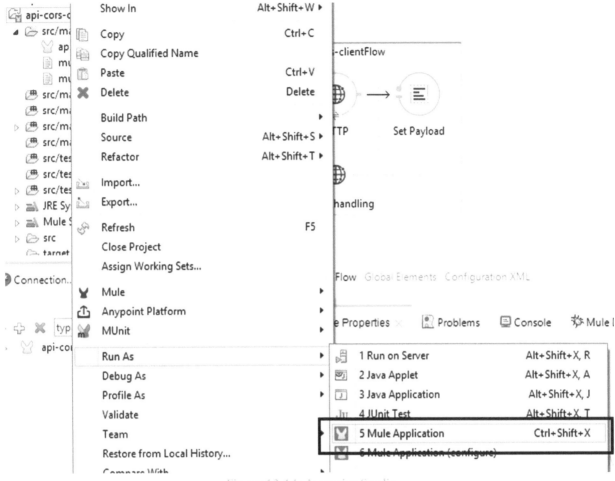

Figure 13.14: Anypoint Studio

9. By default, application will run port 8081. Notice that it is the same port which is provided in the list of allowed origins in API Gateway while applying the policy as in step A.11.

10. Following message will be seen in the console of the Studio if application is deployed successfully.

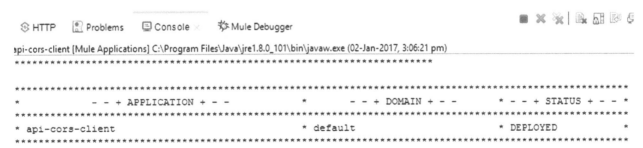

Figure 13.15: Studio Console

11. Open http://localhost:8081 in a browser and open browser console.
12. If CORS policy is applied for salesforce_order API, following will be the output in the browser:

Figure 13.16: Output

13. If CORS policy is not applied for salesforce_order API, following will be the output in the browser:

Figure 13.17: Output

Anticipated Issues

1. Allowed origin may not be given properly while applying the policy. Hence make sure to put the exact URL **http://localhost:8081** in the policy configuration.

References

1. https://docs.mulesoft.com/api-manager/cors-policy
2. https://www.w3.org/TR/cors

RECIPE 14

API Traffic Management Using SLA and Throttling Policies

API management is the process of publishing, analysing, documenting and overseeing APIs in a secure and scalable environment. Traffic management is one of the core pillars that influence the design of a good API, not only because outsiders can access the server, but also because malicious traffic through an API can bring down a server if the API isn't built to withstand big spikes[4]. Few goals of API Traffic Management are:

- To protect APIs from overuse and abuse
- To regulate inbound and outbound traffic according to infrastructure availability

Two ways of imposing restrictions on incoming traffic are:

- Rate Limiting
- Throttling Policy

A **Service Level Access** (SLA) tier is a category of user access that one can define for an API.

Rate limiting specifies the maximum value for the number of messages processed per time and reject any messages beyond the maximum.

SLA-based rate limiting restricts the number of requests by an application to API based on the configuration of an SLA tier. In other words, it is used to limit the requests based on source application identified by client id and token.

Throttling works similar to Rate Limiting Policy except that any requests received beyond the limit are not rejected right way but are put in a queue instead and processed with delays.

SLA-based throttling restricts the number of requests beyond a limit by putting in queue requests by an application to API based on the configuration of an SLA tier.

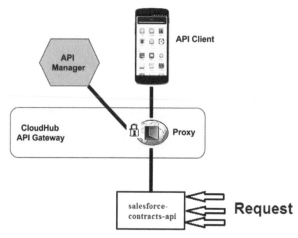

Figure 14.1: Main Flow

In this recipe, we will learn how to apply Rate Limiting Policy and Rate Limiting SLA-based Policy, Throttling Policies and Throttling SLA-based Policy on any application on CloudHub. The objective of this recipe is to impose a limit on requests to control traffic on API through these policies.

Exported deployable archive of this recipe:
https://github.com/WHISHWORKS/mule-api-recipes/tree/publish_v1.0/deploy-api-proxy

Pre-requisites

1. MuleSoft Anypoint Studio 6.1 or latest version (https://www.mulesoft.com/lp/dl/studio) installed
2. MuleSoft CloudHub Account with admin privileges (https://anypoint.mulesoft.com)
3. Source folder of application book-catalogue is available at https://github.com/WHISHWORKS/mule-api-recipes/tree/publish_v1.0/book-catalogue
4. MySQL Database accessible from cloud with admin rights to create database and users (Refer to Recipe 'WHISHWORKS_APIRecipes_Implementing_a_New_API' for more information)
5. SQL file for the book-catalogue app, designed in MuleSoft API Designer (<GitHub location of this recipe>/book-catalogue/src/main/sql/book-catalogue.sql)

Process
High Level Steps:

A. Deploy Mule application book-catalogue on CloudHub
B. Create a Proxy API
C. Configure an API proxy & Deploy to CloudHub
D. Apply Rate Limiting Policy
E. Configure SLA Tiers and Rate Limiting SLA-based Policy
F. Configure Throttling Policies
G. Configure Throttling SLA-based Policy

A. Deploy Mule application salesforce-contracts on CloudHub
1. Download deployable zip file from GitHub location of this recipe or, export book-catalogue application (which is mentioned in pre-requisite) as a deployable archive zip file(Refer to recipe 'WHISHWORKS_APIRecipes_Implementing_a_New_API') and save it to computer.

2. Login to Anypoint Platform https://anypoint.mulesoft.com/. Select Runtime Manager.

Figure 14.2: Anypoint Home - Runtime Manager

3. **Runtime Manager** page appears. Click on **Deploy Application** as shown below:

Figure 14.3: Runtime Manager – Deploy Application

4. The **Deploy Application** page opens:
   a. Write a unique name in the **Application Name** i.e. **book-catalogue-impl**
   b. Click on **Choose file** to select archive (.zip) file which is saved to computer as mentioned in step A.1.
   c. Change **Worker size** to 0.1 vCores.
   d. Retain the rest of the fields as populated by default.
   e. Click on **Deploy Application**.

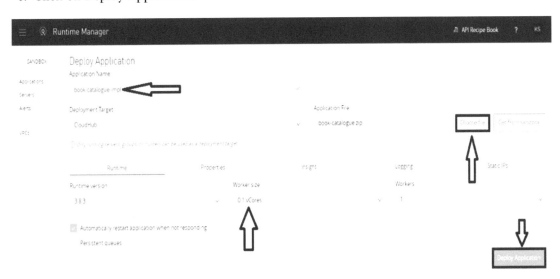

Figure 14.4: Deploy Application

5. Now the application deployment will start as shown below with the status as **Deploying.**

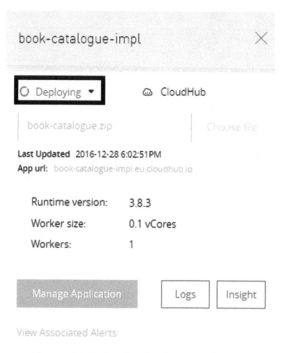

Figure 14.5: Deploy In-Progress Status

6. After some time, the status will change to **green icon** with **Started** as shown below:

Figure 14.6: Deploy Started Status

7. Once the project is deployed, copy the following URL which is shown in the above image (*book-catalogue-impl.eu.cloudhub.io*).
NOTE: This URL may vary depending on the cloud instance.

8. Now, it's time to create a proxy API.

B. **Create a Proxy API**

1. Click on the icon shown below:

Figure 14.7: Runtime Manager

2. Select API Manager.

Figure 14.8: Anypoint Platform Menu

3. API Manager page appears. Click Add new API.

Figure 14.9: API Manager

4. The Add API page will be displayed. Fill the fields as follows:
   a. Enter the **API name** as **Book Catalogue UX.**
   b. Enter the **Version name** as **1.0.**
   c. Leave the API Endpoint blank for now.
   d. Enter the description as **User Experience API to access book catalogue Application.**
   e. Click **Add.**

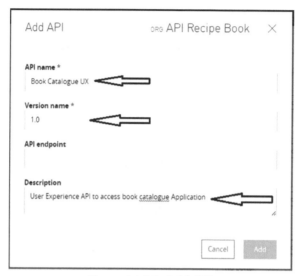

Figure 14.10: Add API

5. The API administration page for newly created API appears.

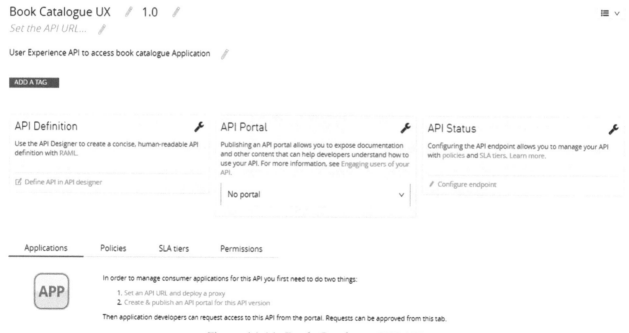

Figure 14.11: Book Catalogue UX API

6. It's time to configure an API Proxy with this API.

C. Configure an API proxy & Deploy to CloudHub
1. Back in the API Administration page, click on Configure endpoint under API Status as shown below:

Figure 14.12: API Status

2. Fill the details as follows:
   a. Select **Endpoint with a proxy.**
   b. Leave the **Type** to the default HTTP URL.
   c. Set the **Implementation URI** to: http://book-catalogue-impl.eu.cloudhub.io/api.
   d. Check the checkbox **Configure proxy for CloudHub,** since it will be deployed to Anypoint Platform CloudHub service.
   e. Retain the rest of the fields as populated by default.
   f. Click **Save** & **Deploy.**

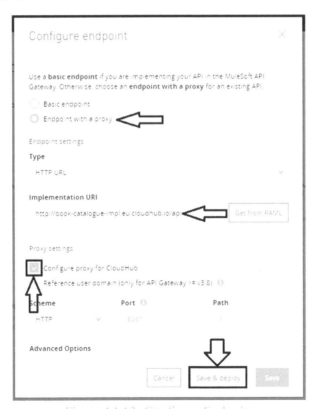

Figure 14.13: Configure Endpoint

3. Deploy Proxy dialogue would be displayed. Click on Deploy Proxy as shown below:

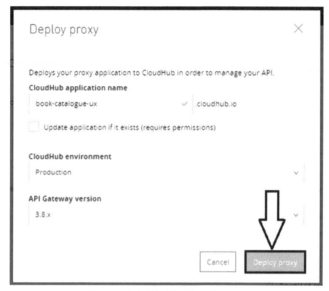

Figure 14.14: Deploy Proxy

4. Proxy API deployment will initiate. The Deploy Status would indicate Starting Application.

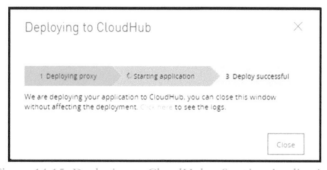

Figure 14.15: Deploying to CloudHub – Starting Application

5. After some time, the status should change to Deploy Successful as shown below:

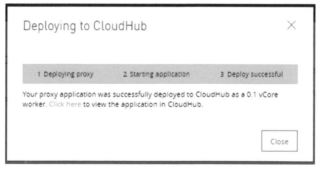

Figure 14.16: Deploying to CloudHub – Deploy Successful

6. Click on Close button.
7. Once the API is deployed, API Status content will be shown as below. Copy the API URL under API Status (*book-catalogue-ux.eu.cloudhub.io*).

Figure 14.17: API Status – After Proxy API Deployment

D. **Apply Rate Limiting Policy**
    a. Click the **Policies** tab.

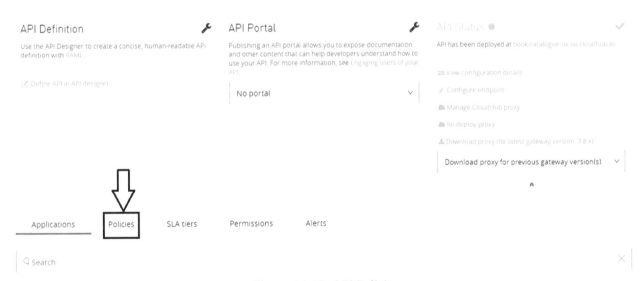

Figure 14.18: API Policies

b. Click on Apply for the Rate Limiting Policy under available policies as shown below:

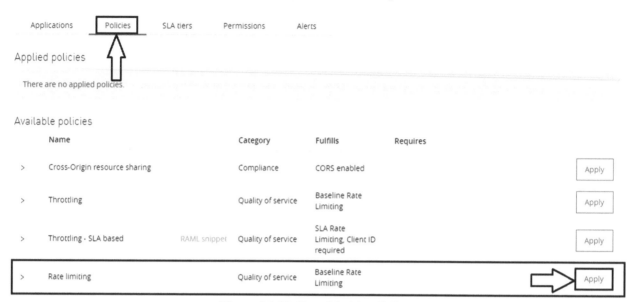

Figure 14.19: Rate Limiting Policy

c. **Apply 'Rate Limiting policy'** dialogue appears. Write the number of maximum requests per any time period like **2** Reqs per **minute** and click **Apply.**

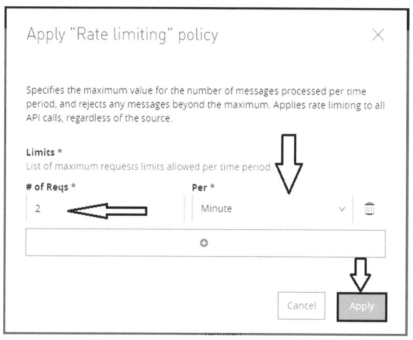

Figure 14.20: Apply Rate Limiting Policy

d.   This policy will be listed in Applied policies as shown below:

Figure 14.21: Applied Policies - Rate Limiting

e.   Testing
a.   Open a browser and go to this URL http://book-catalogue-ux.eu.cloudhub.io/catalogue/books/24.

Figure 14.22: Rate Limiting Testing

[{"Title":"Matilda","Price":"$5.21","Author":"Rohald Dahl","Id":24}]

b.   Test it again by reloading the browser **2 times**.
c.   On the 3rd invocation, a message indicating **API Calls Exceeded** will be displayed as shown below. This demonstrates that Rate Limiting policy has been applied.

Figure 14.23: Rate Limiting Testing Success

E. **Configure SLA Tiers and Rate Limiting SLA-based Policy**
    1.   Click on SLA tiers.

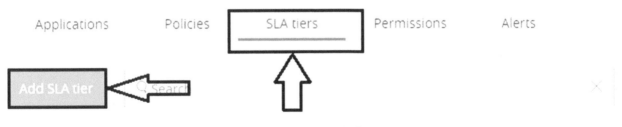

Figure 14.24: SLA tiers

2. Click on Add SLA tiers to add any number of SLA tiers.
3. Add SLA Tiers dialogue appears. Fill the following informations.
   a. **Write** Name **as** Gold
   b. Provide **Description** as **To control traffic**
   c. Retain **Approval** as **Manual** by default
   d. Give **Limits** as **3 Reqs** per **Minute**
   e. Leave **visible** as checked which is by default
   f. Click on **Add**

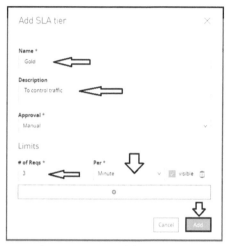

Figure 14.25: Add SLA Tiers

4. Gold tier will be listed as below:

Figure 14.26: Gold SLA Tier

5. Click **Policies** tab.
6. Under **Policies** tab, click Remove to remove Rate Limiting Policy as shown below:

Figure 14.27: Remove Rate Limiting Policy

7. Click on **Remove** in Remove Policy dialogue.

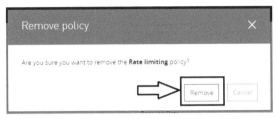

Figure 14.28: Remove Dialogue - Rate Limiting

8. Click on **Apply** for the Rate Limiting – SLA Based Policy under Available policies as shown below:

Available policies

Name		Category	Fulfills	Requires	
> Cross-Origin resource sharing		Compliance	CORS enabled		Apply
> Throttling		Quality of service	Baseline Rate Limiting		Apply
> Throttling - SLA based	RAML snippet	Quality of service	SLA Rate Limiting, Client ID required		Apply
> Rate limiting		Quality of service	Baseline Rate Limiting		Apply
> Rate limiting - SLA based	RAML snippet	Quality of service	SLA Rate Limiting, Client ID required		Apply

Figure 14.29: Rate Limiting – SLA based

9. Click **Apply** in Apply Rate limiting SLA-based policy dialogue to accept the default configuration for the Rate limiting SLA-based policy.

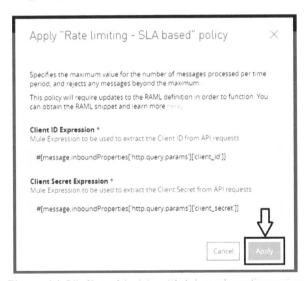

Figure 14.30: Rate Limiting SLA based configuration

10. **Applied Policies** list will be updated as shown below:

11. Create a basic API portal to configure the application for Gold SLA Tier that needs to access the Rate Limited SLA-based policy.
12. Under API Portal, choose **Create new Portal** from dropdown as shown below:

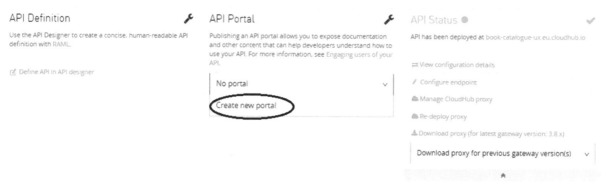

Figure 14.32: API Portal

13. Portal home page appears.
14. Select the checkbox next to the Home page. Make the page visible by clicking the 👁 (visible) icon.

API administration   Book Catalogue UX · 1.0

Book Catalogue UX

Figure 14.33: Book Catalogue Portal

15. Make the Portal Public by clicking on the eye toggle tool.

Figure 14.34: Portal Access

16. Click on  Live portal . It will be redirected to Developer portal page for the application as shown below:

Figure 14.35: Book Catalogue Developer Portal

17. In the top right corner of the portal, select **Request API Access.** Request API access to Book Catalogue UX - 1.0 dialogue opens.
    a. Click on **New Application.**

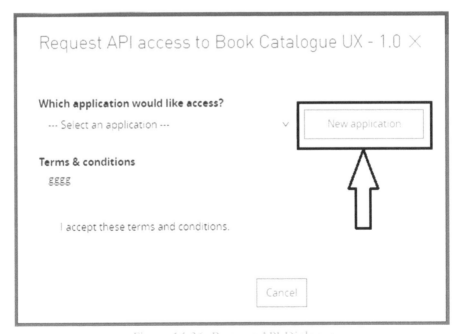

Figure 14.36: Request API Dialogue

b. **Add Application** dialogue opens.
  i. Write **Name** as **Book Application Traffic Management.**
  ii. Write **Description** as **To manage traffic of Book application with Gold SLA tier.**
  iii. Retain other fields as it is.
  iv. Click on **Add** button.

Figure 14.37: New Application

c. Select SLA tier as Gold.
d. Check the checkbox to accept terms and conditions.

Figure 14.38: Request API Access

e. Click on **Request API Access.**

f. Click on **Application Details** in **Request API access** dialogue as shown below:

Figure 14.39: Request API Access - Pending

18. **Book Application Traffic Management** application page appears where **client ID** and **client secret** will be shown as below. Copy those values on Notepad as they will be used later as URI parameters. API name under this application appears as Pending. This API should be approved for SLA-based traffic management.

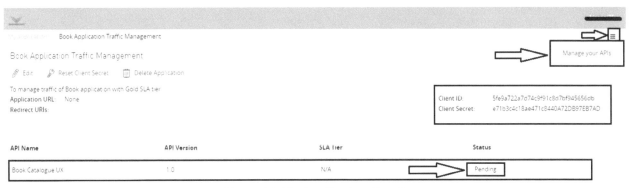

Figure 14.40: Application Details

19. Click on ≡ icon and then click on Manage your APIs. API Manager Page appears listing all APIs. Click on 1.0.

Figure 14.41: API Manager

20. Under API Administration, Book Application Traffic Management application will be listed as shown below. Click on Approve button to approve this SLA-based application.

Figure 14.42: Request API Access – Approve

21. After clicking on Approve button, this application will be approved as shown below:

Figure 14.43: Application Approved

22. Testing
    a. Open a browser and go to this URL http://book-catalogue-ux.eu.cloudhub.io/catalogue/books/24 as same as Step D.5.

Figure 14.44: Rate Limiting SLA Based Testing

    b. Testing will fail with the message **Unable to retrieve client_id from message**. This is because the Rate Limiting - SLA policy is applied.
    c. Now add two URI parameters - client_id and client_secret in the URL (client_id and client_secret is copied earlier in step E.18).
    d. For Example: http://book-catalogue-ux.eu.cloudhub.io/catalogue/books/24?client_id= 5fe9a722a7d 74c9f91c8d7bf945656db&client_secret= e71b3c4c18ae471c8440A72DB97EB7AD
    e. Hit this link in browser.

Figure 14.45: Rate Limiting SLA Based Testing with ID and secret

[{"Title":"Matilda","Price":"$5.21","Author":"Rohald Dahl","Id":24}]

   f. Test it again by reloading the browser **3 times**.

   g. On the 4th invocation, a message indicating **API Calls Exceeded** will be shown as shown below. This demonstrates that Rate Limiting – SLA based policy has been applied.

Figure 14.46: Rate Limiting SLA Based Testing – Success

F. Configure Throttling Policy

1. Click **Policies** tab.
2. Under Policies tab, click **Remove** to remove **Rate Limiting – SLA based** Policy as shown below:

Figure 14.47: Remove Rate Limiting SLA Based Policy

3. Click on **Remove** in **Remove Policy** dialogue.

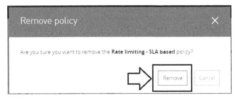

Figure 14.48: Remove Dialogue - Rate Limiting SLA Based Policy

4. Click on **Apply** for the **Throttling Policy** as shown below:

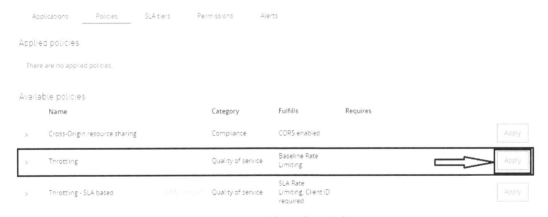

Figure 14.49: Throttling Policy

5. Configure as 3 requests to be processed per minute and click on **apply**.

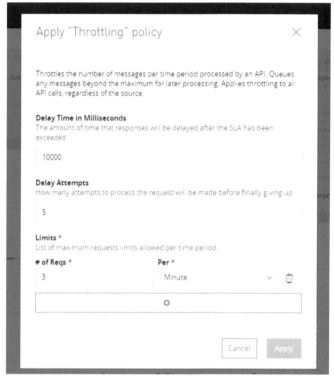

Figure 14.50: Applying Throttling Policy

6. Testing
   a. Open a browser and go to this URL http://book-catalogue-ux.eu.cloudhub.io/catalogue/books/24.

Figure 14.51: Throttling Policy Testing

```
[{"Title":"Matilda","Price":"$5.21","Author":"Rohald Dahl","Id":24}]
```

   b. Test it again by reloading the browser **3 times.**
   c. Any request that exceeds the limits will not be rejected. Fourth request in the same minute will be put in queue and processed in the next minute. After the current minute is exhausted, response will be rendered on the bowser in the next minute. This demonstrates that Throttling policy has been applied.

G. **Configure Throttling SLA-based Policy**
   1. Click on **SLA tiers.**
   2. **Gold tier** is already listed as below:

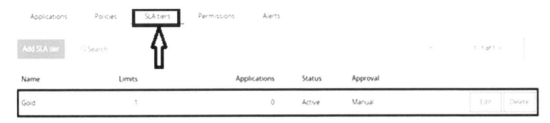

Figure 14.52: GOLD SLA Teirs

3. Click **Policies** tab.

4. Under Policies tab, click **Remove** to remove **Throttling Policy** as shown below:

Figure 14.53: Removing Throttling Policy

5. Click on **Remove** in **Remove Policy** dialogue.

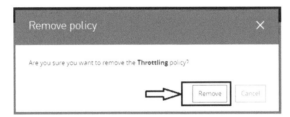

Figure 14.54: Removing Dialogue Throttling Policy

6. Click on **Apply** for the **Throttling – SLA Based Policy** as shown below:

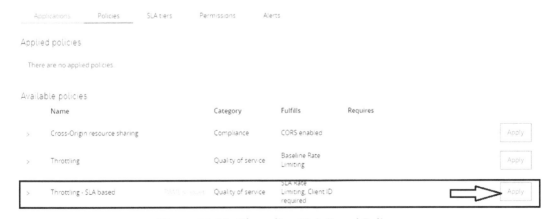

Figure 14.55: Throttling SLA Based Policy

7. Click **Apply** in **Apply Throttling-SLA based policy** dialogue to accept the default configuration for the **Throttling SLA based** policy.

Figure 14.56: Apply Throttling SLA Based Policy

8. **Applied Policies** list will be updated as shown below:

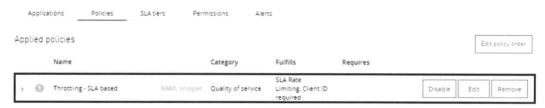

Figure 14.57: Applied Policies - Throttling SLA Based Policy

9. The application for Gold SLA tier that needs to access the Throttling SLA-based policy is already configured. Application is already created and approved in Step E.

10. Testing

a. Open a browser and go to this URL http://book-catalogue-ux.eu.cloudhub.io/catalogue/books/24 as same as Step F.6.

Figure 14.58: Throttling SLA Based Policy Testing

b. Testing will fail with the message **Unable to retrieve client_id from message**. This is because the Throttling - SLA policy is applied, resultantly the proxy is checking for Client ID in the query parameters as per the default configuration in step 7.

c. Now add two URI parameters - client_id and client_secret in the URL (**client_id** and **client_secret** is copied earlier in step E.18).

   For Example: http://book-catalogue-ux.eu.cloudhub.io/catalogue/books/24?client_id= 5fe9a722a7d74c 9f91c8d7bf945656db&client_secret= e71b3c4c18ae471c8440A72DB97EB7AD

d. Hit this link in browser

[{"Title":"Matilda","Price":"$5.21","Author":"Rohald Dahl","Id":24}]

Figure 14.59: Throttling SLA Based Policy Testing with ID and Secret

```
[{"Title":"Matilda","Price":"$5.21","Author":"Rohald Dahl","Id":24}]
```

e. Test it again by reloading the browser **3 times**.
f. Any request that exceeds the limits will not be rejected. Fourth request in the same minute will be put in queue and processed in the next minute. After the current minute is exhausted, response will be rendered on the bowser in the next minute. This demonstrates Throttling policy – SLA based has been applied.

Anticipated Issues

1. When both Rate Limiting and SLA-based Rate Limiting policies are applied on the API, they restrict the number of requests by application to API with the minimum value of allowed requests in Rate Limitng and SLA-based Rate Limiting per unit time. While the client id and client secret is required in all the requests as SLA-based Rate Limiting policy is applied.

References

1. http://raml.org/
2. https://docs.mulesoft.com/apikit/apikit-tutorial
3. https://sites.google.com/a/mulesoft.com/api-led-connectivity-workshop
4. https://www.upwork.com/hiring/development/api-traffic-management-basics/

RECIPE 15

Securing an API with OAuth2

OAuth 2.0 is a method to allow an application to have controlled access to a protected resource via a 3rd-party web service. The responsibility of an OAuth2 web service provider is to control access to protected APIs.

The objective of this recipe is to secure a RAML-based API using any OAuth2 provider. However, in this recipe Google OAuth 2.0 security is being used.

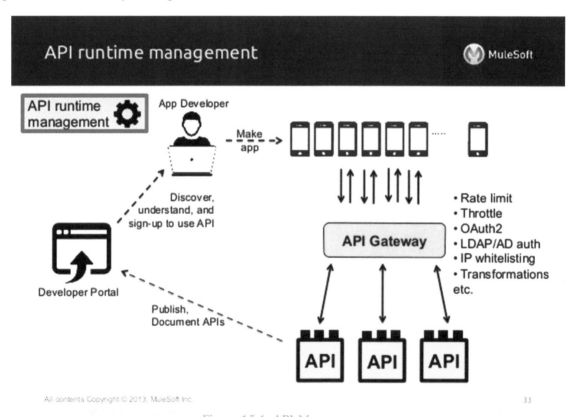

Figure 15.1: API Management

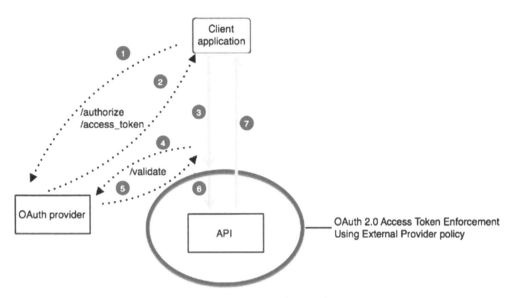

Figure 15.2: OAuth 2.0 Flow

The processes are:
1. The client application requests a token from the provider.
2. The provider returns a token.
3. The client application includes the token either as an authentication header or a query parameter in a request to the API.
4. The OAuth 2.0 Access Token Enforcement using External Provider Policy intercepts this request and communicates with the provider to validate the token.
5. The validated token is whitelisted and kept on record until expiration. Any further requests that contain this token are not validated against the OAuth provider.
6. If the token is valid, the request is forwarded to the API.
7. The API responds to the client application.

GitHub location of this recipe
https://github.com/WHISHWORKS/mule-api-recipes/tree/publish_v1.0/salesforce-contracts

Pre requisites
1. MuleSoft Anypoint Studio 6.1 or above (https://www.mulesoft.com/lp/dl/studio) installed
2. MuleSoft CloudHub Account (https://anypoint.mulesoft.com)
3. OAuth 2.0 Provider - Google OAuth from URL https://console.developers.google.com/
4. Postman plugin for Chrome installed from https://www.getpostman.com/docs/introduction
5. Application salesforce-contracts is available on the above GitHub location .
6. RAML file with examples and schema JSON files are available on GitHub (<GitHub location of this recipe>/src/main/api).
7. It is assumed that the application salesforce-contracts is deployed on CloudHub with Access URL salesforce-contracts.eu.cloudhub.io/
8. It is assumed that the proxy API salesforce-contracts-api is developed and deployed on CloudHub with proxy URL salesforce-contracts-api.eu.cloudhub.io/. The access URL to get contracts data is http://salesforce-contracts-api.eu.cloudhub.io/contracts/800280000006RvO

Process

High Level Steps:

A. Enabling OAuth 2.0 Provider - to ensure that the API requires valid OAuth tokens through the simple application of policies on-the-fly using Anypoint API Manager
B. Applying OAuth 2.0 Policy
C. Testing OAuth 2.0 Security provider on API

A. Enabling OAuth 2.0 Provider
  1. Open the Browser.
  2. Login on https://console.developers.google.com/ with Gmail account or click **Create account** to create a developer account if account not available as shown below:

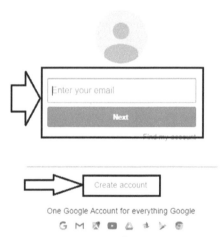

Figure 15.3: Google Account Login

  3. Click **CREATE PROJECT.**

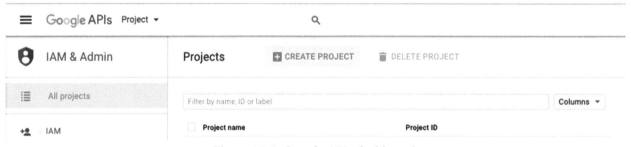

Figure 15.4: Google APIs dashboard

4. Enter the project name **oauth2-test-provider** as shown below:

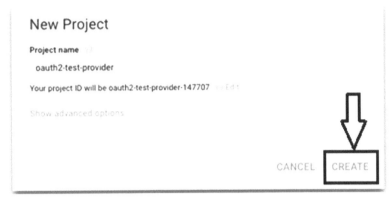

Figure 15.5: New Project

5. Provide the project name as **oauth2-test-provider** and click **CREATE.**
6. Now, Google will create the project and this might take a couple of minutes.
7. Click **Credentials** as shown below:

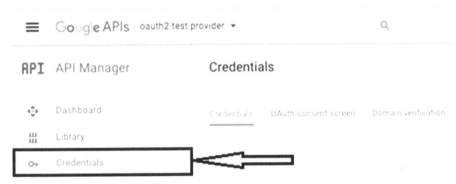

Figure 15.6: Google API Manager

8. Click **Create credentials.**

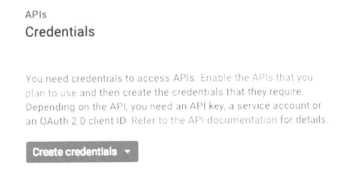

Figure 15.7: APIs Credentials

9. Select **OAuth client ID** from dropdown as shown below:

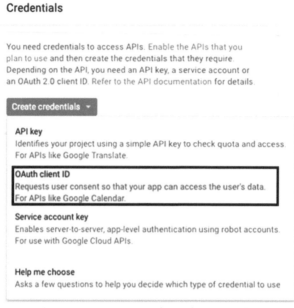

Figure 15.8: APIs Credentials – OAuth

10. **Create Client ID** will be loaded. Click **Configure consent screen.**

Figure 15.9: Create Client ID Home

11. Provide a name for **Product name shown to users** as **OAuthProvider_Test** and click **Save.**

Figure 15.10: OAuth Consent Screen

12. After Configuration, Select **Web Application**
    a. Fill the field Name as OAuthProvider_Test.
    b. Provide valid API URLs in Authorised redirect URL
    http://salesforce-contracts-api.eu.cloudhub.io/contracts/800280000006RvO
    NOTE: This URL might change based on the actual API access URL
    c. Click **Create.**

Figure 15.11: Client ID Details

13. **Client ID** and **Client Secret** will be generated. Copy and keep them safe to be used later. Click **OK**.

OAuth client

Here is your client ID

704929733002-doog9bedmoogqgt7ol6sr4062m4e2kkb.apps.googleusercontent.co

Here is your client secret

cdGI17UfzY0RRINrsqnukHeQ

OK

Figure 15.12: OAuth Client Id and Secret

14. New credentials would be created with the Client ID and Client Secret as shown below:

Credentials

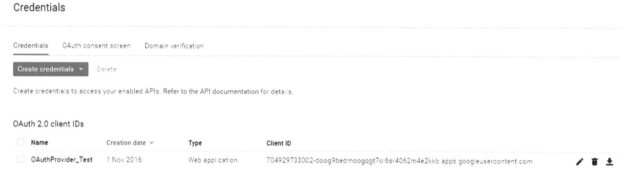

Credentials   OAuth consent screen   Domain verification

Create credentials ▾   Delete

Create credentials to access your enabled APIs. Refer to the API documentation for details.

OAuth 2.0 client IDs

Name	Creation date ∨	Type	Client ID			
OAuthProvider_Test	1 Nov 2016	Web application	704929733002-doog9bedmoogqgt7ol6sr4062m4e2kkb.apps.googleusercontent.com	✎	🗑	⬇

Figure 15.13: OAuth 2.0 Client IDs

15. Using the Client ID and Client Secret, those were generated above in step 13, form the following URL as below and open it in a new browser window.

Format:
https://accounts.google.com/o/oauth2/auth?scope=email%20profile&redirect_uri=<Redirect URI specified in Step 12.b>&response_type=token&client_id=<Client ID generated in Step 13>

Example:
https://accounts.google.com/o/oauth2/auth?scope=email%20profile&redirect_uri=http://salesforce-contracts-api.eu.cloudhub.io/contracts/800280000006RvO&response_type=token&client_id=704929733002-doog9bedmoogqgt7ol6sr4062m4e2kkb.apps.googleusercontent.com

16. Google OAuth Provider would ask to give/allow permissions to the client ID represented by **OAuthProvider_Test,** which is created above, to agree to the terms of authorization. Click **Allow.**

Figure 15.14: OAuth 2.0 Permission

17. The API URL opens and the OAuth 2.0 provider is set. Next, apply this to the actual API endpoint which needs to be secured.

B. Apply OAuth2 Policy on the API
1. Open the Browser.
2. Go to https://anypoint.mulesoft.com/login/#/signin and sign in to Anypoint Platform as shown below:

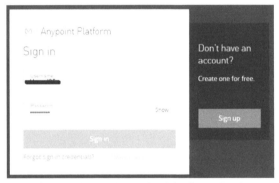

Figure 15.15: Anypoint Platform Login

3. Click on **API Manager.**

Figure 15.16: Anypoint Home

4. The **API administration** page appears, if there is any and which the user is authorized to see.
5. Search for the API over which the **OAuth 2.0** policy needs to be applied. (E.g. **salesforce-contracts-api** depicted below for demonstration)

Figure 15.17: API Manager

6. Click on the version as indicated above (1.0 in this case).
7. API administration screen shall be presented to the user as shown below:

Figure 15.18: Salesforce contracts API

8. Click on **Policies** tab that appears as you scroll down the API administration page.

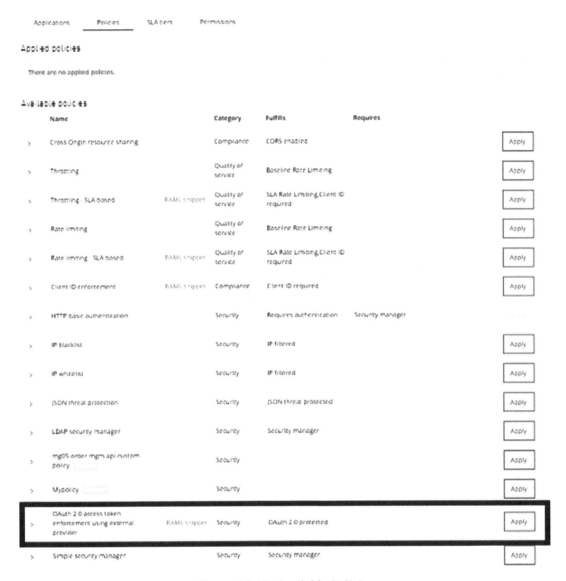

Figure 15.19: Available Policies

9. Select **OAuth 2.0 access token enforcement using external provider** from the list of available policies and click **Apply.**

Figure 15.20: OAuth 2.0 Policy

10. OAuth 2.0 dialogue opens. Since the OAuth provider for this illustration is Google, fill the field Access Token validation endpoint URL as **https://accounts.google.com/o/oauth2/tokeninfo** and click **Apply** (leave the value for Scopes empty).

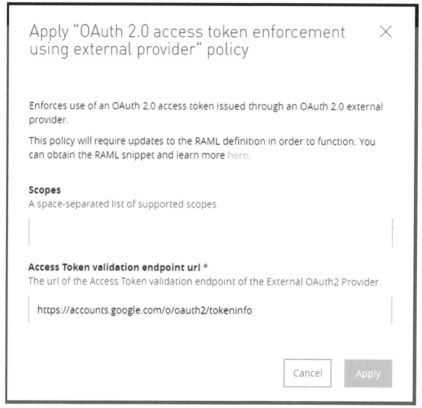

Figure 15.21: OAuth 2.0 Configuration

11. The policy is added and it appears in the Applied policies section as shown below:

Figure 15.22: Applied policies - OAuth 2.0

C. Testing the OAuth 2.0 Security Provider on API

- Testing in Browser
1. Get the access token by passing Client ID, Client Secret, Scope, and redirect URIs which are configured at step A.13.

Format:
https://accounts.google.com/o/oauth2/auth?client_id=<replace with client id>&response_type=token&scope= email&redirect_uri=<replace with Redirect URI>

Example:
https://accounts.google.com/o/oauth2/auth?client_id=704929733002-doog9bedmoogqgt7ol6sr4062m4e2kkb. apps.googleusercontent.com&response_type=token&scope=email&redirect_uri=http://salesforce-contracts-api. eu.cloudhub.io/contracts/800280000006RvO

2. While hitting URL in browser, it will be redirected to redirect URL with **access token separated by '#'**. Redirected URL:
    http://salesforce-contracts-api.eu.cloudhub.io/contracts/800280000006RvO#access_token=ya29.Ci-KA 11U0NXHit9nL7bMPge-BRJ90nrH-5EzKTV2p3bYcQaSFiboBk-jo4S6sEpPUQ&token_type=Bearer& expires_in=3600

3. Copy 'Access token' and keep it safe to be used later.
4. The browser will display an error on autoloading of redirected URL.
5. Ignore the error. Since the access token should be passed as a query parameter, replace '#' with '?' to make access_token as a parameter and load the same with the URL as:
    http://salesforce-contracts-api.eu.cloudhub.io/contracts/800280000006RvO?access_token=ya29.Ci-KA 11U0NXHit9nL7bMPge-BRJ90nrH-5EzKTV2p3bYcQaSFiboBk-jo4S6sEpPUQ&token_type=Bearer &expires_in=3600

← C ⌂ ① salesforce-contracts-api.eu.cloudhub.io/contracts/800280000006RvO?access_token=ya29.Ci-KA11U0NXHit9nL7bMPge-BRJ90nrH-5EzKTV2p3bYcQaSFiboBk-jo4S6sEpPUQ&token_type=Be ☆ ⋮

[{"StartDate":"2016-05-05","Status":"Draft","AccountId":"0012800000v06C7AAI","Id":null,"type":"Contract"}]

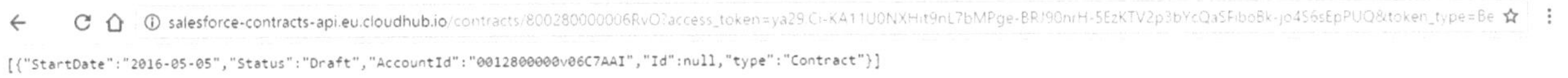

Figure 15.23: Testing Result- OAuth 2.0

The result will be displayed as shown in the figure above. The JSON output from the API protected by OAuth2 policy should be as below, only sample and actual response might vary based on the API being protected:

```
[
{
    "StartDate":"2016-0505",
    "Status":"Draft",
    "AccountId":"0012800000v06C7AAI",
    "Id":null,
    "type":"Contract"
    }
]
```

- Testing in Postman
1. Pass the access_token (from point **a** above) as a query parameter with **Redirect URL** as written below:

Format:
<replace with Redirect URI>?access_token=<replace with access token>

Example:
http://salesforce-contracts-api.eu.cloudhub.io/contracts/ 800280000006RvO?access_token=ya29.Ci-KA9A2Xt N0xVrIqvuhUvK0GCQ2CIF2w4F9QFVfxbqJjWOfR-kAxs8mjWmsS5qrqQ

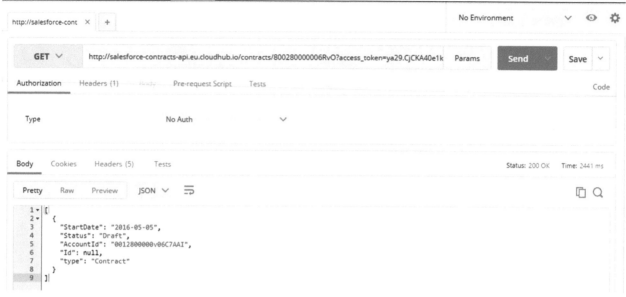

Figure 15.24: Postman Testing - OAuth 2.0

Anticipated Issues

1. If an invalid access_token is passed, the following error response "invalid_token" should be shown. Please validate and confirm that right access_token is used.

Figure 15.25: Postman Testing Error - OAuth 2.0

References

1. https://docs.mulesoft.com/anypoint-platform-for-apis/building-an-external-oauth-2.0-provider-application

RECIPE 16

Exposing legacy SOAP-based Web Service as RESTful API

With the growing demand for RESTful services it has become increasingly difficult to integrate them with the legacy SOAP-based web services. SOAP-based web services are designed with the intent of exposing pieces of application logic as services. The information returned by the SOAP web services could be so huge, making it an overhead for the consumers requesting only a small subset of the information. In such cases, REST architectural style provides an advantage by enabling to request only the information needed as well as in various data formats.

In situations where there is a need for SOAP and REST-based services to co-exist, the SOAP-based services can be exposed as RESTful API to enable easy retrieval of data without affecting other consumers of the SOAP services.

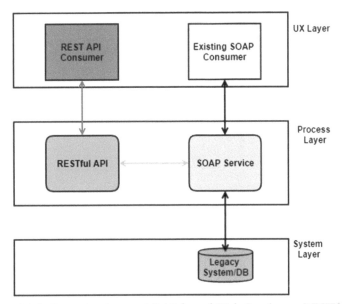

Figure 16.1: Exposing legacy SOAP-based Web Service as RESTful API

A RESTful API can act as a proxy/wrapper web service layer that sits in between the consumer and the legacy SOAP-based service, enabling flexibility in payload formats.

This recipe elaborates how to expose a legacy SOAP-based web service as a RESTful API using Anypoint Studio.

GitHub location of this recipe:
https://github.com/WHISHWORKS/mule-api-recipes/tree/publish_v1.0/soap-to-rest

Pre-requisites
1. Mule runtime version 3.8.0 or above
2. Mulesoft Anypoint Studio 6.1 or above (https://www.mulesoft.com/lp/dl/studio) installed

Process
High Level Steps:
The process for exposing the RESTful service can be divided into the following main tasks:
A. Understanding Legacy SOAP service WSDL
B. Designing RESTful API based on WSDL
C. Importing API into Anypoint Studio
D. Integrating with WSDL

A. Understanding Legacy SOAP service WSDL
1. SOAP services view every task as a service that can be dynamically discovered and organized by hitting the server.
2. For this API, create a WSDL file as **Employee.wsdl,** which holds necessary information like name, id, address of employees.
3. Code for **Employee.wsdl**which is used in this API is as below:

```xml
<?xml version="1.0" encoding="UTF-8"?>
<wsdl:definitions xmlns:soap="http://schemas.xmlsoap.org/wsdl/soap/"
    xmlns:tns="http://www.example.org/contract/Employee"
    xmlns:emp="http://www.example.org/schema/Employee"
    xmlns:wsdl="http://schemas.xmlsoap.org/wsdl/"
    xmlns:xsd="http://www.w3.org/2001/XMLSchema" name="Employee"
    targetNamespace="http://www.example.org/contract/Employee">
    <wsdl:types>
        <xsd:schema targetNamespace="http://www.example.org/schema/Employee">
            <xsd:simpleType name='NameDataType'>
                <xsd:restriction base='xsd:string'>
                    <xsd:maxLength value='20' />
                </xsd:restriction>
            </xsd:simpleType>
            <xsd:complexType name="addressType">
              <xsd:sequence>
<xsd:element name="addressLine1" type="emp:NameDataType" />
                <xsd:element name="addressLine2" type="emp:NameDataType" />
<xsd:element name="addressLine3" type="emp:NameDataType" />
                <xsd:element name="town" type="emp:NameDataType" />
<xsd:element name="state" type="emp:NameDataType" />
<xsd:element name="country" type="emp:NameDataType" />
```

```xml
                </xsd:sequence>
            </xsd:complexType>
            <xsd:complexType name="EmployeeRecordType">
                <xsd:sequence>
                    <xsd:element minOccurs="0" name="Id" type="xsd:int"/>
                    <xsd:element name="Lastname" type="emp:NameDataType" />
                    <xsd:element name="Firstname" type="emp:NameDataType" />
                    <xsd:element name="gender" type="emp:NameDataType" />
                    <xsd:element name="dateOfBirth" type="emp:NameDataType" />
                    <xsd:element name="address" type="emp:addressType"/>
                </xsd:sequence>
            </xsd:complexType>
            <xsd:complexType name="EmptyResponse">
                <xsd:sequence />
            </xsd:complexType>
            <xsd:element name="GetEmployeeDetails"
                type="xsd:int" />
            <xsd:element name="GetEmployeeDetailsResponse"
                type="emp:EmployeeRecordType" />
            <xsd:element name="BasicFault">
                <xsd:complexType>
                    <xsd:sequence>
                        <xsd:element name="errorDetails" type="xsd:string" />
                    </xsd:sequence>
                </xsd:complexType>
            </xsd:element>
        </xsd:schema>
    </wsdl:types>
    <wsdl:message name="GetEmployeeDetailsRequest">
        <wsdl:part element="emp:GetEmployeeDetails" name="parameters" />
    </wsdl:message>
    <wsdl:message name="GetEmployeeDetailsResponse">
        <wsdl:part element="emp:GetEmployeeDetailsResponse" name="parameters" />
    </wsdl:message>

    <wsdl:message name="DataProcessingError">
        <wsdl:documentation>
        </wsdl:documentation>
        <wsdl:part element="emp:BasicFault" name="BasicFault" />
    </wsdl:message>
    <wsdl:portType name="GetEmployeeInformationPortType">
        <jaxws:bindings xmlns:jaxws="http://java.sun.com/xml/ns/jaxws">
            <jaxws:enableWrapperStyle>false</jaxws:enableWrapperStyle>
        </jaxws:bindings>
        <wsdl:operation name="GetEmployeeDetails">
            <wsdl:input message="tns:GetEmployeeDetailsRequest" />
            <wsdl:output message="tns:GetEmployeeDetailsResponse" />
```

```
        <wsdl:fault message="tns:DataProcessingError" name="DataProcessingError"
/>
        </wsdl:operation>
    </wsdl:portType>
     <wsdl:binding name="EmployeeBinding" type="tns:GetEmployeeInformationPortT
ype">
        <soap:binding style="document"
           transport="http://schemas.xmlsoap.org/soap/http" />
        <wsdl:operation name="GetEmployeeDetails">
           <soap:operation soapAction="" />
           <wsdl:input>
              <soap:body use="literal" />
           </wsdl:input>
           <wsdl:output>
              <soap:body use="literal" />
           </wsdl:output>
           <wsdl:fault name="DataProcessingError">
              <soap:fault name="DataProcessingError" use="literal" />
           </wsdl:fault>
        </wsdl:operation>

    </wsdl:binding>
    <wsdl:service name="EmployeeService">
       <wsdl:port name="EmployeePort" binding="tns:EmployeeBinding">
      <soap:address location="http://localhost:8081/employee/getEmployeeDetails"
/>
       </wsdl:port>
    </wsdl:service>
</wsdl:definitions>
```

B. Designing RESTful API based on WSDL

In this part, an API will be designed to expose RESTful web service.

1.   Login (Sign Up, if first time user) to Mule Anypoint Platform.

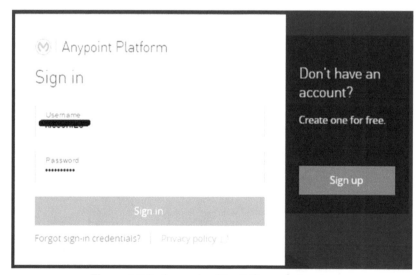

Figure 16.2: Anypoint iPaaS Console Login

2. Select **API Manager** as shown below:

Figure 16.3: Select API Manager

3. Click on **"Add new API"** and enter the API details.

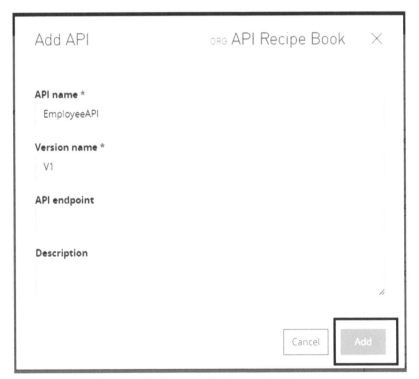

Figure 16.4: API Administration Screen

4. Click on **Define API** in API Designer and define the structure for your API using RESTful API Modeling Language (RAML).

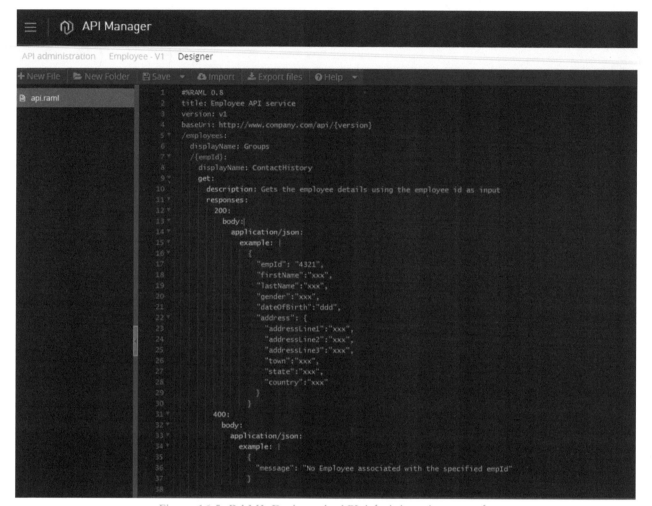

Figure 16.5: RAML Designer in API Administration console

5. Above Figure illustrates a RAML file to retrieve an organization's employee details using employee ID. The sample RAML code is as below:

```
#%RAML 0.8
title: Employee API service
version: V1
baseUri: http://www.company.com/api/{version}
/employees:
  displayName: Groups
  /{empId}:
    displayName: ContactHistory
    get:
      description: get the employee details using the employee id as input
      responses:
        200:
          body:
            application/json:
              example: |
                {
                "empId":"4321",
                "firstname":"xxx",
                "lastname":"xxx",
                "gender":"xxx",
                "dateOfBirth":"ddd",
                "address":{
                  "addressLine1":"xxx",
                  "addressLine2":"xxx",
                  "addressLine3":"xxx",
                  "town":"xxx",
                  "state":"xxx",
                  "country":"xxx"
                  }
                }
        400:
          body:
            application/json:
              example: |
                {
                "error":"No employee associated with the specified empId"
                }
```

6. Save the file as employee.raml. Download the file to your computer to proceed with further steps.

C. Importing API into Anypoint Studio

1. Open the **Anypoint Studio** and create a new Mule project and provide the project details as name **soap-to-rest**. Select the **Add APIkit Components** and then browse the RAML file to be used in **API Definition**.

Figure 16.6: Anypoint Studio, create a new project

2. The Anypoint Designer automatically creates the required flows based on the RAML.

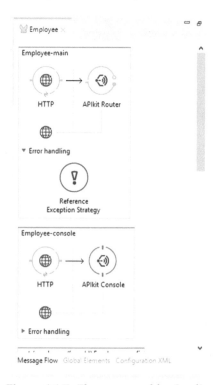

Figure 16.7: Flows created by Studio

3. Now, in order to expose the legacy SOAP web service as a RESTful service, the REST input and output have to be transformed to SOAP input and output parameters. To do that, use **Web Service Consumer** in the project. Drag and drop the component to "/get/employees/{empId}:Employee-config" flow in the Anypoint Studio.

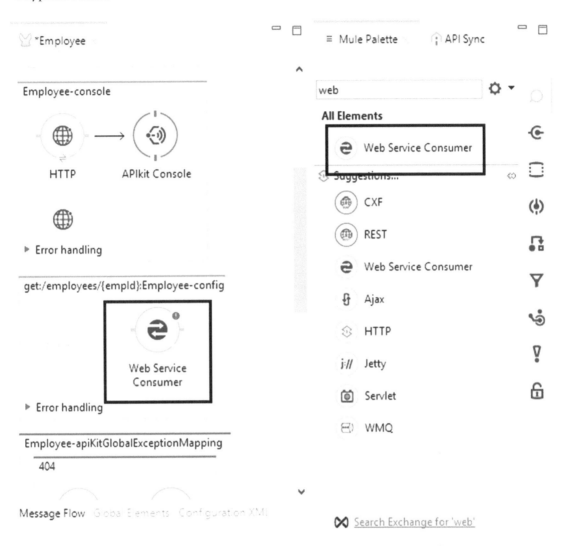

Figure 16.8: Adding Web Service Consumer component to flow

D. Integrating with WSDL

1. Add a WSDL file **Employee.wsdl** for SOAP service at src/main/resource location in the project. **WSDL location** has to be provided as part of Connector configuration in the Web Service Consumer properties. Note – The code for Employee.wsdl file is the same which was created in step A.3.

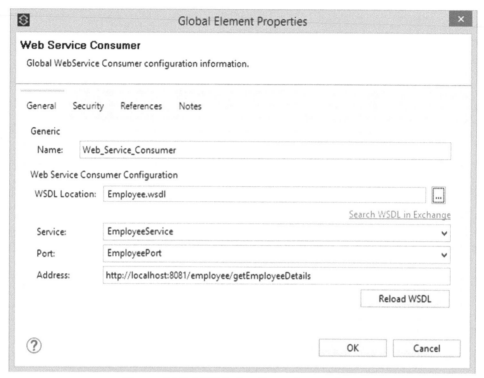

Figure 16.9: WSDL Configuration settings

2. Once the WSDL has been loaded successfully, the input and output of the SOAP has to be transformed using the **Transform Message** Component in Mule.

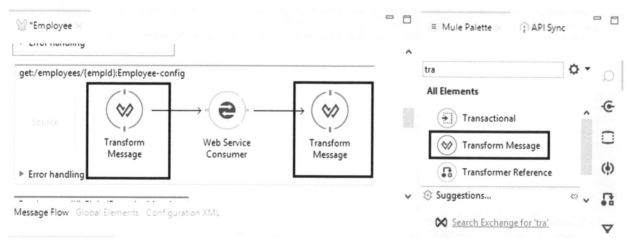

Figure 16.10: Message transformation

3. Map the Transform Message for input and output accordingly. For REST to SOAP Message Transformation, refer the below image and code.

Figure 16.11: REST to SOAP Message Transformation

4. For reference purpose, code for payload is as below:

```
%dw 1.0
%output application/xml
---
{
ns0#GetEmployeeDetailsRequest: {
      ns0#id: flowVars.empId
      }
}
```

5. For SOAP to REST Message Transformation, refer the below image and payload code:

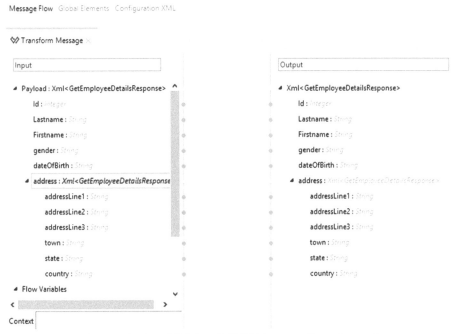

Figure 16.12: SOAP to REST Message Transformation

⟲ Transform Message ✕

Output Payload ▾ ≡₊ ✎ 🗑   ⊞ ⊟ ▢ | Preview

```
1  %dw 1.0
2  %output application/xml
3  %namespace
4  ---
5  {
6      GetEmployeeDetailsResponse: {
7      Id: payload.    GetEmployeeDetailsResponse.Id,
8      Lastname: payload.    GetEmployeeDetailsResponse.Lastname,
9      Firstname: payload.    GetEmployeeDetailsResponse.Firstname,
10     gender: payload.    GetEmployeeDetailsResponse.gender,
11     dateOfBirth: payload.    GetEmployeeDetailsResponse.dateOfBirth,
12     address: {
13         addressLine1: payload.    GetEmployeeDetailsResponse.address.addressLine1,
14         addressLine2: payload.    GetEmployeeDetailsResponse.address.addressLine2,
15         addressLine3: payload.    GetEmployeeDetailsResponse.address.addressLine3,
16         town: payload.    GetEmployeeDetailsResponse.address.town,
17         state: payload.    GetEmployeeDetailsResponse.address.state,
18         country: payload.    GetEmployeeDetailsResponse.address.country
19     }
20     }
21  }
```

Figure 16.13: SOAP to REST Message Transformation output payload

6.   For reference purpose, code for payload is as below:

```
{
     ns0#GetEmployeeDetailsResponse: {
          Id: payload.ns0#GetEmployeeDetailsResponse.Id,
          Lastname: payload.ns0#GetEmployeeDetailsResponse.Lastname,
          Firstname: payload.ns0#GetEmployeeDetailsResponse.Firstname,
          gender: payload.ns0#GetEmployeeDetailsResponse.gender,
          dateOfBirth: payload.ns0#GetEmployeeDetailsResponse.dateOfBirth,
          address: {
               addressLine1: payload.ns0#GetEmployeeDetailsResponse.address.
addressLine1,
               addressLine2: payload.ns0#GetEmployeeDetailsResponse.address.
addressLine2,
               addressLine3: payload.ns0#GetEmployeeDetailsResponse.address.
addressLine3,
               town: payload.ns0#GetEmployeeDetailsResponse.address.town,
               state: payload.ns0#GetEmployeeDetailsResponse.address.state,
               country: payload.ns0#GetEmployeeDetailsResponse.address.country
          }
     }
}
```

7.   Now, running the application from within the studio should automatically open the API console to test the application.

Employee API service

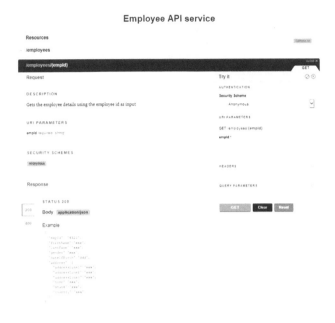

8. Entering a valid value for empId (4321 in our example case) URI parameter and clicking on **GET** button would yield the result as below. Notice that the input is provided through the REST interface and transformed to the Web Service request by Mule Runtime. The SOAP response is transformed back to REST and returned as output. Thus, the Mule's Anypoint Platform can be used to expose complex SOAP services as REST APIs and make integration simple.

WHISHWORKS™

Anticipated Issues

1. Any security configuration required by the SOAP service needs to be done on the Web Service Consumer.

References

1. https://docs.mulesoft.com/anypoint-platform-for-apis/apikit-tutorial
2. https://docs.mulesoft.com/mulc-user-guide/v/3.7/publishing-and-consuming-apis-with-mule
3. http://raml.org/

RECIPE 17

JSON & XML Threat Protection of APIs

APIs exposed to end users could be subjected to malicious XML and JSON threats. A recursive loop of JSON or XML nested elements could increase the object size and thus impact the API performance. This could lead to APIs being unable to respond to genuine client requests. The Mule Anypoint Platform provides out-of-the-box policies that can be applied to the APIs that are vulnerable to these threats. This recipe shows how to safeguard JSON/XML based APIs using JSON/XML Threat Protection Policy.

GitHub location of this recipe:
https://github.com/WHISHWORKS/mule-api-recipes/tree/publish_v1.0/json-xml-threat-protection

Pre-requisites
1. MuleSoft CloudHub Account (https://anypoint.mulesoft.com)
2. API on which policies need to be applied or Book Listing API (used in the document below whose code can be found as book-listing-api.raml in GitHub for reference)
3. Knowledge of Applying Policies
4. Postman plugin for Chrome is installed from (https://www.getpostman.com/docs/introduction)

Process
High Level Steps:
A. JSON Threat Protection Policy configuration, application with the restriction on maximum container depth and testing
B. XML Threat Protection Policy configuration, application with the restriction on maximum container depth and testing

A. JSON Threat Protection Policy
JSON Threat Protection can be achieved by configuring the policy in Anypoint CloudHub Platform with certain input parameters and applying the policy on the desired APIs.
1. Configure the JSON Threat Protection Policy

The policy configuration contains several input parameters:
- **Maximum Container Depth** - Specifies the maximum allowed nested depth. JSON allows you to nest the containers (object and array) in any order to any depth.
- **Maximum String Value Length** - Specifies the maximum length allowed for a string value.

- **Maximum Object Entry Name Length** - Specifies the maximum string length allowed for an object's entry name.
- **Maximum object Entry Count** - Specifies the maximum number of entries allowed in an object.
- **Maximum Array Element Count** - Specifies the maximum number of elements allowed in an array.

2. Apply the Policy

   a. The API administration page lists all active APIs. Search for the API on which the policy is to be applied as given below. This recipe shows policies being applied on the 'Book Listing API'.

Figure 17.1: Selection of API

b. Click on version **1.0** as in this case.
   API administration screen shall be presented as shown below:

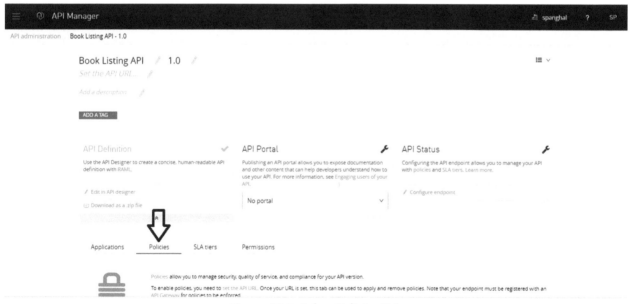

Figure 17.2: Select Policies Tab

c. Click on the **Policies** tab and Select **"JSON Threat Protection"** from the list of available policies and click on **Apply**.

| > | IP whitelist | Security | IP filtered | Apply |
| v | JSON threat protection | Security | JSON threat protected | Apply |

Status   Not applied

Description   Protects against malicious JSON in API requests.

Figure 17.3: Select JSON Threat Protection Policy

d. The **"JSON threat protection"** dialogue appears.

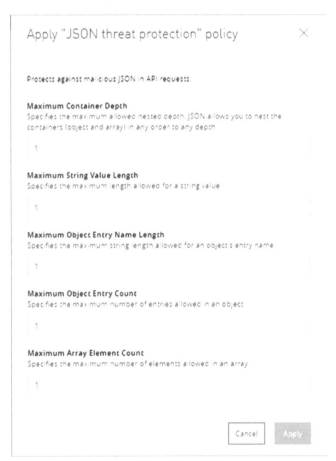

Figure 17.4: JSON threat protection Policy dialog

e. Configure JSON Threat policy with the below values and **Apply**.

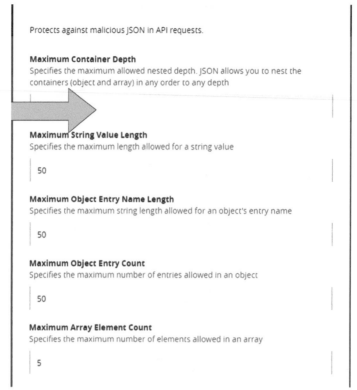

Protects against malicious JSON in API requests.

Maximum Container Depth
Specifies the maximum allowed nested depth. JSON allows you to nest the containers (object and array) in any order to any depth

Maximum String Value Length
Specifies the maximum length allowed for a string value

50

Maximum Object Entry Name Length
Specifies the maximum string length allowed for an object's entry name

50

Maximum Object Entry Count
Specifies the maximum number of entries allowed in an object

50

Maximum Array Element Count
Specifies the maximum number of elements allowed in an array

5

Figure 17.5: Configure JSON threat protection Policy

Here in the above policy the **Maximum Container Depth** field is set to **2**. It specifies the maximum allowed nested depth to 2. So it should result in an error when the input JSON has nesting greater than 2.

3. Test the Policy
   a. Launch Postman and provide API URL: http://booklistinguxapi.cloudhub.io/api/AddBooks (this could change depending on the CloudHub account and API).
   b. Take a simple JSON Input and try to execute the POST service.

```
{
"id": 24,
  "title": "Matilda",
  "author": "Marcella Hazen",
  "price": "$20.99"
}
```

c. POST service is executed successfully with this input.

Figure 17.6: Successful Output

d.   In the sample input below, the JSON has more than two nesting elements. Hence the policy prevents such payload and gives "invalid_json" error.

e.   Input:

```
{
  "books": {
    "genre": {
      "fiction": [
        {
          "classic": {
            "id": "24",
            "title": "Pilgrim's Progress",
            "author": "John Bunyan",
            "price": "$19.21"
          },
          "mystery": [
            {
              "Crime": {
                "id": "24",
                "title": "The Cartel",
                "author": "Don Winslow",
                "price": "$16.45"
              }
            }
          ]
        }
      ]
```

```
            }
        ],
        "non fiction": [
            {
                "Art": {
                    "id": "24",
                    "title": "Ways of Seeing",
                    "author": "John Berger",
                    "price": "$20.99"
                },
                "Cooking": [
                    {
                        "Italian": {
                            "id": "24",
                            "title": "Essentials of Classic Italian Cooking",
                            "author": "Rohald Dahl",
                            "price": "$5.21"
                        },
                        "Mexican": {
                            "id": "24",
                            "title": "Pati'sMexicanTable",
                            "author": "PatiJinich",
                            "price": "$8.46"
                        }
                    }
                ]
            }
        ]
    }
}
```

f. Output:

```
{
    "error": "invalid_json",
    "description": "Container depth has been exceeded. Maximum allowed is: 2"
}
```

Figure 17.7: Output after applying JSON threat protection Policy

Magnified image of output is below:

Figure 17.8: Magnified image of output

B. XML Threat Protection Policy

XML Threat protection can be achieved by configuring the policy in Anypoint CloudHub Platform with certain input parameters and applying the policy on the desired APIs.

1. Configure the XML Threat Protection policy

The policy configuration contains several input parameters:
- **Maximum Node Depth** - Specifies the maximum node depth allowed in the XML.
- **Maximum Attribute Count Per Element** - Specifies the maximum number of attributes allowed for any element. Note that the attributes used for defining namespaces are not counted.
- **Maximum Child Count** - Specifies a limit on the maximum number of children allowed for any element in the XML document.
- **Maximum Text Length** - Specifies a limit on the maximum length, in characters, of any text nodes present in the XML document.
- **Maximum Attribute Length** - Specifies a limit on the maximum length, in characters, of any attributes

for any element in the XML document.
- **Maximum Comment Length** - Specifies a limit on the maximum number of comment characters in the XML document.

2. Apply the Policy
   Navigate to the **Policies** tab of an API. Click **Apply** on **XML Threat Protection policy**. The **Apply "XML threat protection"** dialogue appears. Please fill all required fields. Configure XML Threat Protection policy with the below values and Apply policy to the already configured API. Here in the above policy, we may set the field Maximum Container Depth to 3. It specifies the maximum allowed nested depth to 3. So it should result in an error when the input JSON has nesting greater than 3.

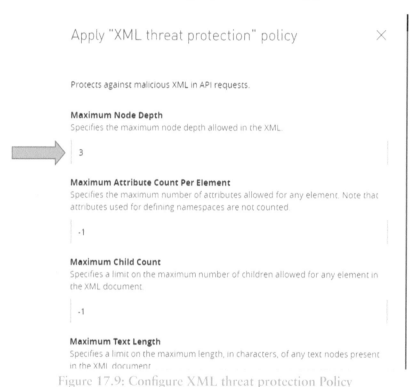

Figure 17.9: Configure XML threat protection Policy

3. Test the Policy
   a. Launch Postman and provide API URL: http://booklistinguxapi.cloudhub.io/api/AddBooksXML (this could change depending on the CloudHub account and your API)
   b. Take a simple XML Input and try to execute the POST service.

```
<classic>
 <id>24</id>
 <title>Pilgrim Progress</title>
 <author>John Bunyan</author>
 <price>$19.21</price>
</classic>
```

c. POST service is executed successfully with this input.

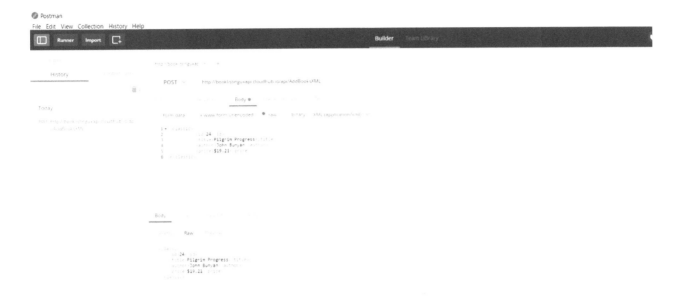

Figure 17.10: Successful XML Input

d. In the sample input below, the XML has more than three nesting elements. Hence the policy prevents such payload and gives "invalid_xml" error.

e. Input:

```
<?xml version="1.0" encoding="UTF-8" ?>
<books>
  <genre>
    <fiction>
      <classic>
        <id>24</id>
        <title>Pilgrim&#x27;s Progress</title>
        <author>John Bunyan</author>
        <price>$19.21</price>
      </classic>
      <mystery>
        <Crime>
          <id>24</id>
          <title>The Cartel</title>
          <author>Don Winslow</author>
<price>$16.45</price>
        </Crime>
      </mystery>
    </fiction>
    <non fiction>
      <Art>
```

```
            <id>24</id>
            <title>Ways of Seeing</title>
            <author>John Berger</author>
            <price>$20.99</price>
          </Art>
          <Cooking>
            <Italian>
              <id>24</id>
              <title>Essentials of Classic Italian Cooking</title>
              <author>Rohald Dahl</author>
              <price>$5.21</price>
            </Italian>
            <Mexican>
              <id>24</id>
              <title>Pati&#x27;sMexicanTable</title>
              <author>PatiJinich</author>
              <price>$8.46</price>
            </Mexican>
          </Cooking>
        </non fiction>
      </genre>
</books>
```

f. Output:

```
{
"error": "invalid_xml",
  "description": "Node depth count has been exceeded. Maximum allowed is: 3"
}
```

Figure 17.11: Output after applying XML threat protection Policy

Magnified image of output is below:

Figure 17.12: Magnified Image of Output

References

1. https://docs.mulesoft.com/api-manager/json-xml-threat-policy

RECIPE 18

Insight – Tracking APIs

Insight is a feature that is currently available for applications/APIs deployed to CloudHub workers. It gives you in-depth visibility into business transactions and events on Mule applications that are deployed to CloudHub. By tracking the data as it is processed at each step in an application, Insight makes information searchable and helps to find and recover from any errors that occurred during message processing and replay any failed transactions instantly.

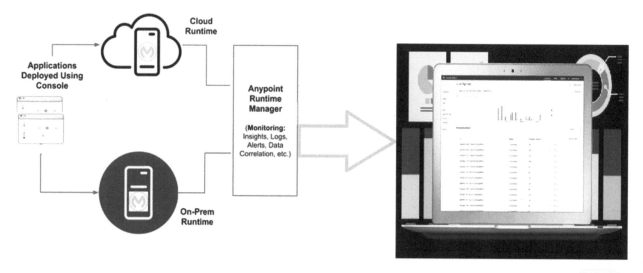

Figure 18.1: Main Flow

Insight helps to answer questions about your integrated apps, such as:
- What happened with a particular transaction or synchronization?
- When did the transaction occur? How long did it take?
- What was the result of a transaction?
- If something went wrong during processing, at what point did the failure occur?

GitHub location of this recipe:
https://github.com/WHISHWORKS/mule-api-recipes/tree/publish_v1.0/book-catalogue

Pre requisites

1. RAML file with book catalogue operations, designed in MuleSoft API Designer (<GitHub location of this recipe>/src/main/api/book-catalogue.raml)
2. MuleSoft Anypoint Studio 6.1 or above (https://www.mulesoft.com/lp/dl/studio) installed
3. MuleSoft CloudHub Account (https://anypoint.mulesoft.com)
4. Access to a deployed Application **book-catalogue-impl** whose deployable code can be accessed as book-catalogue.zip file available at
https://github.com/WHISHWORKS/mule-api-recipes/tree/publish_v1.0/deploy-api-proxy
5. MySQL Database accessible from cloud with Admin rights to create database and users (Refer to Recipe **'WHISHWORKS_APIRecipes_Implementing_a_New_API'** for more information)

Process

High Level Steps:

A. Insight Setup on an Application
B. Testing

A. **Insight Setup on Application**
1. Open a browser.
2. Go to https://anypoint.mulesoft.com/.
3. Login to **Anypoint Platform** and click on **Runtime Manager** shown as below:

Figure 18.2: Anypoint Home

4. The Runtime Manager Page appears, listing all deployed applications and APIs.
5. Search the existing deployed Application **book-catalogue-impl.**
6. Select that application. It will display additional information on the right side (as shown below):

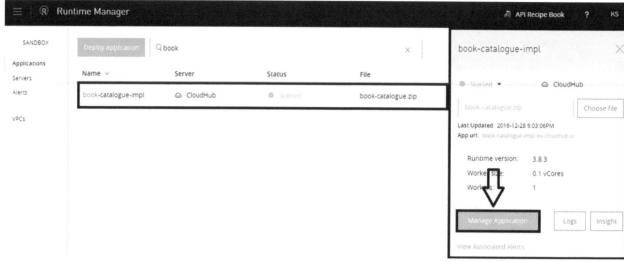

Figure 18.3: Runtime Manager

7. Click **Manage Application** to see the application's dashboard and settings page.

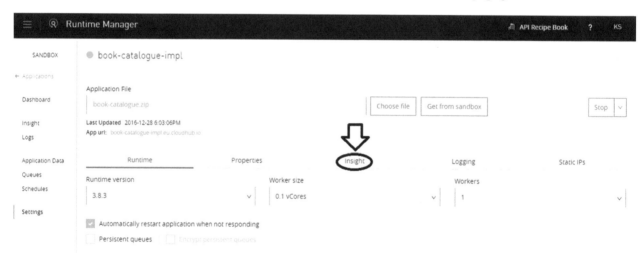

Figure 18.4: Book Catalogue Application

8. In the **Settings** menu, select the **Insight** tab.

Figure 18.5: Insight options

9. Select one of the tracking options:
    a. Disabled – to not use Insight
    b. Metadata - to simply track events
    c. Metadata and Replay - to track events and enable the ability to instantly replay a transaction from the console
10. Select third option and click **Apply Changes.**
11. After the changes are applied, confirmation will be shown as below:

Figure 18.6: Insight option Confirmation

12. After enabling Insight, the following events are tracked by default:
    a. Data that passes through endpoints (inbound and outbound) in Mule applications
    b. Flow initiation and completion

B. **Testing**
   1. Open the browser
   2. Hit this URL http://book-catalogue-ux.eu.cloudhub.io/catalogue/books/24 and get book information.
   3. Again go to **Anypoint platform** which is shown in step A.5.
   4. Click on **Insight** as shown below:

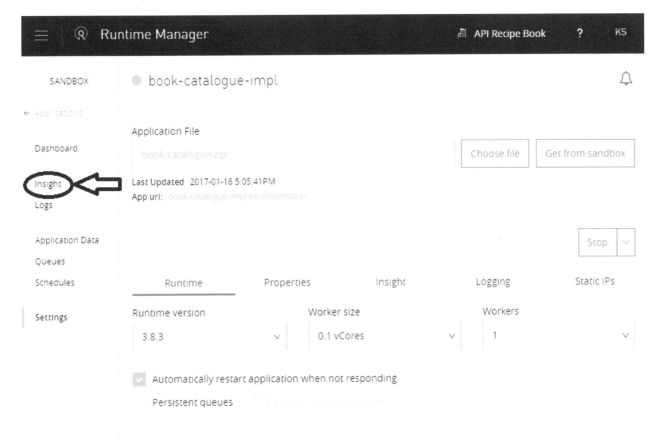

Figure 18.7: Runtime Manager - Insight

5. Insight dashboard screen appears. Here, events within the flow will be tracked that handle your business transaction.

6. Transaction list will be updated as shown below:

Figure 18.8: Insight Dashboard

7. Select the transaction and get low level details of the transaction like event details, metadata, etc.

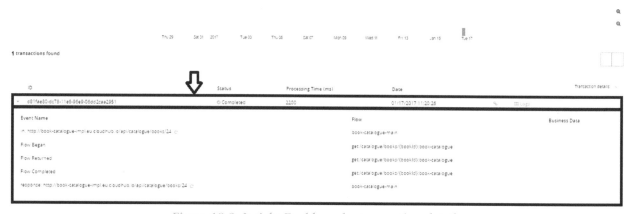

Figure 18.9: Insight Dashboard – transaction details

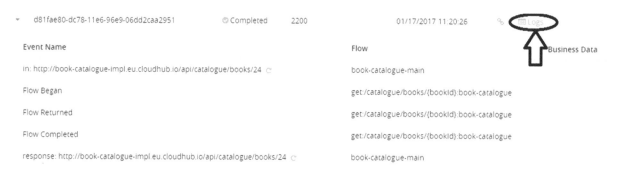

| d81fae80-dc78-11e6-96e9-06dd2caa2951 | Completed | 2200 | 01/17/2017 11:20:26 | | Logs |

Event Name	Flow	Business Data
in: http://book-catalogue-impl.eu.cloudhub.io/api/catalogue/books/24	book-catalogue-main	
Flow Began	get:/catalogue/books/{bookId}:book-catalogue	
Flow Returned	get:/catalogue/books/{bookId}:book-catalogue	
Flow Completed	get:/catalogue/books/{bookId}:book-catalogue	
response: http://book-catalogue-impl.eu.cloudhub.io/api/catalogue/books/24	book-catalogue-main	

Figure 18.10: Transaction details Zoom

8. Logs can be checked for any transaction by clicking the **Logs** link as shown above.

● book-catalogue-impl   Search Results   △

`1/17 11:20 - 1/17 11:20 ✕`   Q Search   Advanced ˅

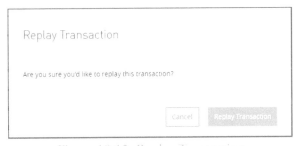

```
11:20:28.351    01/17/2017    Worker-0    [book-catalogue-impl].book-catalogue-httpListenerConfig.worker.04
    INFO
Fetched the record

11:20:34.498    01/17/2017    Worker-0    [book-catalogue-impl].book-catalogue-httpListenerConfig.worker.04
    INFO
Fetched the record
```

Figure 18.11: Log info for completed transaction

9. After investigating the logs and resolving the issue that caused the transaction failure, transaction can be replayed with ⟳ icon.
    Note: Replay only works for flows that have inbound endpoints.
10. The confirmation message for replay appears on click of the **replay** icon.

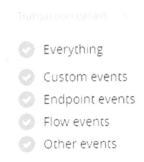

Figure 18.12: Replay Transaction

11. Click on **Replay Transaction.**

Figure 18.13: Replay Transaction Confirmation

12. Within transactions, use the **Transaction Details** to further refine the types of events that Insight displays for each transaction. Click the **Transaction Details dropdown** to reveal possible filter criteria.

Transaction details ˅

✓ Everything

✓ Custom events

✓ Endpoint events

✓ Flow events

✓ Other events

Figure 18.14: Transaction Filter

Anticipated Issues

1. Replay only works for flows that have inbound endpoints.

References

1. https://docs.mulesoft.com/runtime-manager/insight
2. http://blogs.mulesoft.com/dev/anypoint-platform-dev/announcing-cloudhub-insight-real-time-visibility-message-replay-and-root-cause-analysis/

RECIPE 19

Enabling Custom Business Events to Track Incoming Requests on the API

All businesses demand that key events within the business processes should be tracked and made visible to the IT Operations or business heads.

Custom business events can be designed and implemented to provide insights into runtime transactions. This enables administrators, support personnel and business users to identify points of failure and address them either reactively or proactively.

Mule provides two out-of-the-box options to track business events:
1. Custom business events at specific points within a flow
2. Default event tracking

As a design recommendation, **Default event tracking** should be enabled only after considering performance requirements of the services. When default events are enabled, all the data is tracked by the Mule Runtime and hence it may become a performance overhead.

Alternately, **custom business events** provide flexibility to the architects and developers to capture and track only such business data which provides traces with minimal performance impact.

This recipe explains how custom business events can be generated and tracked with Mule Anypoint Platform.

GitHub location of this recipe: https://github.com/WHISHWORKS/mule-api-recipes/tree/publish_v1.0/business-events

Pre-requisites
A. RAML file with book catalogue operations, designed in MuleSoft API Designer (<GitHub location of this recipe>/src/main/api/business-events.raml)
B. MuleSoft Anypoint Studio 6.1 or above (https://www.mulesoft.com/lp/dl/studio) installed
C. MySQL Database accessible from cloud with admin rights to create database and users
D. MySQL Connector/J connector JAR (mysql-connector-java-5.1.18) to connect database available from https://dev.mysql.com/downloads/connector/j/
E. MuleSoft CloudHub Account (https://anypoint.mulesoft.com)
F. Knowledge of Insights[1]
G. Install Postman plugin in Chrome from chrome webstore

Process
High Level Steps:

A. Implementation of the API - demonstrate POST method implementation
B. Deploying to CloudHub
C. Create Proxy and Configure proxy with Implementation URL
D. Configure an API proxy & Deploying to CloudHub
E. Tracking business events with Insights

A. Implementation of the API

1. Download the **MySQL DDL script** from <GitHub location of this recipe>/src/main/sql/business-events.sql.
2. From the command line on the MySQL server system execute
   mysql –u[admin _user] –p[admin_password] < [/path/to/]business-events.sql.

```
# business-events.sql
CREATE USER 'bc_user'@'%' IDENTIFIED BY 'password';
CREATE DATABASE business_events CHARACTER SET utf8;
GRANT ALL PRIVILEGES ON business_events.* TO 'bc_user'@'%' IDENTIFIED BY 'password';
USE book_catalogue;
CREATE TABLE orders (id int, order_status varchar(255), operator varchar(255),
price varchar(255));
```

NOTE: This MySQL database should be accessible from cloud.

3. Download mysql-connector-java-5.X.XX.zip from https://dev.mysql.com/downloads/connector/j/ as mentioned in pre-requisites.
4. Download the **RAML file** from GitHub location as mentioned in pre-requisites above.
5. Launch **Mule Anypoint Studio** and create a new Mule Project as shown below:
   File > New > Mule Project

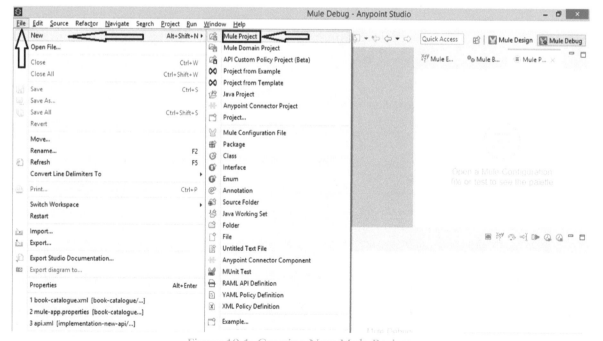

Figure 19.1: Creating New Mule Project

6.   In the **New Mule Project** dialogue that comes up, provide the **Project Name** as **business-events.** Select the checkbox **Add APIkit components** and provide the path of the **business-events.raml** file downloaded above. Click **Finish.**

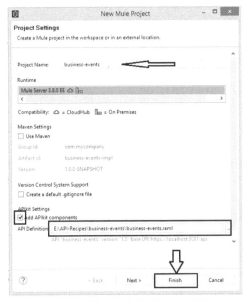

Figure 19.2: New Mule Project Wizard

7.   This will create a skeleton project and skeleton Mule Flows for each of the HTTP operations PUT, GET, POST and DELETE along with a main APIkit Router flow and APIkit Console flow based on the RAML definition.

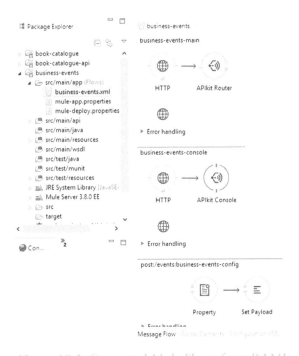

Figure 19.3: Generated Mule Flows from RAML

8. Create and configure the **Global Component** for MySQL Database as shown below:
9. Click on **Global Elements** as shown above.
    a. Click on **Create** button.

Figure 19.4: Global Mule Configuration Elements

b. **Choose Global Type** dialogue appears. Search for **MySQL** in Filter field for **MySQL Database Connector.**

Figure 19.5: Choose Global Type

c. Select **MySQL Configuration** that appears under **Connector Configuration** as shown below and click **OK.**

Figure 19.6: Global Element - Connector Configuration

d. **Global Element Properties** dialogue would be displayed.

e. Fill **Host** [mysql_server_IP or DNS], **Port** [default 3336], **User** [bc_user], **Password** [password] and **Database** [book_catalogue] details in MySQL configuration as shown below:
   NOTE: The User, Password and Database should match as given in MySQL DDL script file A.2 above.

f. Click **Add File** to add **MySQL connector driver** to connect to MySQL Database. Select the **zip/jar file** downloaded in step A.3 above.

g. Click **Test Connection** to check that the database connector is configured correctly and is able to successfully connect to MySQL.

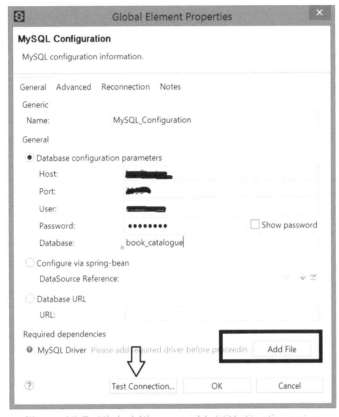

Figure 19.7: Global Element - MySQL Configuration

h. Successful connection message should be shown as below. Click **OK** on the Test connection dialogue.

Figure 19.8: Test Connection

i.   Click **OK** button in the **Global Element Properties** dialogue.

j.   The configured MySQL element should appear in **Global Elements** tab as shown below:

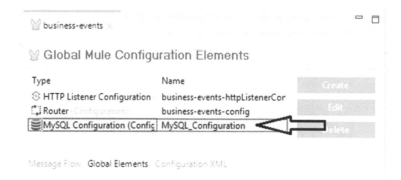

Figure 19.9: Global Element

10.   Navigate to **Message Flow** tab.

    a. The skeleton Mule Flow for POST will look as below:

Figure 19.10: POST Method Skeleton

b.   Click on the **Configuration XML** tab and search with the flow name i.e. post:/events:business-events-config. The corresponding POST Mule Flow XML content should look like:

```
<flow name="post:/events:business-events-config">
  <set-property propertyName="Content-Type"
value="application/json" doc:name="Property"/>
  <set-payload value="{&#xA;
&quot;id&quot;:&quot;2345&quot;,&#xA;
&quot;order_status&quot;: &quot;FAILED&quot;,&#xA;
&quot;operator&quot;: &quot;Savings&quot;,&#xA;
&quot;price&quot;: &quot;25.25&quot;&#xA;}" doc:name="Set Payload"/>
</flow>
```

11.   Implement the HTTP POST method in **post:/events:business-events-config** flow.

    a. In this POST Mule Flow replace the XML with the following XML content:

```
<flow name="post:/events:business-events-config">
<json:json-to-object-transformer returnClass="java.util.HashMap" doc:name="JSON
to Object" />
<db:insert config-ref="MySQL_Configuration" doc:name="Insert Into DB">
      <db:parameterized-query><![CDATA[insert into orders (id, order_status,
operator, price) VALUES (#[payload.id],#[payload.order_status],#[payload.
operator],#[payload.price])]]></db:parameterized-query>
</db:insert>
<db:select config-ref="MySQL_Configuration" doc:name="read from db">
      <db:parameterized-query><![CDATA[Select * fromorders]]></db:parameterized-
query>
</db:select>
<logger message="#[payload[1].order_status]" level="INFO" doc:name="Logger"/>

<tracking:custom-event event-name="Retrieved Orders 1" doc:name="Retrieved
Orders 1">
      <tracking:meta-data key="Order Id" value="#[payload[0].ID]" />
      <tracking:meta-data key="Order Status" value="#[[payload[0].order_
status]]" />
      <tracking:meta-data key="Charge Amount" value="#[[payload[0].price]]" />
</tracking:custom-event>
<tracking:custom-event event-name="Retrieved Orders 2" doc:name="Retrieved
Orders 2">
      <tracking:meta-data key="Order Id" value="#[payload[1].ID]" />
      <tracking:meta-data key="Order Status" value="#[[payload[1].order_
status]]" />
      <tracking:meta-data key="Charge Amount" value="#[[payload[1].order_status]]"
/>
</tracking:custom-event>
</flow>
```

b.   In the code above, the request JSON is received and transformed to database object type. The database then inserts the data into orders table using the statement 'insert into orders (id, order_status, operator, price) VALUES (#[payload.id],#[payload.order_status], #[payload.operator],#[payload.price])'. The second DB component is used to read all data from table orders. Two custom business events component is used in this example to track success and failure with respect to number of data sets in orders table.

c.   **Save** the file and click on **Mule Flow** tab. The corresponding POST Mule Flow should now look like:

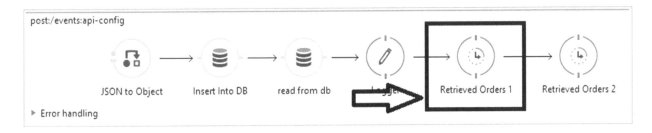

Figure 19.11: POST Mule Flow

221

d. In the same flow, the custom business event element is highlighted by the arrow. Set the Key Performance Indicators (KPIs) to capture business-related information that needs to be tracked from the payload. In this example, order id, order status and order amount will be tracked as shown below. This will be used at a later stage.

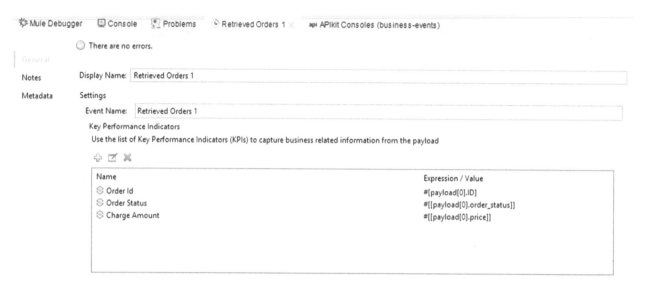

Figure 19.12: Custom Business component configuration

e. The flow consists of two business events which will populate the first and second row of orders table of the database. If orders table has more than or equal to two rows, then it will not return any error, but if it consists of less than two rows then custom business event will return an error accordingly.

12. Similarly, DELETE method can be completed. A sample implementation can be found at 'GitHub location of this recipe'.

13. Now, all the flows are completed. It's time to build and deploy the application to CloudHub.

14. Right click on the **business-events** project and **Export** the zip file of the project as shown below:

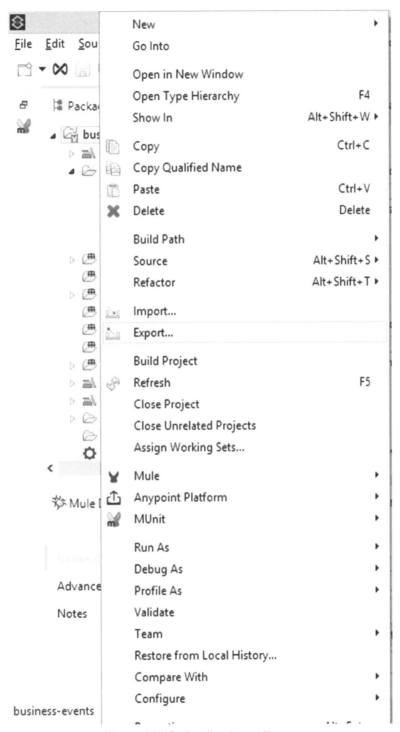

Figure 19.13: Application – Export

15. Select **Mule > Anypoint Studio Project to Mule Deployable Archive (includes Studio metadata)** and click **Next.**

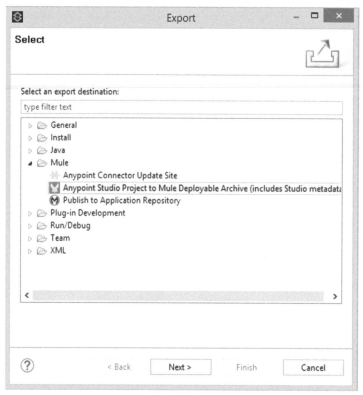

Figure 19.14: Export Dialogue

16. Select the path on the computer where the archive should be saved. Uncheck **Attach profile source** checkbox as shown below. Click **Finish.**

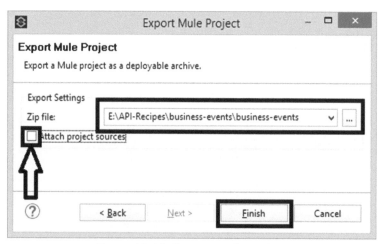

Figure 19.15: Export Mule Project

B. **Deploying to CloudHub**
   1. Open a browser and login to Anypoint platform https://anypoint.mulesoft.com/.
   2. Select **Runtime Manager.**

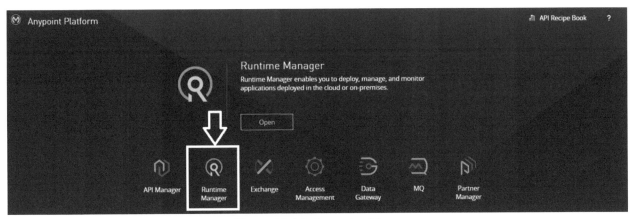

Figure 19.16: Anypoint Home

3. **Runtime Manager** Page appears. Click on **Deploy Application**.

Figure 19.17: Runtime Manager

4. The Deploy Application page opens:
   a. Fill a unique name in **Application Name** i.e. business-events-impl.
   b. Click on **Choose file** to select archive (.zip) file which is exported from Anypoint Studio in step A.15 above.
   c. Change Worker size to 0.1 vCores.
   d. Retain the rest of the fields as populated by default.
   e. Click on **Deploy Application.**

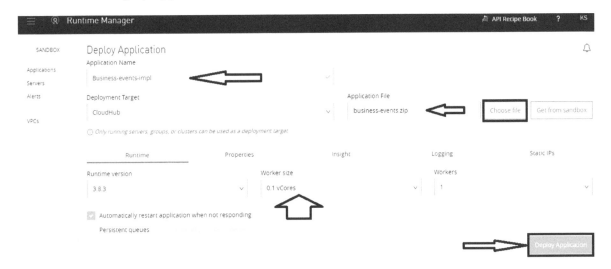

Figure 19.18: Deploy Application

5. After some time, a green icon will be displated with the status **Started** as shown below:

Figure 19.19: Application Deployed Status

6. Once the project is deployed, copy the **App url:** as shown above (business-events-impl.eu.cloudhub.io). NOTE: This URL may vary depending on the cloud instance.

7. Click **Manage Application** to see the application's dashboard and settings page.

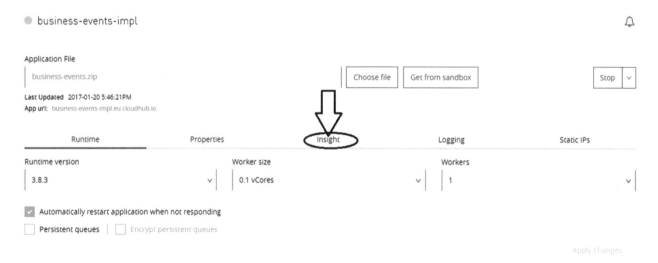

Figure 19.20: Application Dashboard

8. Click on **Insight** tab.
9. Select **Metadata and Replay** radio button and click **Apply Changes**.

Figure 19.21: Application Dashboard – Insight

10. It will track business events and enable the ability to instantly replay a transaction from the console as shown below:
11. Check the Insight dashboard without hitting the application from browser or Postman. Click on **Insight** as shown below:

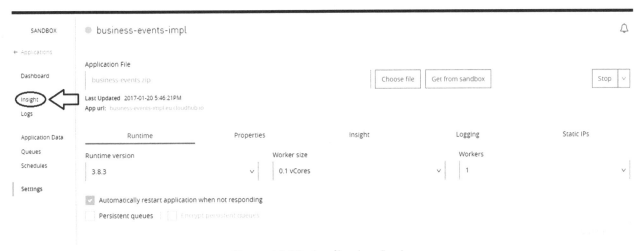

Figure 19.22: Application Setting

12. Insight dashboard will be shown as below:

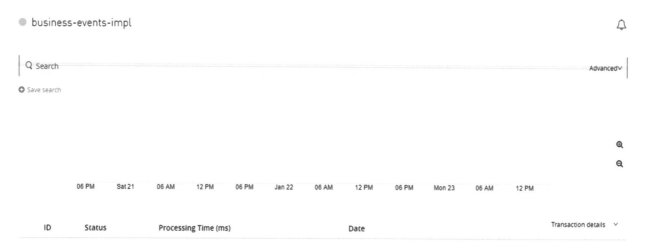

Figure 19.23: Insight Dashboard

13. Now, it's time to create a proxy API.

C. **Create Proxy and Configure proxy with Implementation URL**
   1. Click on the icon shown below:

Figure 19.24: Runtime Manager

2. Select **API Manager.**

Figure 19.25: Anypoint Platform Menu

3. API Manager Page appears. Click **Add new API.**

Figure 19.26: API Manager

4. The Add API page will be displayed. Fill the fields as follows:
   a. Enter the API name of **Custom Business Events UX.**
   b. Enter Version name as **1.0.**
   c. Leave the API Endpoint blank for now.
   d. Enter the description as **Illustrate custom business events tracking.**
   e. Click **Add.**

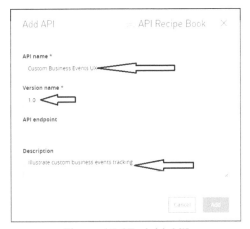

Figure 19.27: Add API

5. The API administration page for newly created API appears.

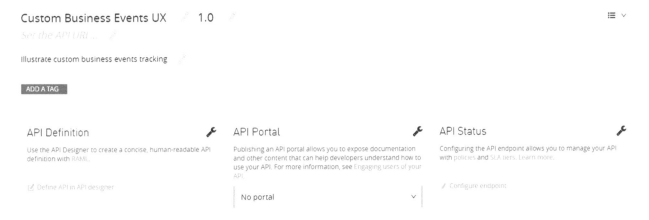

Figure 19.28: Custom Business Events UX

6. It's time to configure an API Proxy with this API.

D. Configure an API proxy & Deploying to CloudHub
1. Back in the API Administration page, click on **Configure endpoint** under API Status as shown below:

Figure 19.29: API Status

2. Fill the information as follows:
   a. Select **Endpoint with a proxy**.
   b. Leave the Type to the default HTTP URL.
   c. Set the Implementation URI to: http://business-events-impl.eu.cloudhub.io/api.
   d. Check the checkbox **Configure proxy for CloudHub,** since we will be deploying to Anypoint Platform CloudHub service.
   e. Retain the rest of the fields as populated by default.
   f. Click **Save** & **Deploy.**

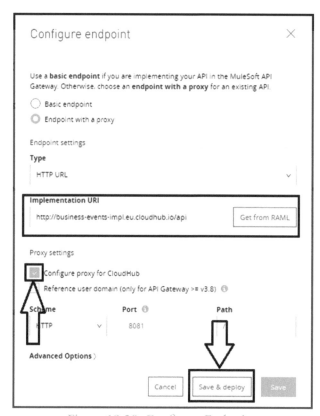

Figure 19.30: Configure Endpoint

3. Deploy Proxy dialogue would be displayed. Click on **Deploy Proxy** as shown below:

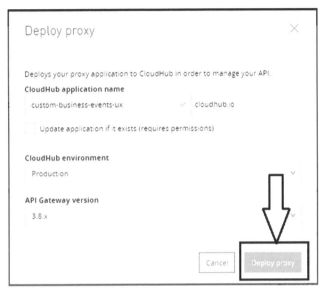

Figure 19.31: Deploy Proxy

4. Proxy API deployment will initiate. The deploy status would indicate **Starting Application.**

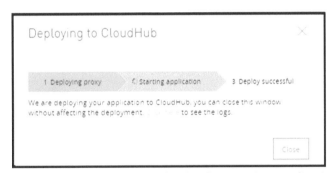

Figure 19.32: Deploying to CloudHub – Starting Application

5. After some time, the status should change to **Deploy Successful** as shown below:

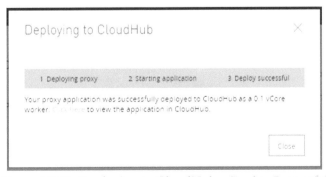

Figure 19.33: Deploying to CloudHub – Deploy Successful

6. Click on **Close** button.
7. Once the API is deployed, API Status content will be shown as below. Copy the API URL under API Status (custom-business-events-ux.eu.cloudhub.io).

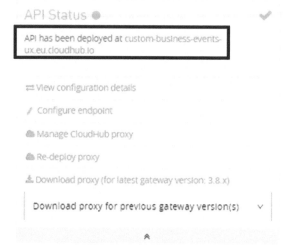

Figure 19.34: API Status – After Proxy API Deployment

E. **Testing and Tracking business events**
   1. Launch Postman Chrome Application as mentioned in pre-requisites.

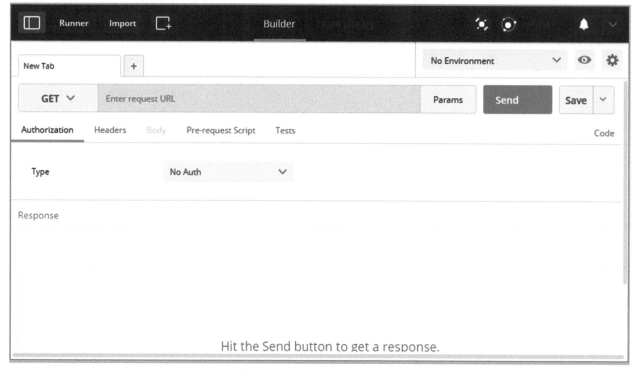

Figure 19.35: Postman Home

2. Select **POST** Method which has to be tested from the dropdown.
    a. Provide URL (Copied URL + /events) http://custom-business-events-ux.eu.cloudhub.io/events to post a business event as shown below:

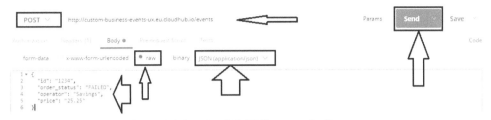

Figure 19.36: 1st POST Request in Postman

b. Click **Body**. Select **raw** and then select **JSON (application/json)** from dropdown.
c. Provide Event details sample data as shown below:

```
{
  "id": "1234",
  "order_status": "FAILED",
  "operator": "Savings",
  "price": "25.25"
}
```

d. Click **Send** to invoke the API.
e. Click **Raw** and the response will be shown as below:

```
Execution of the expression "payload[1].order_status" failed. (org.mule.api.
expression.ExpressionRuntimeException).
```

Figure 19.37: 1st POST Response in Postman

f. The reason for this error is already explained in step A.11.e.
g. Post second event data by providing input as shown below:

Figure 19.38: Second POST Request in Postman

h.   Provide Event details sample data as shown below:

```
{
  "id": "2345",
  "order_status": "SUCCESS",
  "operator": "Savings",
  "price": "5.25"
}
```

i.   Click **Raw** and the following response will be shown:

```
[
{"price":"25.25","operator":"Savings","order_status":"FAILED","id":1234},
{"price":"5.25","operator":"Savings","order_status":"SUCCESS","id":2345}
]
```

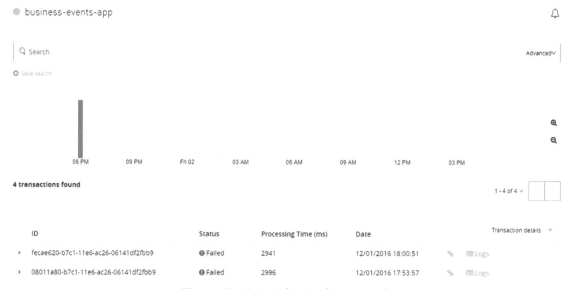

Figure 19.39: Second POST Response in Postman

3.   Again go to **Anypoint Platform** which is shown in step B.11.
4.   Select the **Insight** tab on the left side. It shows the Custom Business Events tracked for the application as shown below. It provides information like ID, Status, Processing time, Date. It also shows a timeline when the various transactions have occurred.
5.   Click on **Insight**. The corresponding screen appears as shown as below:

Figure 19.40: Insight Tracking Details

6. In the first case, if the order table has only one row, then the second business event element will return an error as shown below:

Figure 19.41: Insight Dashboard – Failed event

7. As explained in step A.11.e, if the orders table has two rows then both the business events elements will return a value accordingly.

Figure 19.42: Insight Dashboard – completed event

8. Logs can be checked for any transaction on click of Logs where you can analyse the root cause of failure for any event of transaction. It also helps to recover from any errors that might have occurred.

Anticipated Issues

1. Replay only works for flows that have inbound endpoints.

References

1. https://docs.mulesoft.com/mule-management-console/v/3.7/business-events-use-cases
2. https://www.mulesoft.com/exchange#!/tracking-custom-business-event
3. https://docs.mulesoft.com/mule-user-guide/v/3.6/business-events#best-practices

RECIPE 20

Manage Anypoint MQ with its APIs

A nypoint MQ is an enterprise multi-tenant, cloud messaging service that performs advanced asynchronous messaging scenarios between applications. Anypoint MQ is fully integrated with Anypoint Platform, offering role-based access control, client application management, and connectors. It provides fully hosted and managed queues and message exchanges in the cloud.

This recipe would boost your confidence level on MuleSoft Anypoint Platform for how easy and quick it is to implement a messaging service via AnypointMQ and deploy to MuleSoft's cloud platform CloudHub.

GitHub location of this recipe: https://github.com/WHISHWORKS/mule-api-recipes/tree/publish_v1.0/anypoint-mq-api

Pre-requisites
1. RAML file with book catalogue operations, designed in MuleSoft API Designer (<GitHub location fo this recipe>/src/main/api/mq.raml)
2. MuleSoft Anypoint Studio 6.1 or above (https://www.mulesoft.com/lp/dl/studio) installed
3. MuleSoft CloudHub Account with admin privileges (https://anypoint.mulesoft.com)

Process

High Level Steps:
A. Setup Anypoint MQ Access Environment
B. Create Queue in Anypoint MQ
C. Implementation of API
D. Deploying to CloudHub
E. Testing

A. Setup Anypoint MQ Access Environment
1. Open a browser and login to Anypoint platform https://anypoint.mulesoft.com/.
2. Click **Access Management** from the left navigation bar or from the main Anypoint Platform screen.

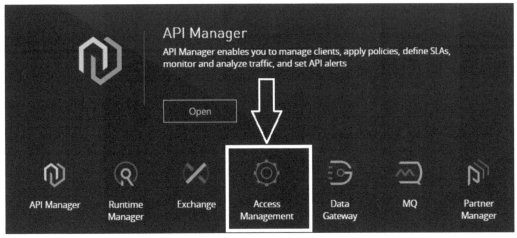

Figure 20.1: Anypoint Platform Home

3. **Access Management** page appears. Click **Users**.
4. Click **Username** value as shown below:

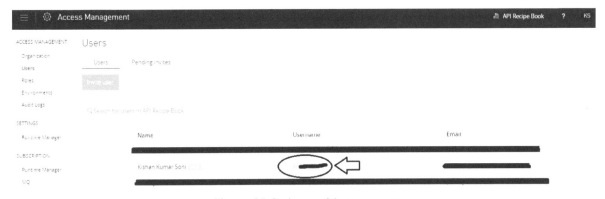

Figure 20.2: Access Management

5. Click **MQ** and set the environment and permissions.

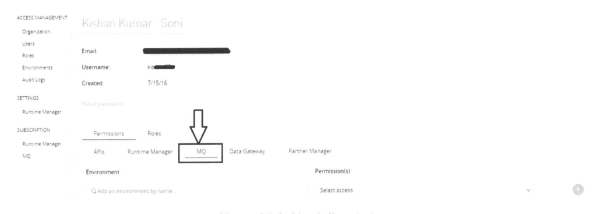

Figure 20.3: User's Permission

6. Select **Environment** as **Sandbox** from the Environment dropdown. For permissions, click **Select all** to set all permissions in **Permission(s)** dropdown as shown below:

Figure 20.4: MQ Permissions

7. Click **plus icon** to add permissions and environment as shown above.
8. Selected accesses have been added as shown below:

Figure 20.5: Added Permissions

B. Create Queue in Anypoint MQ

1. Click on **Menu** icon as shown below:

Figure 20.6: Menu icon

2.   Select **MQ** from the Menu as shown below:

Figure 20.7: MQ Menu

3.   Select **Environment** as **Sandbox**. Then, click **Select** as shown below:

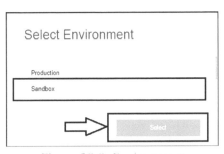

Figure 20.8: Environment

4.   MQ home page appears. Click **Destinations** as shown below:

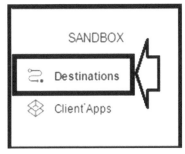

Figure 20.9: MQ Home

5. Click the **blue plus** icon.
6. In the drop-down, click **Queue** as shown below:

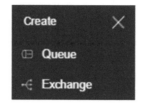

Figure 20.10: Create

7. **Create Queue** dialogue opens.
   a. Write a **unique Id** as sample-recipe-mq.
   b. Retain the rest of the fields as populated by default.
   c. Click on **Save Changes.**

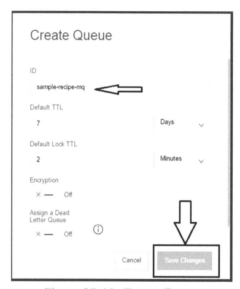

Figure 20.11: Create Queue

8. Queue **sample-recipe-mq** will be created in queue list as shown below:

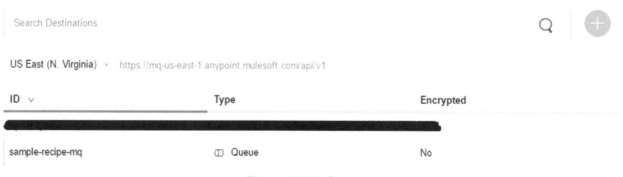

Figure 20.12: Queues

9. Click on the row to view details about a queue and to delete a queue as shown below:

10. Number of messages (now 0 in **In Queue**) can be seen under queue details on right side of the above image.
11. Now, click on **Client Apps** as shown below:

12. Click the **blue plus** icon.
13. **Create Client App** dialogue opens.
    a. Enter the **Name** as **sample-client-app.**
    b. Click on **Save Changes.**

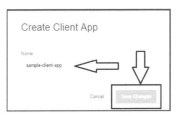

14. Client app **sample-client-app** will be created in the list as shown below:

Figure 20.16: Client App list with Id and secret

15. Copy **Client id** and **Client Secret** for later use.

C. Implementation of API

1. Download the RAML file from GitHub location as mentioned in pre-requisites above.
2. Launch Mule Anypoint Studio and create a new Mule Project as shown below:
   File > New > Mule Project

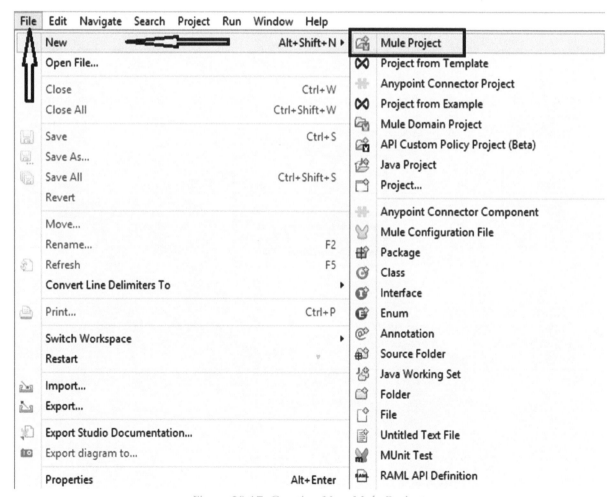

Figure 20.17: Creating New Mule Project

3. In the New Mule Project dialogue that comes up, provide the **Project Name** as **anypoint-mq-api**. Select the checkbox **Add APIkit components** and provide the path of the mq.raml file downloaded above. Click **Finish.**

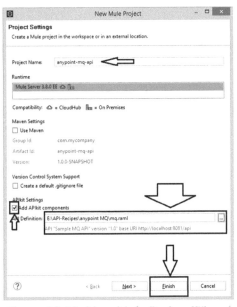

Figure 20.18: New Mule Project Wizard

4. This will create a skeleton project and skeleton Mule Flows for each of the HTTP operations PUT, GET, POST and DELETE along with the main APIkit Router flow and APIkit Console flow based on the RAML definition.

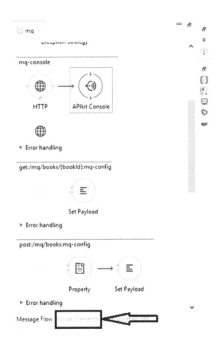

Figure 20.19: Generated Mule Flows from RAML

5. Create and configure the Global Connector for AnypointMQ as shown below:
6. Click on **Global Elements** as shown in Figure above.
a. Click on **Create** button.

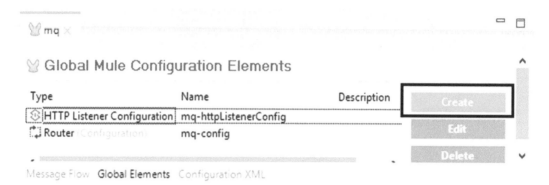

Figure 20.20: Global Elements

b. **Choose Global Type** dialogue appears. Search for anypoint in Filter field for Anypoint MQ Connector.
c. Select **AnypointMQ Configuration** that appears under Connector Configuration as shown below and click **OK**.

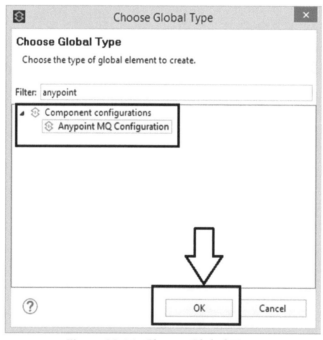

Figure 20.21: Choose Global Type

d. **Global Element Properties** dialogue would be displayed. Fill **Client App Id** and **Client Secret** which has been copied earlier. Retain remaining fields as default. Click **OK.**

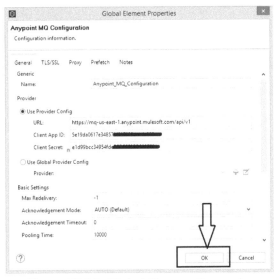

Figure 20.22: Global Element Properties

e. Global Elements will be updated as shown below:

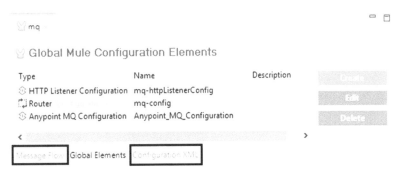

Figure 20.23: Updated Global Element

7. Navigate to **Message Flow** tab.
   a. The skeleton Mule Flow for POST will look as below:

Figure 20.24: POST flow Skeleton

b. Click on the **Configuration XML** tab and search with the flow name i.e. post:/mq/books:mq-config. The corresponding POST Mule Flow XML content should look like:

```
<flow name="post:/mq/books:mq-config">
<set-property propertyName="Content-Type"
value="application/json" doc:name="Property"/>
<set-payload value="{&#xA; &quot;Id&quot;: &quot;24&quot;,&#xA;
&quot;Title&quot;: &quot;Matilda&quot;,&#xA;
&quot;Author&quot;: &quot;Rohald Dahl&quot;,&#xA;
&quot;Price&quot;: &quot;$5.21&quot;&#xA;}" doc:name="Set Payload"/>
</flow>
```

8. Implement the HTTP POST method in post:/mq/books:mq-config flow.
   a. In this POST Mule Flow, replace the XML with the following XML content:

```
<flow name="post:/mq/books:mq-config">
<set-payload value="#[payload]" doc:name="Input Data"/>
<anypoint-mq:publish config-ref="Anypoint_MQ_Configuration" destination="sample-
recipe-mq" doc:name="Anypoint MQ"/>
<logger message="Message ID: #[messageId] -- -- Payload: #[payload]" level="INFO"
doc:name="Message Id logger"/>
<set-payload value="#[messageId]" doc:name="Message Id Return"/>
</flow>
```

In the code above, the request JSON is received and pushed into Anypoint MQ queue i.e. sample-recipe-mq. This flow returns Message Id of the pushed message. With the help of this Message Id, data can be received from the queue.

b. **Save** the file and click on **Mule Flow** tab. The corresponding POST Mule Flow should now look like:

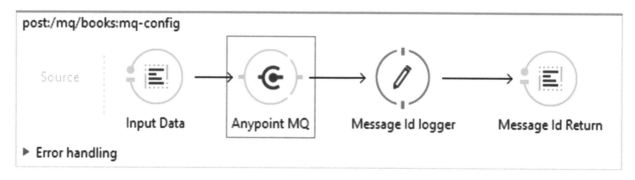

Figure 20.25: POST Mule Flow

9. Similarly, the GET methods can be implemented. A sample implementation can be found at GitHub location of this recipe provided above.
10. Now that all the flows are completed It's time to build and deploy the application to CloudHub.

D. Deploying to CloudHub

1. Right click on the **anypoint-mq-api** project and **Export** the zip file of the project as shown below:

Figure 20.26: Export Option

2. Select **Mule > Anypoint Studio Project to Mule Deployable Archive (includes Studio metadata)** and click **Next.**

Figure 20.27: Export Dialogue

3. Select the path on the computer where the archive should be saved. Uncheck **Attach project sources** checkbox as shown below. Click **Finish.**

Figure 20.28: Export Mule Project

4. Open a browser and login to Anypoint Platform https://anypoint.mulesoft.com/.
5. Select **Runtime Manager.**

Figure 20.29: Anypoint Platform Home - Runtime

6. **Runtime Manager** Page appears. Click on **Deploy Application.**

Figure 20.30: Runtime Manager – Deploy Application

7. The Deploy Application page opens:
   a. Fill a unique name in **Application Name** i.e. **anypoint-mq-api.**
   b. Click on **Choose file** to select archive (.zip) file which is exported from Anypoint Studio in step B.3 above.

c. Change **Worker size** to 0.1 vCores.
d. Retain the rest of the fields as populated by default.
e. Click on **Deploy Application.**

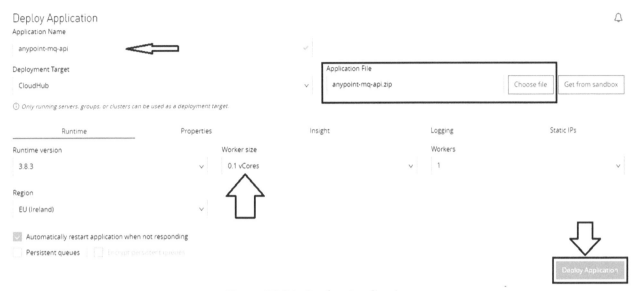

Figure 20.31: Deploy Application

8. Now the application deployment will start as shown below with the status **Deploying.**

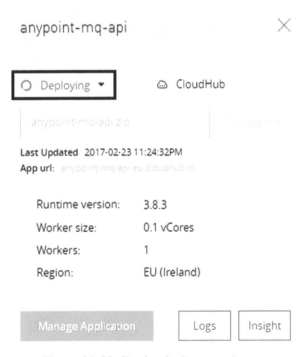

Figure 20.32: Deploy In-Progress Status

9. After some time, status should change to green icon with the status **Started** as shown below:

Figure 20.33: Application Deployed Status

10. Once the project is deployed, copy the **App url:** as shown above (anypoint-mq-api.eu.cloudhub.io). NOTE: This URL may vary depending on the cloud instance.

E. Testing

1. Open a browser and access deployed API anypoint-mq-api.eu.cloudhub.io/console/.

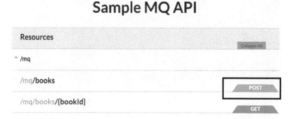

Figure 20.34: Sample MQ Console - POST

The test console is launched with all the methods and resources available for the Anypoint-mq-api.

2. Test **POST** method for resource **/mq/books**:

a. Click on **POST** button as shown above. Use the **default data** (sample as shown below) that is populated in the body.

```
{
  "Id": "24",
  "Title": "Matilda",
  "Author": "Rohald Dahl",
  "Price": "$5.21"
}
```

Figure 20.35: POST Method Request

b.   Click **POST** button to invoke the API. This should return JSON response.

```
"41750f75-24c3-4511-854e-56a02a3ae7f0"
```

Figure 20.36: POST Method Response

c. It will push books data into **sample-recipe-mq** and return Message Id to be retrieved from the queue. Copy this Message Id for later use.

d. Number of messages will be increased from 0 to **1** in **sample-mq-queue.** It can be seen in Anypoint Platform as explained earlier in step B.9 and B.10.

3. Test GET method for resource **/mq/books/{bookId}** with URI parameter **bookId** as **messageId** which is copied in step E.2.c.

a. Click on **GET** in the same screen as shown below:

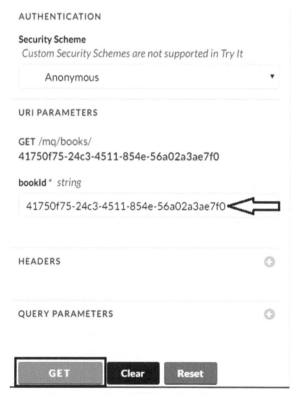

Figure 20.37: Sample MQ Console - GET

b. Provide **bookId** as shown below:

Figure 20.38: GET Method Request

c. Click **GET** to invoke the API. Book details would be returned as shown below:

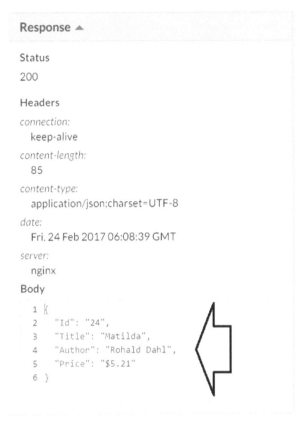

Figure 20.39: GET Method Response

d. This should return JSON as shown below:

```
{
"Id": "24",
"Title": "Matilda",
"Author": "Rohald Dahl",
"Price": "$5.21"
}
```

Note that this is the catalogue created in **POST** method in step E.2.b.

Anticipated Issues

1. Anypoint MQ connector may not provide the ID directly into payload for use. But, it may store it in a variable named as **messageId.**

References

1. https://docs.mulesoft.com/anypoint-mq/
2. https://docs.mulesoft.com/anypoint-mq/mq-tutorial

RECIPE 21

Handle Salesforce Streaming Content with an API

Streaming API works differently from a normal HTTP API. In case of a streaming API, the data is more continuous and event-driven. The objective of this recipe is to create a flow which can consume streaming data from sources like Twitter, Facebook, and Salesforce. For this recipe, Salesforce Connector is used as a streaming inbound connector. The data from Salesforce would be stored in a database.

In **Salesforce**, a PushTopic should be created through which the streaming data can be consumed. Below are the steps to enable streaming in Salesforce (referred from Salesforce Developer's Guide [(3)]):

1. Create a PushTopic based on a **Salesforce Object Query Language (SOQL)** query. This defines the channel.
2. Clients subscribe to the channel.
3. A record is created, updated, deleted, or undeleted (an event occurs). The changes to that record are evaluated.
4. If the record changes match the criteria of the PushTopic query, a notification is generated by the server and received by the subscribed clients.

From the Mule Flow, the Salesforce Streaming Inbound Connector would be used to consume from the channel.

GitHub location of this recipe: https://github.com/WHISHWORKS/mule-api-recipes/tree/publish_v1.0/streaming-api

Pre requisites
1. **MuleSoft Anypoint Studio** installed https://www.mulesoft.com/lp/dl/studio/
2. Access to **MySQL** database accessible from cloud.
3. **SQL** file for the database table is available at <GitHub location of this recipe>/src/main/sql/streaming-api.sql
4. **MySQL Driver** 5.0.8 jar https://dev.mysql.com/downloads/connector/j/5.0.html
5. **Salesforce** Developer Account https://developer.salesforce.com/
6. **SOQL** basic understanding

Process
High Level Steps:
- A. Create PushTopic in Salesforce
- B. Create Flow in Anypoint Studio
- C. Testing the Flow

A. Create PushTopic in Salesforce

1. Login to Salesforce account https://developer.salesforce.com/.

Figure 21.1: Salesforce Login

2. Go to **My Developer Account** as shown below:

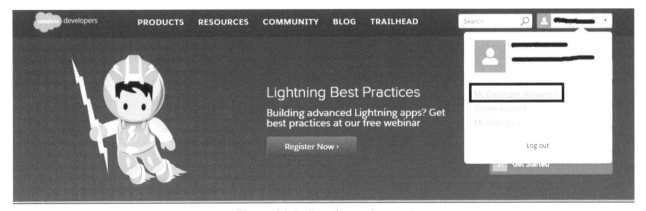

Figure 21.2: Developer Account

3. Click on **Developer Console**.

Figure 21.3: Developer Console

4. A new SOQL window would open. Navigate to **Open Execute Anonymous Window** under Debug as shown below:

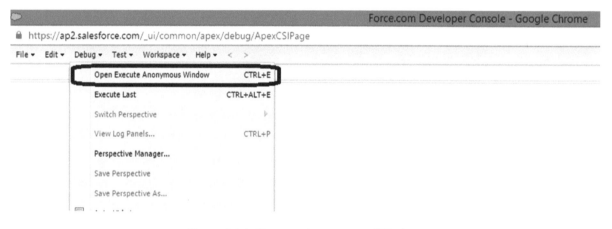

Figure 21.4: Execute Anonymous Window

5. Copy & paste the PushTopic code and **Execute**.

```
PushTopic pushTopic = new PushTopic();
pushTopic.Name = 'ContactTopic';
pushTopic.Query = 'SELECT Id,FirstName,LastName,Email FROM Contact';
pushTopic.ApiVersion = 30.0;
pushTopic.NotifyForOperationCreate = true;
pushTopic.NotifyForOperationUpdate = true;
pushTopic.NotifyForOperationUndelete = true;
pushTopic.NotifyForOperationDelete = true;
pushTopic.NotifyForFields =  'All';
insert pushTopic;
```

Enter Apex Code ▲ ×

```
1    PushTopic pushTopic = new PushTopic();
2    pushTopic.Name = 'ContactTopic';
3    pushTopic.Query = 'SELECT Id,FirstName,Last
4    pushTopic.ApiVersion = 30.0;
5    pushTopic.NotifyForOperationCreate = true;
6    pushTopic.NotifyForOperationUpdate = true;
7    pushTopic.NotifyForOperationUndelete = true
8    pushTopic.NotifyForOperationDelete = true;
9    pushTopic.NotifyForFields = 'All';
10   insert pushTopic;
```

☑ Open Log Execute Execute Highlighted

Figure 21.5: Apex Code

6. After executing this code a new PushTopic is created namely **ContactTopic,** which will execute the Query available in **pushTopic.Query** parameter whenever create, update, or delete happens for **Contact** object in Salesforce.

B. Create Flow in Anypoint Studio

1. Create a new project in Anypoint Studio & name it **streaming_api** as shown below:

Figure 21.6: Anypoint Studio New Project

2. Drag and drop **Salesforce** Connector from **Mule Palette** as shown below:

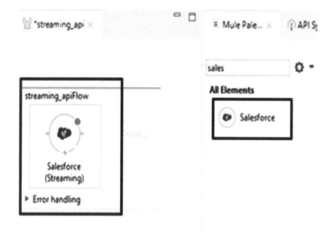

Figure 21.7: Salesforce Connector

3. By default, the connector will be set to streaming mode for inbound operations.

Figure 21.8: Flow

4. In the connector configuration of **Salesforce** connector, click on the **+ sign** to add a new configuration.

Figure 21.9: Salesforce Configuration

5.   Choose **Salesforce Basic Authentication.**

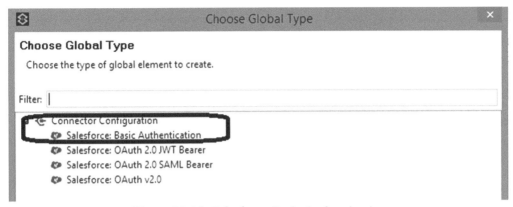

Figure 21.10: Salesforce Basic Authentication

6.   Add the Salesforce account details in **mule-app.properties** file in the format as in <GitHub location of this recipe>/src/main/app/mule-app.properties.

7.   Give the Salesforce login details in the dialogue window as shown:

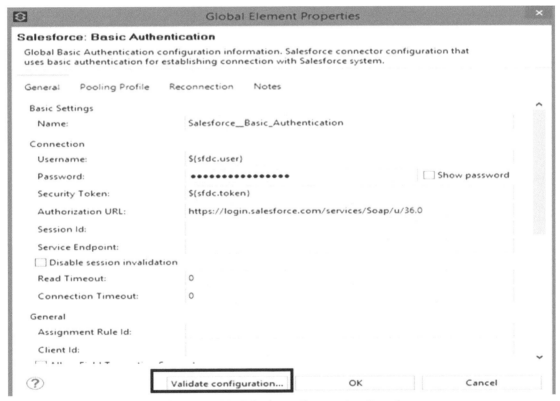

Figure 21.11: Salesforce Connection Details

8.   Click on **Validate Configuration** to check the connection details, following screen shows that the configuration is correct.

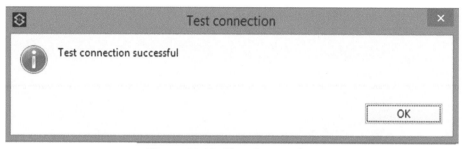

Figure 21.12: Test Connection

9. In the settings of Salesforce connector, choose **Operation** as **Subscribe Topic,** and give the topic name **ContactTopic** in the **Topic** parameter.

There are no errors.

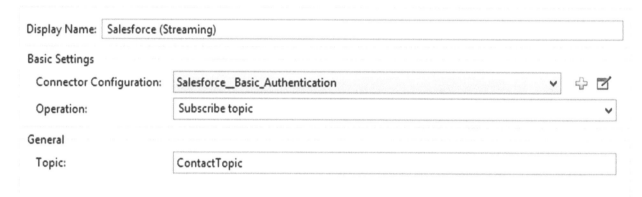

Figure 21.13: Salesforce Operation

10. Drag and drop a **Database** connector from **Mule Palette** as shown below:

Figure 21.14: Database Connector

11. Copy and paste the **mysql-connector-java-5.0.8-bin.jar** from the local computer to the project directory as shown below:

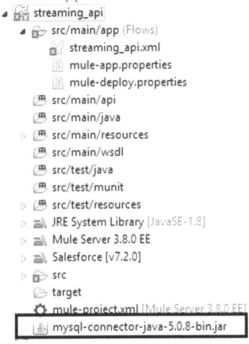

Figure 21.15: MySQL Driver

12. Right click on the **mysql jar** -> **Build Path** -> **Add to build path** as shown below:

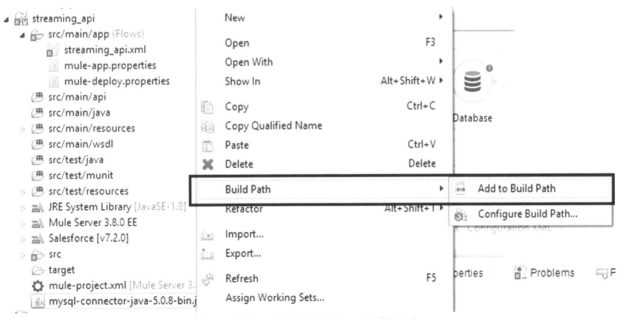

Figure 21.16: MySQL Driver Build Path

13. Select **MySQL configuration** in the connector configuration settings.

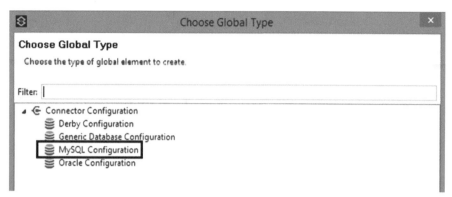

Figure 21.17: MySQL Configuration

14. Add the Database details in **mule-app.properties** file in the format as in <GitHub location of this recipe>/src/main/app/mule-app.properties.
15. Provide the connection details for the database in the dialogue window as shown below:

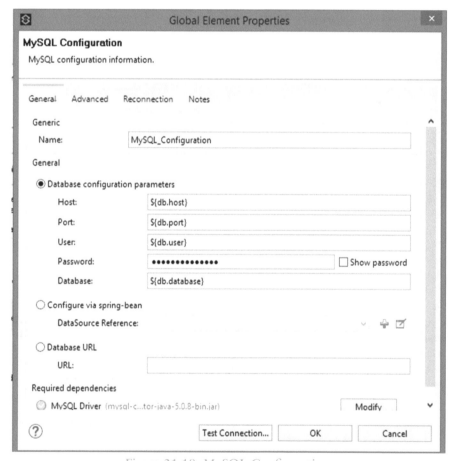

Figure 21.18: MySQL Configuration

16. Click on **Test Connection** to verify the database credentials. Following dialogue shows successful connection.

Figure 21.19: Successful Connection

17. Choose **Insert** operation in the Operation Settings, and copy paste this query:

```
insert into sfdcevent (Id,FirstName, LastName, Email) values (#[payload.Id],
#[payload.FirstName],#[payload.LastName],#[payload.Email])
```

Figure 21.20: Database Configuration

C. Testing the Flow
1. Deploy the application in **Anypoint Platform**.

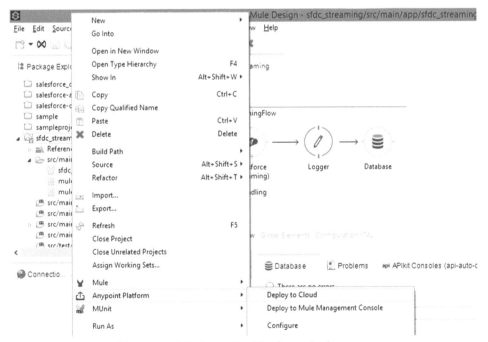

Figure 21.21: Anypoint Platform deployment

2. Once the deployment is done, login again into Salesforce account.
3. Navigate to **Contacts** tab and click **New** to create a new contact.

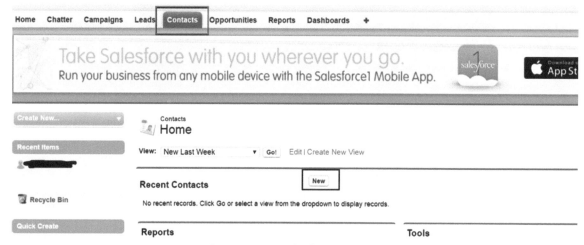

Figure 21.22: Salesforce Contact

4. This should trigger the Mule Flow and update the database. In this case, the values are:
   First Name: Mr. John;
   Last Name: D;
   Email: john@xyz.com

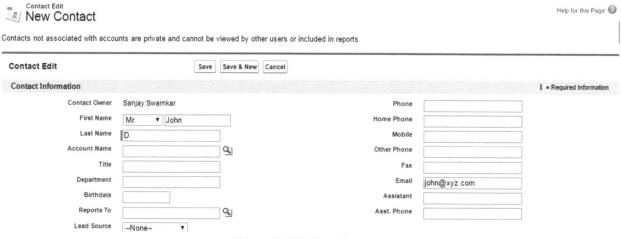

Figure 21.23: New Contact

5. Log shows that the Flow, as it was subscribed to the 'Contact Topic', got triggered as soon as a new contact was created.

```
17:35:32.228    12/01/2016    Worker-0    [sfdc-streaming].sfdc_streamingFlow.stage1.03    INFO
{Email=john@xyz.com, FirstName=John, Id=00328000000idB8JAAU, LastName=D}
```

Figure 21.24: Log Output

6. Also Flow updates the **MySQL** Database as shown: Highlighted area shows the new record created/ updated.

Figure 21.25: Database Updated

NOTE: As an example, only a single change to the 'Contact' object on Salesforce is provided here. Multiple objects and conditions can be added to the PushTopic to stream larger sets of data.

Anticipated Issues

NA

References

1. https://sites.google.com/a/mulesoft.com/sfdc-workshop/lab-4
2. http://blogs.mulesoft.com/dev/news-dev/real-time-web-and-streaming-apis/
3. https://developer.salesforce.com/docs/atlas.en-us.api_streaming.meta/api_streaming/intro_stream.htm

RECIPE 22

Implementing Asynchronous RESTful API

Asynchronous services help in building non-blocking client and server calls. In cases where the client makes a request for a time-consuming activity, the server can complete the task independently. Asynchronous applications are typically easier to scale, allowing for the implementation of reliability patterns and sometimes even reflect use cases in the real world better. Mule, not surprisingly, offers a plethora of opportunities to process messages asynchronously.

Few transports and connectors, like JMS (Java Message Service) or the VM transport, are asynchronous by default. Other transports which are inherently synchronous, like HTTP, need there exchange pattern explicitly set. Setting one-way exchange patterns on these transports allow you to simulate asynchronous behavior with protocols that would otherwise not be asynchronous.

In this design approach, request, processing and response happen in different threads.
GitHub location of this recipe:
https://github.com/WHISHWORKS/mule-api-recipes/tree/publish_v1.0/async-restful-api

Pre-requisites
1. MuleSoft Anypoint Studio 6.1 or above (https://www.mulesoft.com/lp/dl/studio) installed
2. MuleSoft CloudHub Account (https://anypoint.mulesoft.com)
3. JMS Provider Service - Apache ActiveMQ (download ActiveMQ 5.X.X from http://activemq.apache.org/) and refer to URL http://activemq.apache.org/getting-started.html for its installation for any operating system
4. RAML file with Asynchronous RESTful API operations, designed in MuleSoft API Designer (<GitHub location of this recipe>/src/main/api/async-rest.raml)
5. MySQL Database accessible from cloud with admin rights to create database and users
6. MySQL Connector/J connector JAR (mysql-connector-java-5.1.18) to connect database available from https://dev.mysql.com/downloads/connector/j/
7. Install Postman plugin in Chrome from Chrome webstore

Process
High Level Steps:
A. ActiveMQ Setup
B. Implementation of API
C. Process to achieve Asynchronous API

- Asynchronous Using JMS
- Asynchronous Using Status

A. **ActiveMQ Setup**
   1. Download and install the latest version of ActiveMQ as mentioned in pre-requisites.
   2. To verify **ActiveMQ** is running, below steps must be followed:
      a. Open a browser and go to http://localhost:8161/admin. Login with default credentials as **admin/admin** shown as below:

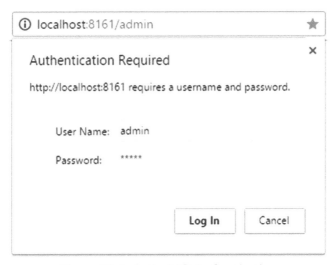

Figure 22.1: ActiveMQ Authentication

   b. The ActiveMQ dashboard will be shown as below :

Figure 22.2: ActiveMQ Dashboard

   3. Next, JMS environment setup is done.

4. Click on **Queue.** Create a queue **AccountQueue** by clicking on **Create** button in ActiveMQ as shown below:

Figure 22.3: ActiveMQ Queue

B. **Implementation of API**
1. Download the MySQL DDL script from **<GitHub location of this recipe>**/src/main/sql/async.sql.
2. From the command line on the MySQL server system execute
   mysql –u[admin _user] –p[admin_password] < [/path/to/]async.sql.

```
# async.sql

CREATE USER 'bc_user'@'%' IDENTIFIED BY 'password';
CREATE DATABASE async_rest CHARACTER SET utf8;
GRANT ALL PRIVILEGES ON async_rest.* TO 'bc_user'@'%' IDENTIFIED BY 'password';
USE async_rest;
CREATE TABLE async_jms_msg (id int, name varchar (255), Type varchar (255),
Address varchar (255));
```

NOTE: This MySQL database should be accessible from cloud
3. Download mysql-connector-java-5.X.XX.zip from https://dev.mysql.com/downloads/connector/j/ as mentioned in pre-requisites.
4. Download the RAML file from GitHub location as mentioned in pre-requisites above.
5. Launch **Mule Anypoint Studio** and create a new **Mule Project** as shown below:
   File > New > Mule Project

Figure 22.4: Creating New Mule Project

6. In the **New Mule Project** dialogue that comes up as shown below, provide the **Project Name** as 'async-restful-api'. Select the checkbox **Add APIkit components** and provide the path of the **async.raml** file downloaded above. Click **Finish.**

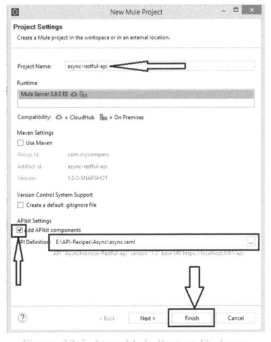

Figure 22.5: New Mule Project Dialogue

7. This will create a skeleton project and skeleton Mule Flows for each of the HTTP operations GET and POST along with a main APIkit Router flow and APIkit Console flow based on the RAML definition as shown below:

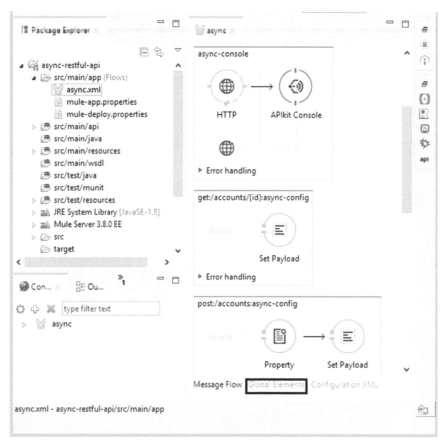

Figure 22.6: Generated Mule Flows from RAML

8. Create and configure the **Global Component** for ActiveMQ as shown below:
9. Click on **Global Elements.**
   a. Click on **Create** button as shown below:

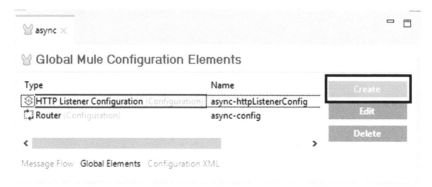

Figure 22.7: Global Mule Configuration Elements

b. **Choose Global Type** dialogue appears as shown below:

Figure 22.8: Choose Global Type

c. Search for **ActiveMQ** in **Filter** field for ActiveMQ connector provider. Select **ActiveMQ** that appears under **Connector Configuration > JMS** as shown below and click **OK**.

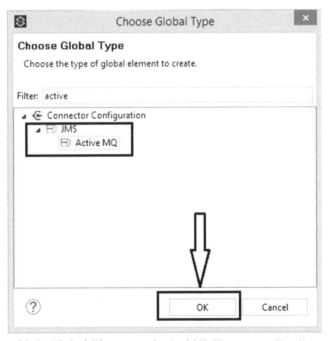

Figure 22.9: Global Element – ActiveMQ Connector Configuration

d. Fill the details as follows as shown below:
- Leave **Broker URL** as default as **tcp://localhost:61616** (Value may vary depend on setup)
- Write **User Name** and **Password** as **admin** and **admin** respectively

Figure 22.10: ActiveMQ Global Element Properties

e. The configured MySQL element should appear in **Global Elements** tab as shown below:

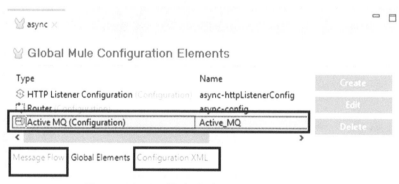

Figure 22.11: Global Element – ActiveMQ

10. Add **Database connection** details in **mule-app.properties** file as given in the GitHub repository.
11. Create and configure the **Global Component** for MySQL Database as shown below:
   a. Click on **Create** button as shown in step B.9.a.
   b. **Choose Global Type** dialogue appears. Search for **MySQL** in **Filter** field for MySQL Database Connector.

c. Select **MySQL Configuration** that appears under **Connector Configuration** as shown below and click **OK.**

Figure 22.12: Global Element – MySQL Configuration

d. **Global Element Properties** dialogue would be displayed.
e. Fill **Host** ${db.host}, **Port** ${db.port}, **User** ${db.user}, **Password** ${db.password} and **Database** ${db.database} details in MySQL configuration as shown in below figure:
   NOTE: The User, Password and Database should match as given in MySQL DDL script file in step B.2.
f. Click **Add File** to add MySQL connector driver to connect to the MySQL Database. Select the zip/jar file downloaded in step B.3.
g. Click **Test Connection** to check that the database connector is configured correctly and is able to successfully connect to MySQL.

Figure 22.13: Global Element Properties- MySQL Configuration

h. Successful connection message should be shown below. Click **OK** on the **Test connection** dialogue.

Figure 22.14: Test Connection

i. Click **OK** button in the **Global Element Properties** dialogue.
j. The configured MySQL element should appear in **Global Elements** tab as shown below:

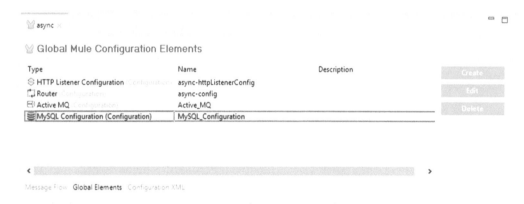

Figure 22.15: Global Element – MySQL

12. To configure this app with **ActiveMQ**, right click on **async-restful-api** and choose **Build Path –> Add External Archives** as shown below:

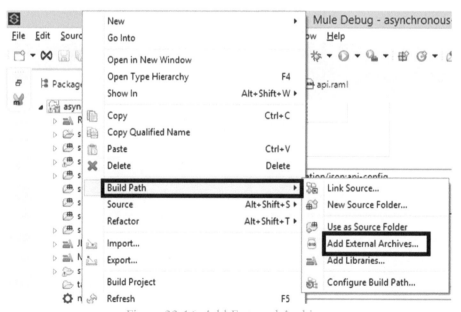

Figure 22.16: Add External Archives

13. Browse to your ActiveMQ installation directory, and from the main folder choose **activemq-all-[5.x.x].jar** as shown below:

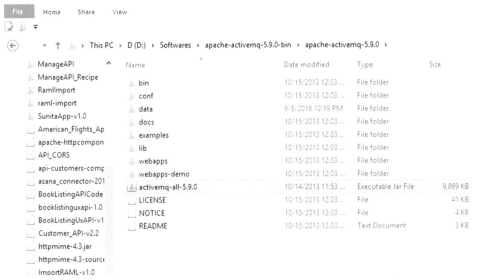

Figure 22.17: ActiveMQ Jar File

C. Configure the asynchronous flow in Anypoint Studio. This can be achieved in many ways. In this recipe, this is achieved by using JMS.

Preferred approach to achieve Asynchronous behavior of a flow is to create asynchronous services to introduce JMS between the client and the server. With JMS in between, the service becomes completely decoupled yet reliable.

1. Navigate to **Message Flow** tab.
2. The skeleton **Mule Flow** for **POST** will look as below:

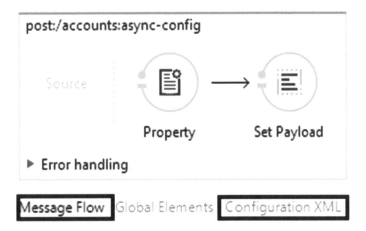

Figure 22.18: POST Method Skeleton

3. Click on the **Configuration XML** tab and search with the flow name i.e. **post:/accounts:async-config**. The corresponding **POST** Mule Flow XML content should look like:

```
<flow name="post:/accounts:async-config">
        <set-property propertyName="Content-Type" value="application/json"
doc:name="Property"/>
        <set-payload value="{&#xA;  status: ok&#xA;}" doc:name="Set Payload"/>
</flow>
```

4. Implement the **HTTP POST** method in **post:/accounts:async-config** flow.
    a. In this POST Mule Flow replace the XML with the following XML content:

```
<flow name="post:/accounts:async-config">
      <set-payload value="#[payload]" doc:name="Set Payload" />
      <set-variable variableName="uniqueId" value="#[function:uuid]" doc:name="Unique
Id" />
      <dw:transform-message metadata:id="a94c1353-f8e4-425e-87e5-636c26f77e41"
doc:name="Transform Message">
         <dw:input-variablemimeType="application/java" variableName="uniqueId"/>
         <dw:set-payload><![CDATA[%dw 1.0
             %output application/json
             ---
             {
                   id: flowVars.uniqueId,
                   name: payload.name,
                   Type: payload.Type,
                   Address: payload.Address
             }]]>
         </dw:set-payload>
      </dw:transform-message>
      <object-to-string-transformer doc:name="Object to String" />
      <jms:outbound-endpoint  queue="AccountQueue"  connector-ref="Active_MQ"
doc:name="JMS"/>

      <logger  message="Data  received  after  JMS:  #[payload]"  level="INFO"
doc:name="Print Data after JMS" />
      <set-payload  value="{  Generated  Id:  #[flowVars.uniqueId],  Status:
Initiated}" doc:name="Set Payload" />
</flow>
```

    b. In the code above, the request JSON is received, transformed and pushed into ActiveMQ queue **AccountQueue** which is created in step A.4. A unique Id is used to generate the Id for each and every message which gets pushed in ActiveMQ.
    c. **Save** the file and click on **Mule Flow** tab. The corresponding POST Mule Flow should now look like as below:

post:/accounts:async-config

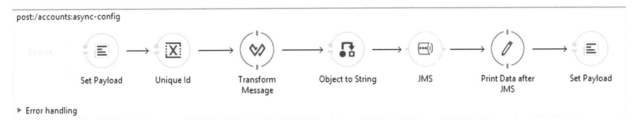

Figure 22.19: POST Method Mule Flow

5. It is required to add a queue listener to receive the account request and push into the database table **async_jms_msg** for further process. It is required to create a flow to add a queue listener in the flow as shown below:

    a. Drag **Flow Element** from Mule Palette and drop into the **Message Flow** as shown below:

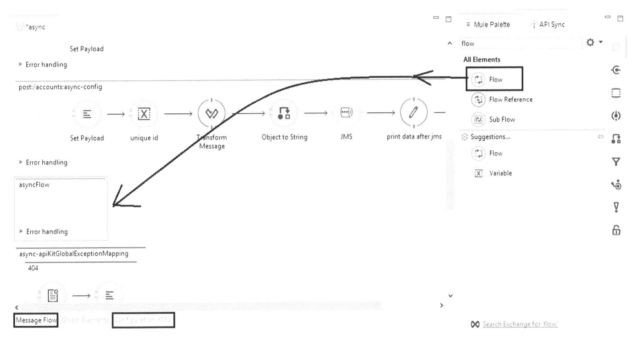

Figure 22.20: Queue Listener Flow Drag

    b. The corresponding XML can be seen in the configuration XML as shown below:

```xml
<flow name="asyncFlow"/>
```

    c. Implement the flow for queue listener. In this Mule Flow replace the XML with the following XML content:

```
<flow name="asyncFlow">
      <jms:inbound-endpoint  queue="AccountQueue"  connector-ref="Active_MQ"
doc:name="Reading message from JMS"/>
      <json:json-to-object-transformer returnClass="java.util.HashMap" doc:name="JSON
to Object" />
      <db:insert config-ref="MySQL_Configuration" doc:name="Insert into Database">
            <db:parameterized-query><![CDATA[insert into async_jms_msg (id, name,
Type, Address) VALUES (#[payload.id],#[payload.name],#[payload.Type],#[payload.
Address])]]></db:parameterized-query>
      </db:insert>
      <logger message="After Insertion: #[payload]" level="INFO" doc:name="Insertion
Status" />
</flow>
```

d.   **Save** the file and click on **Mule Flow** tab. The corresponding Mule Flow should now look like as below:

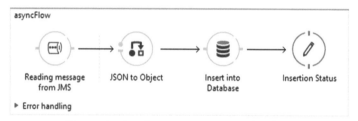

Figure 22.21: Queue Listener Mule Flow

6.   Right click on **async-restful-api** application and hover on **Run As** then click on **Mule Application** as shown below:

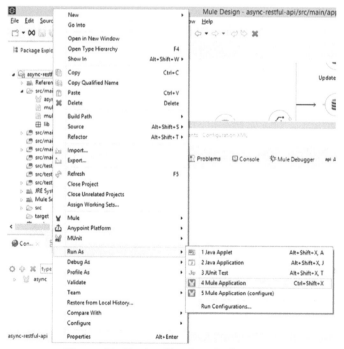

Figure 22.22: Application deployment

7. After some time, the Console will be updated to show the "application is deployed successfully on the local server" as shown below:

Figure 22.23: Application deployed

8. Testing this process
   a. Launch Postman Chrome Application as mentioned in pre-requisites.

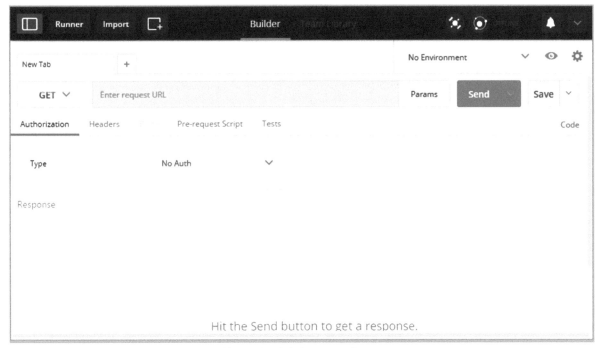

Figure 22.24: Postman Home

b. Post the data using Postman as shown below:
   i. Select **POST** Method which has to be tested from the dropdown.
   ii. Provide URL http://localhost:8081/api/accounts.

Figure 22.25: POST Request in POSTMAN

iii. Click **Body**. Select **raw** and then select **JSON** (**application/json**) from dropdown.
iv. Provide sample data as shown below:

```
{
  "name": "Test",
  "Type": "Saving",
  "Address": "Lokhandwala"
}
```

v. Click **Send** to invoke the API.
vi. Click **Raw** and Response will be as shown below:

Figure 22.26: POST Response in Postman

```
{ Generated Id: 83a60ed0-e84e-11e6-afed-f04da29fb7b6, Status: Initiated}
```

c. Unique Id will be generated for each input data pushed in AccountQueue.
   Note: Copy generated Id for further use in next process.
9. The processor can act on the account request from step C.5 above in a separate thread and there's no requirement on the API to wait.
10. This process enables Async request response pattern. The below figure depicts the steps defined above:

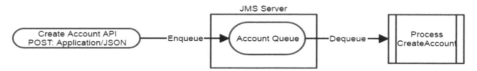

Figure 22.27: Async with JMS Queue

REST resources, methods and HTTP Status codes can be leveraged to process the request asynchronously. Note that HTTP 202 response means that a request is accepted but doesn't indicate if the same is successfully processed by the server.

11. Generated Id will be used to get the status of completion.
12. Response from the POST by the server would be:
    a. HTTP /1.1 202 Accepted
    {Generated Id: 83a60ed0-e84e-11e6-afed-f04da29fb7b6, Status: Initiated}

{ Generated Id: 83a60ed0-e84e-11e6-afed-f04da29fb7b6, Status: Initiated}

Figure 22.28: Status Initiated

13. It is required to create a flow in GET subflow of the same application to get the status as shown below:
    a. Navigate to **Message Flow** tab.
    b. The skeleton **Mule Flow** for **GET** will look as below:

get:/accounts/{id}:async-config

Set Payload

▶ Error handling

Figure 22.29: GET Method Skeleton

c. Click on the **Configuration XML** tab and search with the flow name i.e. **get:/accounts/{id}:async-config**. The corresponding **GET** Mule Flow XML content should look like:

```
<flow name="get:/accounts/{id}:async-config">
<set-payload  value="{&#xA;    &quot;name&quot;:  &quot;API  Account&quot;,&#xA;
&quot;Type&quot;:  &quot;Savings&quot;,&#xA;    &quot;Address&quot;:  &quot;My
Address&quot;&#xA;}"  doc:name="Set Payload"/>
 </flow>
```

14. Implement the **HTTP POST** method in `get:/accounts/{id}:async-config` flow
    a. In this **GET** Mule Flow replace the XML with the following XML content:

```
<flow name="get:/accounts/{id}:async-config">
    <logger          message="#[message.inboundProperties.'http.uri.params'.id]"
level="INFO" doc:name="Logger" />
    <set-variable         variableName="varId"           value="#[message.
inboundProperties.'http.uri.params'.id]" doc:name="Variable" />
    <db:select config-ref="MySQL_Configuration" doc:name="get Data from DB">
        <db:parameterized-query><![CDATA[SELECT counter FROM async_jms_msg
WHERE id = #[flowVars.varId];]]></db:parameterized-query>
    </db:select>
    <choice doc:name="Choice">
        <when expression="#[payload[0].counter==0]">
            <async doc:name="Async">
                <expression-component doc:name="Expression"><![CDATA[
                    Thread.sleep(30000);
                ]]></expression-component>
                <db:update config-ref="MySQL_Configuration" doc:name="In
Progress">
                    <db:parameterized-query><![CDATA[update     async_
jms_msg set counter= 1, status='Approval in progress' where id=#[flowVars.
varId];]]></db:parameterized-query>
                </db:update>
                <db:select config-ref="MySQL_Configuration" doc:name="Getting
Status 1">
                    <db:parameterized-query><![CDATA[select id, status
from async_jms_msg WHERE id = #[flowVars.varId];]]></db:parameterized-query>
                </db:select>
                <set-payload value="#[payload]" doc:name="Set Payload"/>
            </async>
            <db:update config-ref="MySQL_Configuration" doc:name="verification
stage">
                <db:parameterized-query><![CDATA[update    async_jms_msg
set status='Verification started' where id=#[flowVars.varId];]]></db:parameterized
-query>
            </db:update>
            <db:select config-ref="MySQL_Configuration" doc:name="Getting
status">
                <db:parameterized-query><![CDATA[select   id,   status
from async_jms_msg WHERE id = #[flowVars.varId];]]></db:parameterized-query>
            </db:select>
            <set-payload value="#[payload]" doc:name="Set Payload"/>
        </when>
        <when expression="#[payload[0].counter==1]">
            <async doc:name="Async">
                <expression-component doc:name="Expression"><![CDATA[
                    Thread.sleep(30000);
                ]]></expression-component>
                <db:update config-ref="MySQL_Configuration" doc:name="Final
Update">
```

```
                        <db:parameterized-query><![CDATA[update    async_
jms_msg  set  counter=#[payload[0].counter] + 1, status='Application Accepted'
where id=#[flowVars.varId];]]></db:parameterized-query>
                        </db:update>
                        <db:select config-ref="MySQL_Configuration" doc:name="Getting
Status 3">
                            <db:parameterized-query><![CDATA[select id, status
from async_jms_msg WHERE id = #[flowVars.varId];]]></db:parameterized-query>
                        </db:select>
                        <set-payload value="#[payload]" doc:name="Set Payload"/>
                    </async>
                    <db:select  config-ref="MySQL_Configuration"  doc:name="Getting
Status 2">
                        <db:parameterized-query><![CDATA[select   id,    status
from async_jms_msg WHERE id = #[flowVars.varId];]]></db:parameterized-query>
                        </db:select>
                        <set-payload value="#[payload]" doc:name="Set Payload"/>
            </when>
            <when expression="#[payload[0].counter&gt;1]">
                    <db:select  config-ref="MySQL_Configuration"  doc:name="Getting
Status 4">
                        <db:parameterized-query><![CDATA[select   id,    status
from async_jms_msg WHERE id = #[flowVars.varId];]]></db:parameterized-query>
                        </db:select>
                        <set-payload value="#[payload]" doc:name="Set Payload"/>
            </when>
        </choice>
</flow>
```

b. In this above code snippet, a variable is used to set Id which is passed as an input to retrieve the status of input. From the given Id, it is easy to retrieve data from the database which is pushed in step C.8. Choice is used for routing based on completion status. There are three stages in this process like Verification started, Approval in progress and Application accepted. After 'Verification started' status, it will take 30 seconds to update the status to Approval in progress and the same time delay for final status 'Application accepted'. Here, Async scope is used to hold the process and update status accordingly.

c. **Save** the file and click on **Mule Flow** tab. The corresponding **POST** Mule Flow should now look like as below:

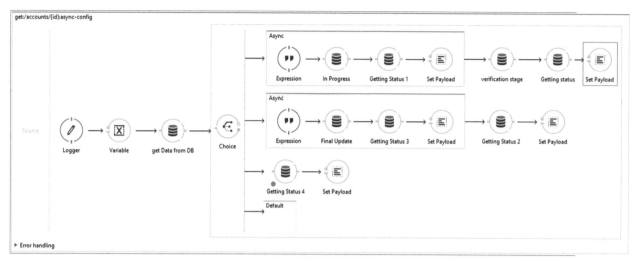

Figure 22.30: GET Method Flow

15. Client can get the status from the location as below:
    {baseURL}/ api/accounts/{id}.
16. Testing this process
    a. Again Launch **Postman** Chrome Application as mentioned in pre-requisites.
    b. Get the data with URL: http://localhost:8081/api/accounts/<id> as shown below:
    c. Select **GET** method which has to be tested from the dropdown.
    d. Provide URL http://localhost:8081/api/accounts/83a60ed0-e84e-11e6-afed-f04da29fb7b6 as shown below:

Figure 22.31: GET Request in Postman

    e. Click **Send** to invoke the API.
    f. The result after the completion of first stage is as shown below:

[{"status":"Verification started","id":"83a60ed0-e84e-11e6-afed-f04da29fb7b6"}]

Figure 22.32: GET Response after First Stage

```
[{"status":"Verification started","id":"83a60ed0-e84e-11e6-afed-f04da29fb7b6"}]
```

g. This will take 30 seconds to change the status. It will show the same status on multiple checks up to 30 seconds. After 30 seconds, the status will change to 'Approval in process' as shown below:

Figure 22.33: GET Response after 2nd Stage

```
[{"status":"Approval in progress","id":"83a60ed0-e84e-11e6-afed-f04da29fb7b6"}]
```

h. This will further take 30 seconds to change the status. It will show the same status on multiple checks up to 30 seconds. After 30 seconds, the status will change to 'Application Accepted' as shown below. Once the processing is complete, the server will respond to the GET request as shown below:

Figure 22.34: GET Response after processing completed

```
[{"status":"Application
Accepted","id":"83a60ed0-e84e-11e6-afed-f04da29fb7b6"}]
```

Note: Apart from the above two approaches, another option is to use the Future class of JDK (java.util.concurrent. Future). This class allows getting the response asynchronously.

Anticipated Issues:

1. Active MQ should be up and running.
2. MySQL Database connection not established: Ensure that the database is accessible from CloudHub.

References

1. Asynchronous processing with Mule:
   http://blogs.mulesoft.com/dev/mule-dev/asynchronous-message-processing-with-mule/
2. Using Future class : https://docs.oracle.com/javase/8/docs/api/java/util/concurrent/Future.html
3. http://farazdagi.com/blog/2014/rest-long-running-jobs/

RECIPE 23

Implementing Custom OAuth Provider

OAuth (Open Authorization) is an open standard for token-based authentication and authorization; it allows an end user's account information to be used by third-party services without exposing the user's password. There are many applications available over the Internet to be used as OAuth service providers like Gmail; although in some cases it is required to have a custom OAuth provider API.

OAuth defines four roles:
- **Resource Owner** is the user who authorizes an application to access their account. The application's access to the user's account is limited to the "scope" of the authorization granted (e.g. read or write access).
- **Client** is the application that wants to access the user's account. Before it may do so, it must be authorized by the user, and the authorisation must be validated by the API.
- **Resource Server** hosts the protected user accounts.
- **Authorization Server** verifies the identity of the user then issues access tokens to the application.

OAuth separates the role of clients from that of resource owner by adding an authorization layer. Instead of using the resource owner's credentials to access protected resources, the client obtains an access token. Access tokens are issued to third-party clients by an authorization server with the approval of the resource owner. The client uses the access token to access the protected resources hosted by the resource server.

In this recipe, an API serves the purpose of both Authorization and Resource Server.

Abstract Protocol Flow

1. Authorization Request

2. Authorization Grant

User
(Resource Owner)

Application
(Client)

3. Authorization Grant

4. Access Token

Authorization
Server

5. Access Token

6. Protected Resource

Resource
Server

Service API

Figure 23.1: OAuth 2 Flow

1. Client application sends an authorization request to the Resource Owner to access the restricted resources.
2. If the resource owner authorizes the request, the application receives an authorization grant.
3. Client then requests for an access token from the authorization server (API) by presenting authentication of its own identity, and the authorization grant.
4. If the application identity is authenticated and the authorization grant is valid, the authorization server (API) issues an access token to the application. Authorization is complete.
5. The application then requests the resource from the resource server (API) and presents the access token for authentication.
6. If the access token is valid, the resource server (API) sends the resource to the application.

The actual flow of this process will differ depending on the authorization grant type in use. Application should be registered with the OAuth server before it can be used to authenticate. In this recipe registration part is assumed that it's already done and **client-id** and **client-secret** have been generated.

There are four ways by which a consumer can obtain authorization to dance with an OAuth service provider.
1. Authorization Code
2. Implicit
3. Resource Owner Password Credentials
4. Client Credentials

The **authorization code** grant type is the most commonly used way because it is optimized for *server-side applications*, where source code is not publicly exposed, and *Client Secret* confidentiality can be maintained. To use this flow, application should be capable of interacting with the *user-agent* (i.e. the user's web browser) and receiving API authorization codes that are routed through the user-agent.

Authorization Code Flow

Figure 23.2: Authorization Code Flow

GitHub location of this recipe:
https://github.com/WHISHWORKS/mule-api-recipes/tree/publish_v1.0/api-custom-oauth/

Pre requisites
1. Anypoint Studio 3.8 installed
https://www.mulesoft.com/lp/dl/studio
2. Mule Standalone Runtime 3.8.2
https://developer.mulesoft.com/download-mule-esb-runtime/

Process
High Level Steps:
A. Create API for Resource/Authorization Server
B. Run Client Application
C. Testing

A. **Create API for Resource/Authorization Server**
1. Open Anypoint Studio and click on **File -> Mule Project** as shown:

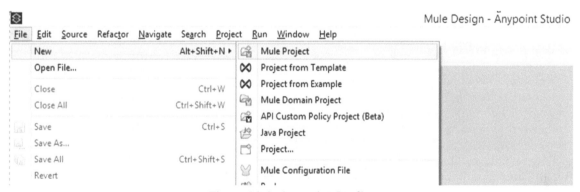

Figure 23.3: Anypoint Studio

2. Give name **OAuthProvider** and click **Finish** as shown below:

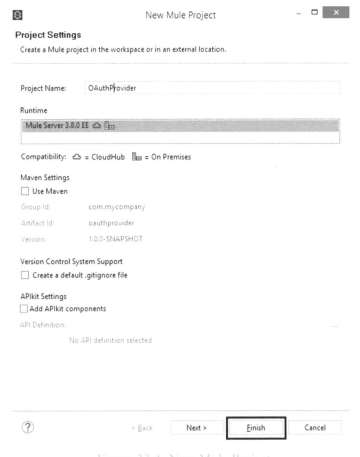

Figure 23.4: New Mule Project

3. Drag and drop an **HTTP** connector from **Mule Palette** as shown:

Figure 23.5: HTTP Connector

4. Click on **HTTP connector** and create a connector configuration. **HTTP connector** dialogue opens up, click **Ok** as shown below:

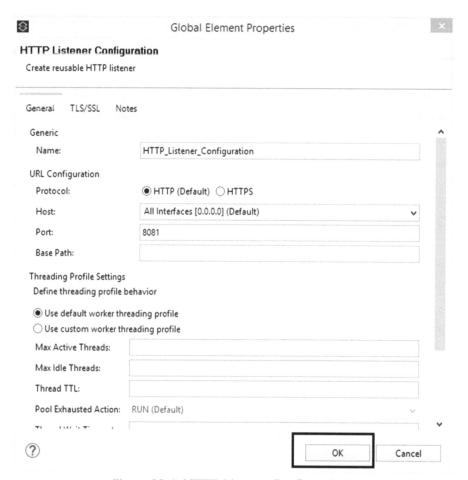

Figure 23.6: HTTP Listener Configuration

5. Drag and drop **an OAuth provider module** from **Mule Palette** as shown below:

Figure 23.7: OAuth Provider Module

6. Click on **OAuth provider module** and create a **Config Reference** as shown below:

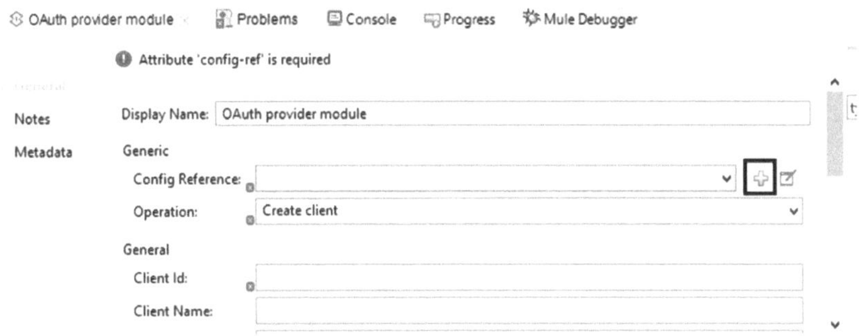

Figure 23.8: OAuth Config Reference

7. In the **Config dialogue box** provide the following details:
   Name: OAuth_provider_module
   Access Token Endpoint Path: oauthprovider/api/token
   Host: localhost
   Provider Name: OAuth Provider
   Authorization Ttl Seconds: 60
   Port: 9999
   Authorization Endpoint Path: oauthprovider/api/authorize
   Scopes: READ_RESOURCE
   Token Ttl Seconds: 15
   Resource Owner Security provider Reference: resourceOwnerSecurityProvider
   Supported Grant Types: AUTHORIZATION_CODE
   Leave rest of the fields as it is and click **Ok** as shown below:

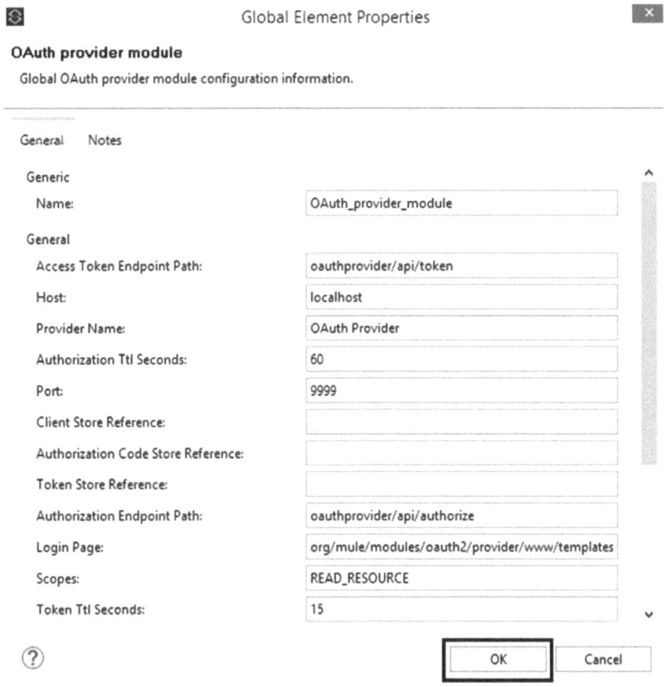

Figure 23.9: OAuth Config Details

8. In the **Operation** drop down of **OAuth provider module** select **Validate** as shown below:

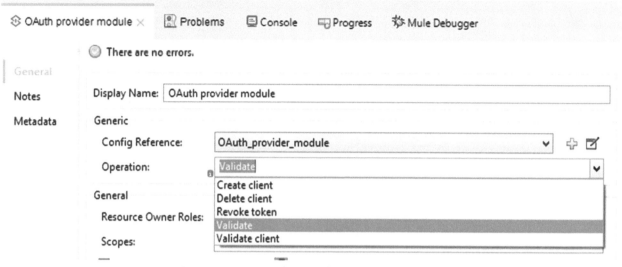

Figure 23.10: OAuth provider module Operation

9. In **General section** provide **Scopes** as **READ_RESOURCE** and also check **Throw Exception on Unaccepted** as shown below:

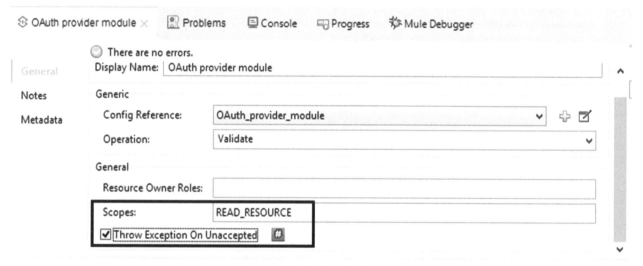

Figure 23.11: OAuth Scopes

10. A user needs to be created which will have access to this application, hence a security manager is to be added which can authenticate users.

11. Add following code in **oauthprovider.xml** after schema location. Here a user with username **john** and password **doe** is added as shown below:

```
<spring:beans>
        <ss:authentication-manager alias="resourceOwnerAuthenticationManager">
          <ss:authentication-provider>
              <ss:user-service id="resourceOwnerUserService">
                              <ss:user   name="john"   password="doe"
authorities="READ_PROFILES"/>
              </ss:user-service>
          </ss:authentication-provider>
        </ss:authentication-manager>
</spring:beans>
<mule-ss:security-manager name="muleSecurityManager" doc:name="Spring Security
Provider">
        <mule-ss:delegate-security-provider name="resourceOwnerSecurityProv
ider"
        delegate-ref="resourceOwnerAuthenticationManager"/>
        </mule-ss:security-manager>
```

12. **Clients** are third party applications which will use this application to authenticate the users trying to login to client application.

13. In this recipe, registration process of clients with the **OAuth provider** application is assumed to be complete and a dummy client-id and client-secret is assigned to the client application.

14. Now the clients which can access this API using OAuth   need to be added. Users and clients are not the same. Users are the users of this application.

15. Below is the configuration for an **OAuth client** in Mule, put this inside **oauth2-provider-config** in **oauthprovider.xml**.

```
<oauth2-provider:clients>
                        <oauth2-provider:client    clientId="${client id}"
secret="${client-secret}"
        type="CONFIDENTIAL" clientName="OAuth Consumer Client"
        description="Test client">
              <oauth2-provider:redirect-uris>
                        <oauth2-provider:redirect-uri>http://localhost*</
oauth2-provider:redirect-uri>
              </oauth2-provider:redirect-uris>
              <oauth2-provider:authorized-grant-types>
                  <oauth2-provider:authorized-grant-type>AUTHORIZATION_
CODE</oauth2-provider:authorized-grant-type>
              </oauth2-provider:authorized-grant-types>
              <oauth2-provider:scopes>
                            <oauth2-provider:scope>READ_RESOURCE</
oauth2-provider:scope>
              </oauth2-provider:scopes>
        </oauth2-provider:client>
          </oauth2-provider:clients>
```

16. Open **mule-app.properties** file and paste the following content:

```
client-id=12345
client-secret=abc
```

Figure 23.12: Mule-app properties file

17. Add the following code inside the flow element in **oauthprovider.xml** as shown below:

```
<logger message="Access token granted" level="INFO" doc:name="Logger"/>
      <set-payload value="Congratulations!!! You are logged in with your OAUTH
Provider account." doc:name="Set Payload"/>
         <catch-exception-strategy doc:name="Catch Exception Strategy">
            <logger message="inside exception " level="INFO" doc:name="Logger"/>
              <set-payload value="Invaild Access Token" doc:name="Set Payload"/>
         </catch-exception-strategy>
```

18. Also add this namespace for **authentication manager** in **oauthprovider.xml**

```
xmlns:ss="http://www.springframework.org/schema/security"
```

19. Complete XML code can be found at < GitHub location of this recipe>/api-oauthprovider/src/main/app/api-oauthprovider.xml/
20. Complete flow looks as shown below:

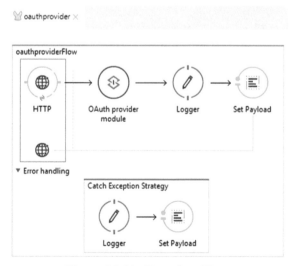

Figure 23.13: Complete Flow

21. Right click on **Project** -> **Run** as -> **Mule Application.**

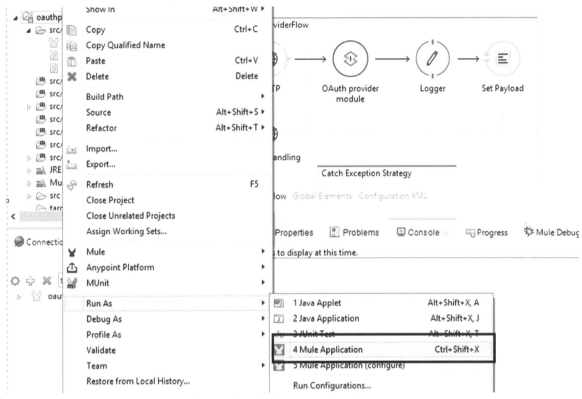

Figure 23.14: Run Mule Application

22. Once the application is successfully deployed, Console output will be as shown below:

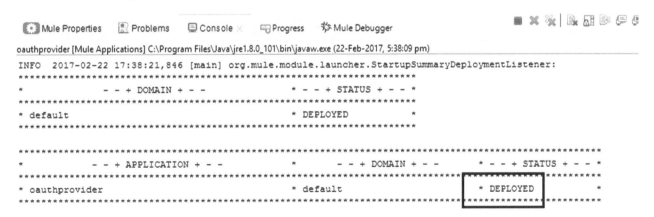

Figure 23.15: Console

B. **Run Client Application**

1. Download the **oauth2-consumer** client application available at <GitHub location of this recipe>/ oauth2-consumer/.

2. Open mule-ee-distribution-standalone-3.8.2 folder.
3. Extract the downloaded application in the ~\mule-ee-distribution-standalone-3.8.2\mule-enterprise-standalone-3.8.2\apps folder as shown below:

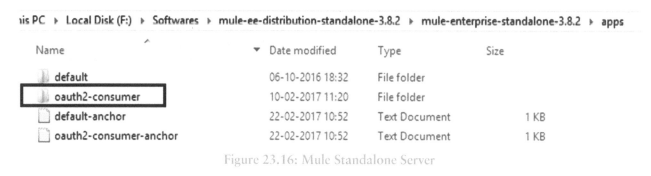

Figure 23.16: Mule Standalone Server

4. Go to the ~\mule-ee-distribution-standalone-3.8.2\mule-enterprise-standalone-3.8.2\bin folder & run the server by opening command prompt. Give command **mule** as shown below:

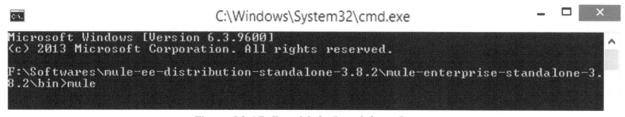

Figure 23.17: Run Mule Standalone Server

5. Following message will appear if the application **oauth2-consumer** is deployed successfully:

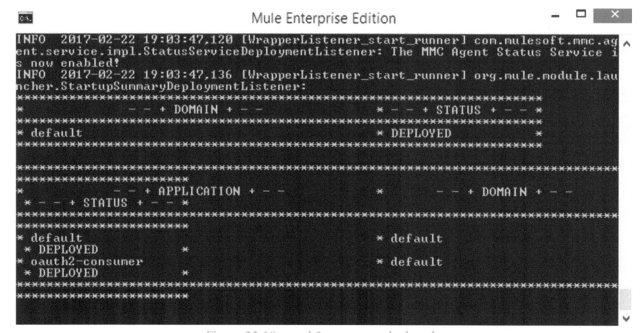

Figure 23.18: oauth2-consumer deployed

C. Testing

1. Start a web browser and open http://localhost:8085/client/index.jsp URL, click on **Your OAuth Service Provider Account** link as shown below:

Figure 23.19: OAuth Consumer Client Login Page

2. This will open OAuth provider login page, enter username: **john** password: **doe** & click on **Login and Authorize** as shown below:

Figure 23.20: OAuth Provider Login

3. If the login is successful, following message comes up on the screen:

Figure 23.21: Login Successful

Anticipated Issues

1. **Client Application** must be registered with OAuth provider application by adding client-id and secret.
2. **OAuth provider** application must be up and running before testing with client application.

References

1. https://oauth.net/2/
2. https://www.digitalocean.com/community/tutorials/an-introduction-to-oauth-2
3. https: //docs.mulesoft.com/mule-user-guide/v/3.8/mule-sts-oauth-2.0-example-application
4. https://dzone.com/articles/oauth-20-mule

RECIPE 24

Implementing Caching Strategy on a Mule Flow

The objective of this recipe is to implement a Caching Strategy on a Mule Flow. The **Cache Scope** in Mule saves on time and processing load by storing and reusing frequently requested data.

The **Caching Strategy** defines the actions a Cache Scope takes when a message enters its sub-flow. If there is no cached response event (a cache "miss"), Cache Scope processes the message. If there is a cached response event (a cache "hit"), Cache Scope offers the cached response event rather than processing the message.

The **Default Caching Strategy** used by **Cache Scope** uses an InMemoryObjectStore, and is only suitable for testing. For example, processing messages with large payloads may quickly exhaust memory storage and slow the processing performance of the flow. In such a case, it is advisable to create a Global Caching Strategy that stores cached responses in a different type of object store and prevents memory exhaustion.

This recipe talks about creating a **Global Caching Strategy** which will use **Redis Server** as an Object Store, so that memory exhaustion can be prevented. Since this is not provided as an out-of-the-box solution by Mulesoft, a java code has to be written to interact with the Redis Server.

GitHub location of this recipe:
https://github.com/WHISHWORKS/mule-api-recipes/tree/publish_v1.0/cache-strategy/

Pre requisites
1. Anypoint Studio installed
   https://www.mulesoft.com/lp/dl/studio/
2. Redis Server installed
   https://redis.io/download/
3. **MySQL** database installed
   https://www.mysql.com/downloads/
4. **Database tables** created as given in the SQL scripts available in the repository
5. **MySQL Driver 5.0.8** jar https://dev.mysql.com/downloads/connector/j/5.0.html/
6. Jedis 2.1.0 jar
   http://www.java2s.com/Code/Jar/j/Downloadjedis210jar.html/

Process
High Level Steps:
  A.   Designing Mule Flow using Cache Scope
  B.   JAVA Class for Redis Cache
  C.   Starting Redis Server
  D.   Testing

A. Designing flow using Cache Scope

  1.   Open **Anypoint Studio,** create a new **Mule Project.**

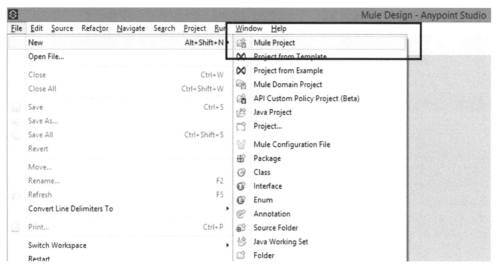

Figure 24.1: Anypoint Studio

  2.   Give **Project Name** as **cache-strategy** and click on **Finish** as shown below:

Figure 24.2: New Mule Project

3. Drag and drop an **HTTP component** from **Mule Palette** as shown below:

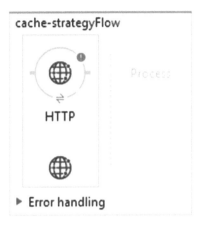

Figure 24.3: HTTP Component

4. Click on **HTTP component**, click on **Add Connector configuration** as shown below:

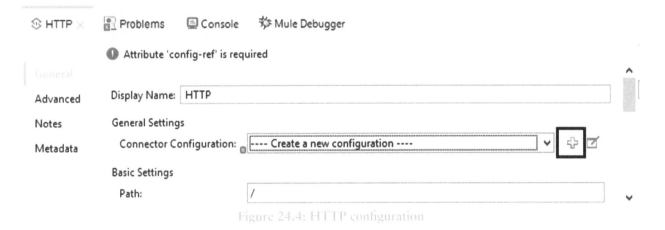

Figure 24.4: HTTP configuration

5. In the HTTP Listener Configuration, a window opens, click **OK** as shown below:

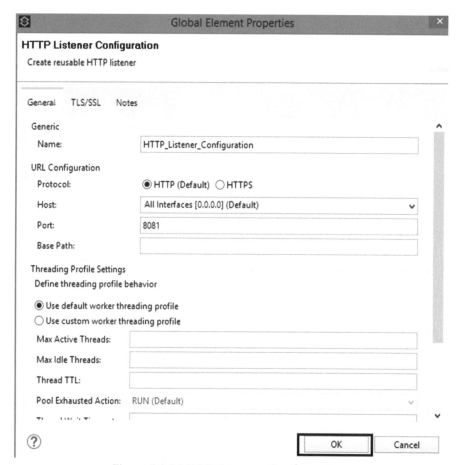

Figure 24.5 HTTP Listener Configuration

6. Give the path in **Basic Settings** as **/api/{id}** and **Allowed Methods** as **GET** as shown below:

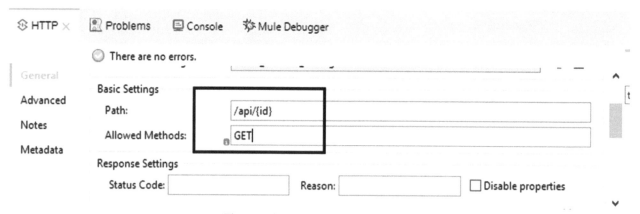

Figure 24.6: HTTP Basic Settings

7. Copy and paste the **mysql-connector-java-5.0.8-bin.jar** from the local computer to the project directory as shown:

Figure 24.7: MySQL Driver

8. Right click on **mysql jar** -> **Build Path** -> **Add to build path** as shown below:

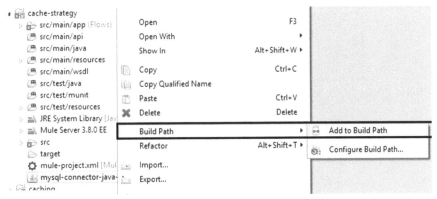

Figure 24.8: Build Path

9. Drag and drop **Set Payload** component from **Mule Palette** as shown below:

Figure 24.9: Set Payload

10. Click on **Set Payload** and give the Value as **#[message.inboundProperties.'http.uri.params'.id]** as shown below:

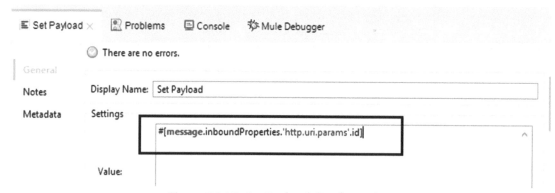

Figure 24.10: Set Payload Configuration

11. Drag and drop a **Cache Scope** component from Mule Palette as shown below:

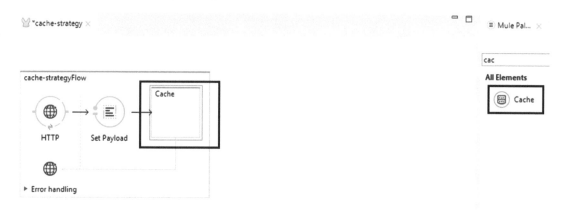

Figure 24.11: Cache Scope

12. Drag and drop **Logger** component from Mule Palette inside the Cache Scope as shown below:

Figure 24.12: Logger

13. Click on **Logger** component and mention **Calling DB for key #[payload]** in the Message settings as shown below:

Figure 24.13: Logger Message

14. Next, drag and drop a **Database connector** from Mule Palette inside the Cache Scope as shown below:

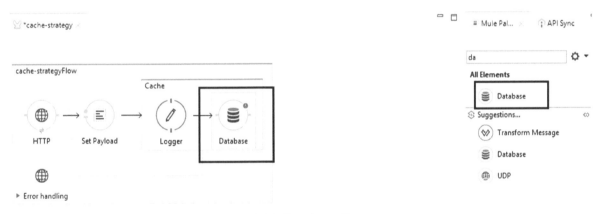

Figure 24.14: Database Connector

15. Click on **Database** -> **Add New Connector Configuration** as shown below:

Figure 24.15: Database Connector Configuration

16. Select **MySQL Configuration** in the dialogue box and click **OK** as shown below:

Figure 24.16: Connector Configuration

17. Give the database details in the dialogue box as shown below:

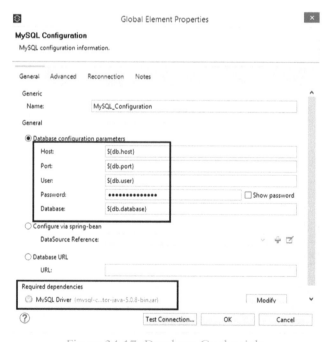

Figure 24.17: Database Credentials

18. Click on **Test Connection** to make sure the database is reachable.

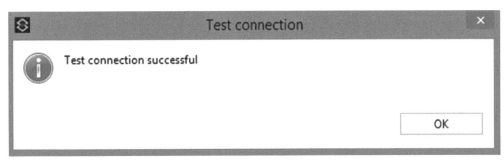

Figure 24.18: Test Connection

19. In the **Operation** option of **Database** component, click on the **drop down** menu and then click **Select** as shown below:

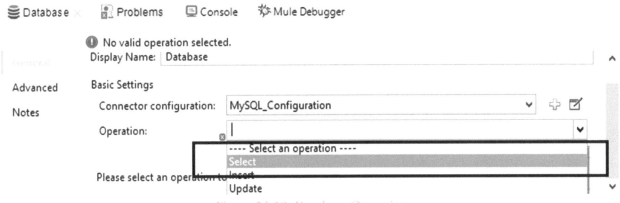

Figure 24.19: Database Operation

20. Give the following query in the Parameterized Query option
select * from apiproject.cachingapi where id = #[payload].

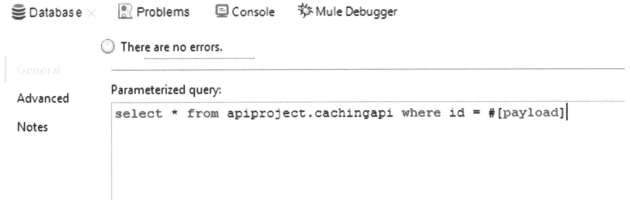

Figure 24.20: SQL Query

21. Drag and drop two Object to JSON components from Mule Palette, one inside the Cache Scope and the other one outside as shown below:

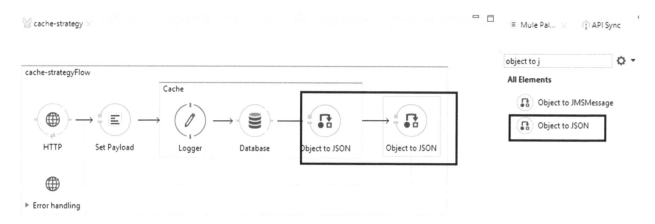

Figure 24.21: Object to JSON

B. JAVA Class for Redis Cache

1. In this recipe, **Jedis API** is used for **Redis** connections. Jedis is a small Redis Java client.
2. Copy and paste **jedis-2.1.0.jar** into the project and include it in the build path as shown:

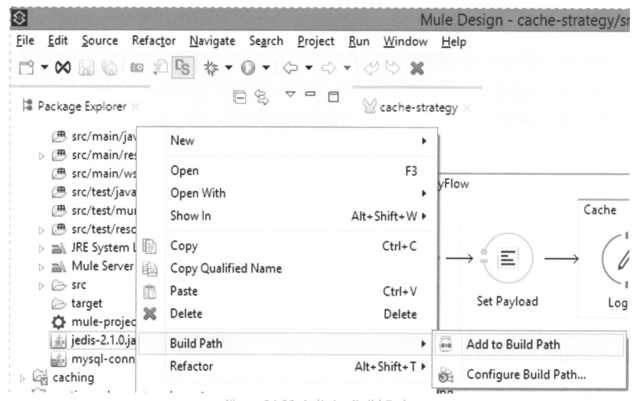

Figure 24.22: Jedis jar Build Path

3. Create a new **Java class RedisCache** in src/main/java directory as shown below:

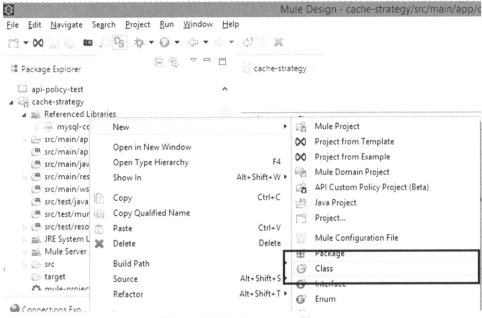

Figure 24.23: New Java Class

4. Give **Package** name as **ww.caching** and **Class** name as **RedisCache** and click **Finish** as shown below:

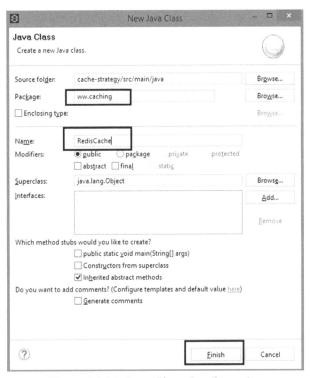

Figure 24.24: Java Class Configuration

5. Following is the class diagram of the Java class:

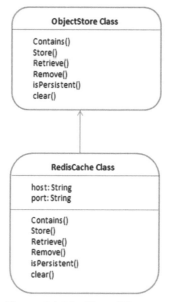

Figure 24.25: Class Diagram

6. Connection with Redis Server can be made using:
   Jedis jedis = new Jedis(host, port);
7. After the connection is made with Redis Server through Jedis API, Jedis object gives getter and setter methods to Read/Write the data.
8. Class in this recipe implements ObjectStore Interface by Mule, which is used to write custom object store.
9. In the Retrieve and Store method of RedisCache class, jedis's set and get methods are implemented so that when Cache Scope is called, it stores the data with a unique key, and if the same data is requested again it will check that the key is available in the Redis database by calling contains method, and if it returns true then the data will be fetched from Redis database and returned to the user.
10. Following code snippet shows the two functions - Store and Retrieve

```java
public synchronized void store(Serializable key, T value)
throws ObjectStoreException {
    // TODO Auto-generated method stub
    Jedis jedis = new Jedis(host, port);

    MuleEvent muleEvent =  (MuleEvent) value;
    String payload = null;
    try {
        payload = muleEvent.getMessageAsString();
    } catch (MuleException e) {
        // TODO Auto-generated catch block
        e.printStackTrace();
    }
```

```
        jedis.set((String)key, payload);
}

@SuppressWarnings({ "unchecked" })
@Override
public synchronized T retrieve(Serializable key) throws ObjectStoreException {

        MuleEvent muleEvent = RequestContext.getEvent( );

        // TODO Auto-generated method stub
        if(contains(key)) {
                Jedis jedis = new Jedis(host, port);
                String value = jedis.get((String)key);
                DefaultMuleMessage msg = new DefaultMuleMessage(value, muleEvent.
getMuleContext() );
                muleEvent.setMessage(msg);
                return  (T) muleEvent;
        }
        return null;
}
```

11. Copy and paste the full JAVA code available at <GitHub location of this recipe >/src/main/java/ww/ caching/RedisCache.java.
12. Click on **Cache Scope** and in **Caching strategy reference** option, select **Reference to a strategy** and click on **Add** as shown below:

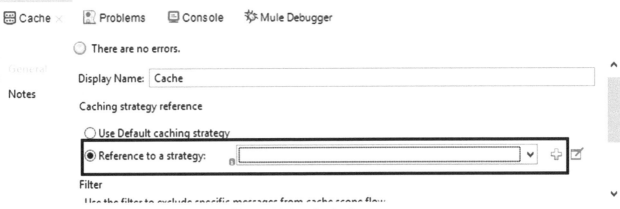

Figure 24.26: Cache Strategy

13. Global Element properties dialogue would appear. Enter **Key Expression** as **#[payload]** and click on **Add Object Store** as shown below:

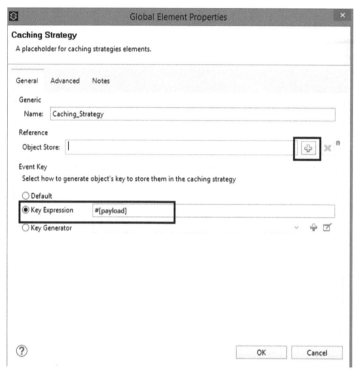

Figure 24.27: Caching Strategy

14. In the dialogue, select **core:custom-object-store** and click **Next** as shown below:

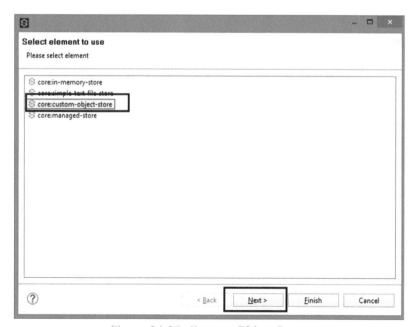

Figure 24.28: Custom Object Store

15. In the next dialogue, click on the **search** icon and search for **RedisCache class** as shown below:

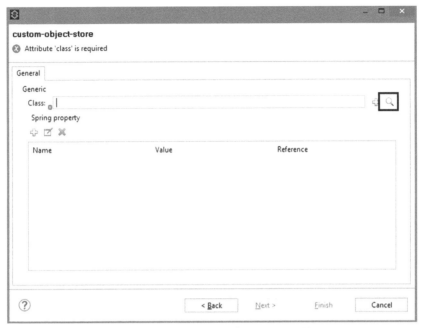

Figure 24.29: Custom Object Store Class

16. Select **RedisCache class** and click **OK** as shown below:

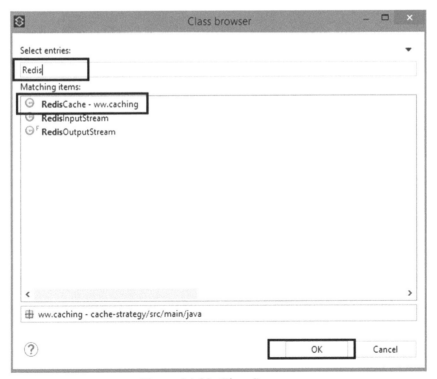

Figure 24.30: Class Browser

17. Click **Finish** in the **Custom Object store** dialogue as shown below:

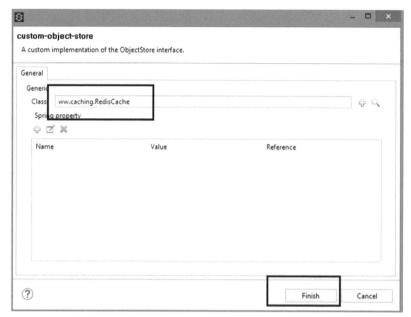

Figure 24.31: Custom-object-store

18. Click **OK** on Caching Strategy.

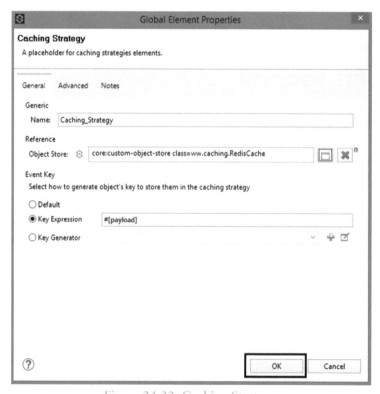

Figure 24.32: Caching Strategy

19. Complete flow looks as shown below:

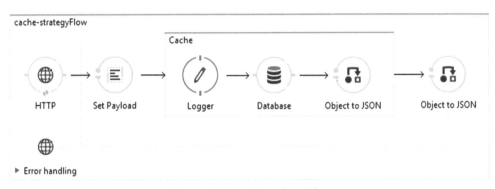

Figure 24.33: Complete Flow

20. XML Code snippet for the above flow is:

```xml
        <http:listener-config  name="HTTP_Listener_Configuration"  host="0.0.0.0"
port="8081" doc:name="HTTP Listener Configuration"/>
    <db:mysql-config name="MySQL_Configuration" host="123.176.38.211" port="3306"
user="apiuser1" password="apiwhish#369" database="apiproject" doc:name="MySQL
Configuration"/>
    <ee:object-store-caching-strategy name="Caching_Strategy" keyGenerationExp
ression="#[payload]" doc:name="Caching Strategy">
        <custom-object-store class="ww.caching.RedisCache"/>
    </ee:object-store-caching-strategy>
    <flow name="cache-strategyFlow">
        <http:listener config-ref="HTTP_Listener_Configuration" path="/api/{id}"
allowedMethods="GET" doc:name="HTTP"/>
        <set-payload value="#[message.inboundProperties.'http.uri.params'.id]"
doc:name="Set Payload"/>
        <ee:cache doc:name="Cache" cachingStrategy-ref="Caching_Strategy">
            <logger message="Calling DB for key #[payload]" level="INFO"
doc:name="Logger"/>
          <db:select config-ref="MySQL_Configuration" doc:name="Database">
                <db:parameterized-query><![CDATA[select * from apiproject.
cachingapi where id = #[payload]]]></db:parameterized-query>
            </db:select>
            <json:object-to-json-transformer doc:name="Object to JSON"/>
        </ee:cache>
        <json:object-to-json-transformer doc:name="Object to JSON"/>
    </flow>
</mule>
```

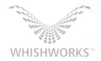

C. Starting Redis Server

1. Open Command prompt and navigate to the **Redis Server directory,** and run **redis-server** as shown below:

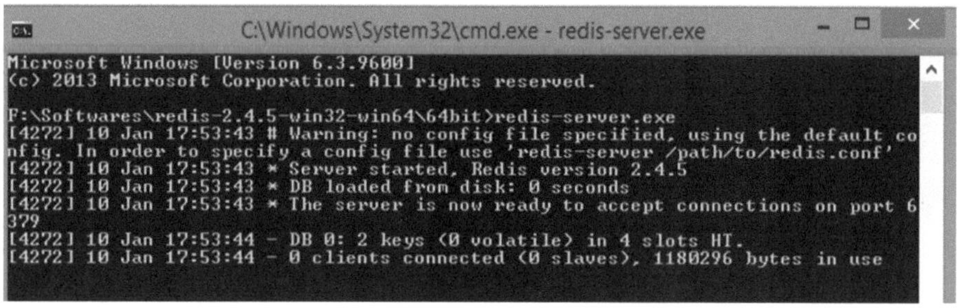

Figure 24.34: Redis Server start

2. In the project, open **mule-app.properties** file in src/main/app location and put the host and port of Redis server as shown:
redis.host=localhost
redis.port=6379

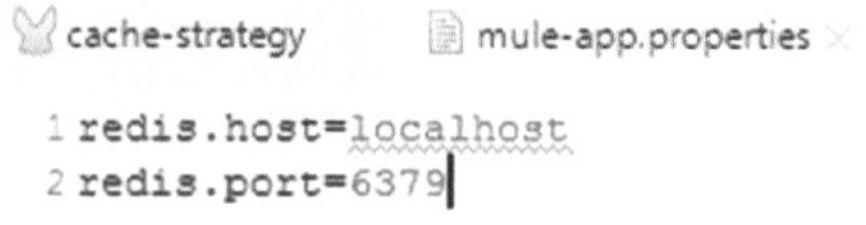

Figure 24.35: Redis Server host & port

D. Testing

1. Right click on the **project,** click **Run As -> Mule Application** as shown below:

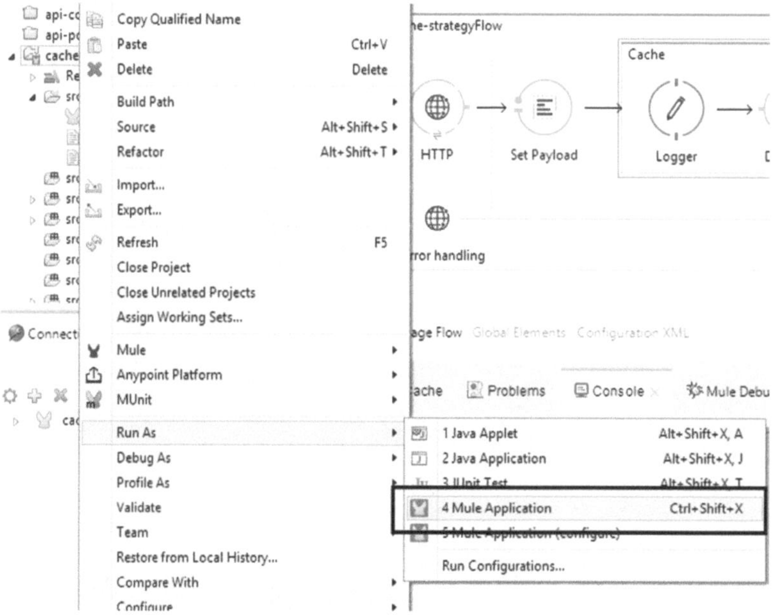

Figure 24.36: Run as Mule Application

2. After the successful deployment of the project, the console should this message:

Figure 24.37: Console

3. Open a browser with URL http://localhost:8081/api/1.
4. Since this was the first time that the request was made for ID 1, flow will call the database and get the response back. At the same time, it will save it in Redis server.

Figure 24.38: Console

5. Flow response:

[{"LastName":"swarnkar","FirstName":"sanjay","Email":"sanjay@abc.com","Id":"1"}]

Figure 24.39: Response

6. Refresh the same page. This time a second request is made for the same data with key 1, hence Cache Scope fetches the response from the Redis server and sends it to the user.

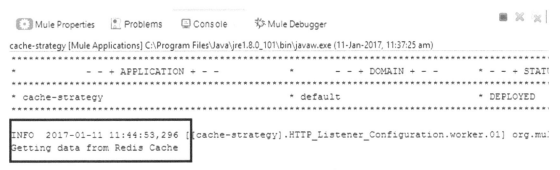

Figure 24.40: Console

`[{"LastName":"swarnkar","FirstName":"sanjay","Email":"sanjay@abc.com","Id":"1"}]`

Figure 24.41: Response

Anticipated Issues
1. Redis Server should be up and running
2. SQL database should be accessible

References
1. https://docs.mulesoft.com/mule-user-guide/v/3.7/cache-scope
2. https://redislabs.com/redis-java
3. https://docs.mulesoft.com/mule-user-guide/v/3.6/mule-object-stores

RECIPE 25

File Upload with REST API

MuleESB carries packages of information (messages) from one system to another, allowing for software integration without the need of the involved systems to know about each other, their transport, protocols or any API changes. When a message originates through an HTTP POST that sends files through a Multipart Request, each file is automatically read by Mule and stored in the message under the **inboundAttachments** property.

This recipe would boost your confidence level on MuleSoft Anypoint Platform to create an API to upload any file and write it at the provided location.

GitHub location of this recipe:
https://github.com/WHISHWORKS/mule-api-recipes/tree/publish_v1.0/file-upload-api

Pre-requisites
1. MuleSoft Anypoint Studio 6.1 or above (https://www.mulesoft.com/lp/dl/studio) installed
2. MuleSoft CloudHub Account (https://anypoint.mulesoft.com)
3. Postman plugin for Chrome is installed from https://www.getpostman.com/docs/introduction

Process
High Level Steps:
 A. Implementation of the API
 B. Testing

A. **Implementation of the API**
 1. Launch Mule Anypoint Studio and create a new **Mule Project** as shown below:
   File > New > Mule Project

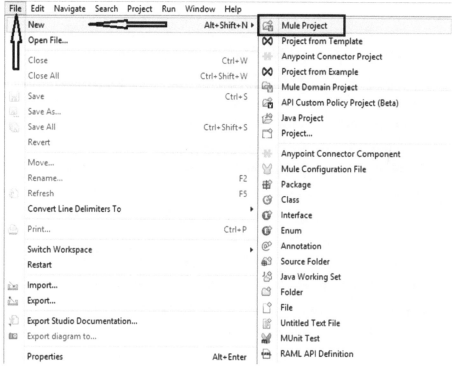

Figure 25.1: Creating New Mule Project

2. In the **New Mule Project** dialogue that comes up, provide the **Project Name** as 'file-upload-api'. Click **Finish.**

Figure 25.2: New Mule Project Wizard

3. This will create a skeleton project.

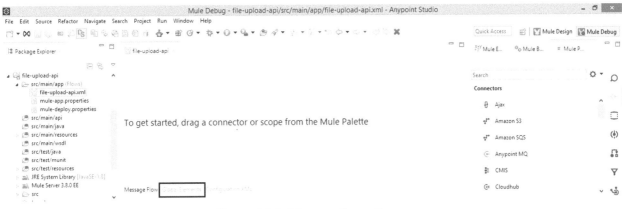

Figure 25.3: Message flow - Empty

4. Click on **Global Elements** as shown in the figure above.
5. **HTTP Connector** should be added as **Global Element**.
a. Click on **Create** button.

Figure 25.4: Global Mule Configuration Elements

b. **Choose Global Type** dialogue appears. Search for HTTP in **Filter** field for **HTTP listener configuration connector.**

Figure 25.5: Choose Global Type

c.   Select **HTTP Listener Configuration** that appears under Connector Configuration as shown below and click **OK.**

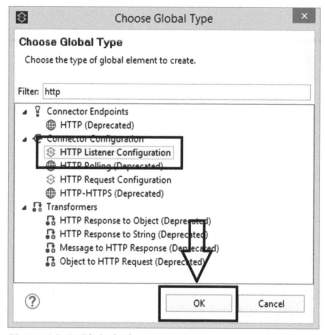

Figure 25.6: Global Element - Connector Configuration

d.   **Global Element Properties** dialogue would be displayed. Click **OK.**

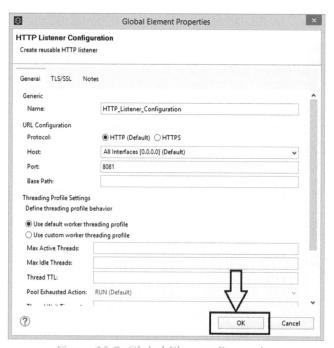

Figure 25.7: Global Element Properties

e. The Global element will be updated in **Global Elements** tab as shown below:

Figure 25.8: Global Element

6. Navigate to **Message Flow** tab as shown above.
   a. Drag **Flow element** from **Mule Palette** and drop it in the Message Flow tab as shown below:

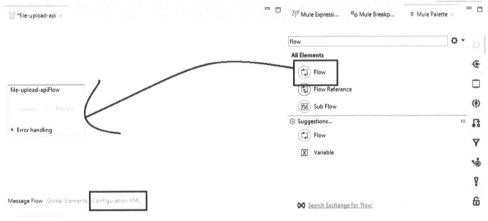

Figure 25.9: Flow Skeleton

b. Search **HTTP Connector** and drag it to the source inside the flow as shown as below:

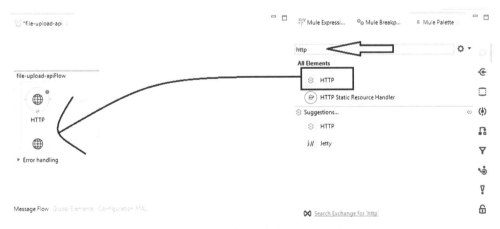

Figure 25.10: Flow Skeleton – HTTP

c. Double click on **HTTP connector,** provide the **Path** as **'/fileupload'** under Basic Setting.

d. Create a Java custom transformer file i.e. **CustomTransformer.java** which will transform file to readable format as shown below:

```
# CustomTransformer.java

package org.mule;
import java.io.IOException;
import java.io.InputStream;
import javax.activation.DataHandler;
import org.mule.api.MuleMessage;
import org.mule.api.transformer.TransformerException;
import org.mule.config.i18n.MessageFactory;
import org.mule.transformer.AbstractMessageTransformer;
public class CustomTransformer extends AbstractMessageTransformer {
    @Override
    public byte[] transformMessage(MuleMessage message, String outputEncoding)
throws TransformerException {
        try {
            DataHandler file = message.getInboundAttachment("file");
            final InputStream in = file.getInputStream();
                    byte[] byteArray=org.apache.commons.io.IOUtils.toByteArray(in);
            return byteArray;
        }catch(IOException ioException){
            thrownew TransformerException(MessageFactory.createStaticMessage("Error
while transforming"), ioException);
        }
    }
}
```

e. Add this file to project at **path src < main < java < org < mule**. Refresh the Application in Anypoint Studio to update it. It looks like as shown below:

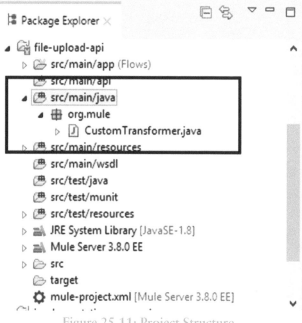

Figure 25.11: Project Structure

f.   Drag **Java transformer** from **Mule Palette** and drop it to flow as shown below:

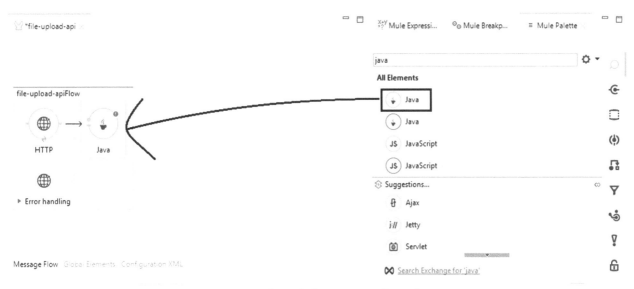

Figure 25.12: Flow Skeleton – Java Transformer

g.   Double click on **Java** transformer element to open its configuration.
     i. Change Display Name **Java** to **Custom Transformer.**
     ii. Click Search icon as shown below:

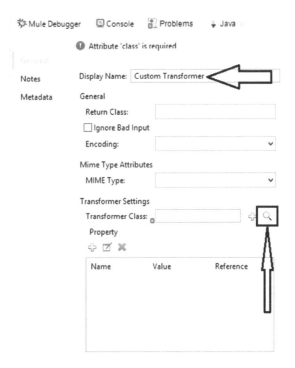

Figure 25.13: Java Transformation Configuration

iii. Search for the **CustomTransformer** Java file in **Transformer Class browser** dialogue as shown below:

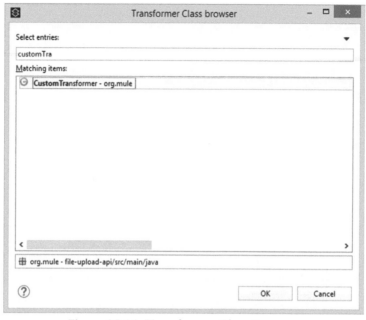

Figure 25.14: Transformer Class Browser

iv. **Select** the file and click **OK.**

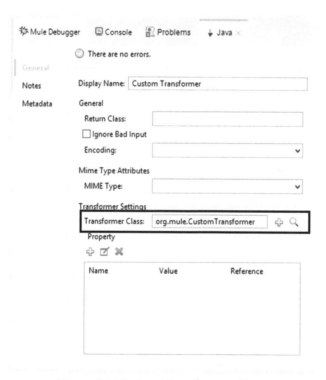

Figure 25.15: Java Transformer Class

h. Drag and drop **File** to write the content(output from CustomTransformation.java file) at specific location as shown below:

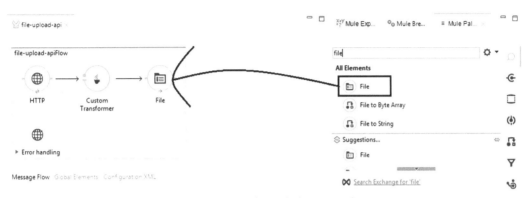

Figure 25.16: Flow Skeleton – File

i. Double click on **Java transformer** element to open its configuration.
   i. Provide the path as any location as per the PC drive (Note: To deploy on CloudHub, use a cloud service path such as Amazon S3).
   ii. Provide File Name/Pattern as **#[message.inboundAttachments['file'].dataSource.part.fileName]**.
   iii. Add **Connector Configuration** on click of **add icon** and click **OK** under Global Element Properties.

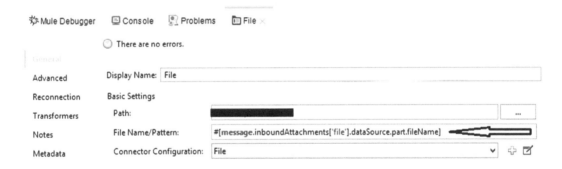

Figure 25.17: File Configuration

j. **Save** the application and navigate to **Configuration XML** tab to cross check XML for the flow.

```
<flow name="file-upload-apiFlow">
    <http:listener   config-ref="HTTP_Listener_Configuration"   path="/fileupload"
doc:name="HTTP"/>
    <custom-transformer   class="org.mule.CustomTransformer"   doc:name="Custom
Transformer"/>
    <file:outbound-endpoint   path="E:\backup\newfolder"   outputPattern="#[message.
inboundAttachments['file'].dataSource.part.fileName]" connector-ref="File" response
Timeout="10000" doc:name="File"/>
    <set-payload   value="File   Uploaded   Successfully...."   doc:name="Success
Message"/>
</flow>
```

k. **Save** the file and click on **Mule Flow** tab. The corresponding **POST** Mule Flow should now look like:

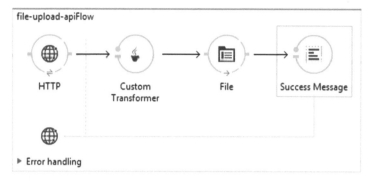

Figure 25.18: Mule Flow

7. Now, the flow is completed. It's time to build and deploy the application.
8. Right click on **project name** and select **Run As > Mule Application** to run this application.

Figure 25.19: Run Application

9. After some time, the application will be initiated as shown below:

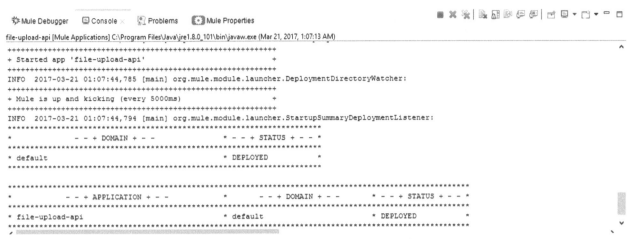

Figure 25.20: Application Started

B. Testing

1. Launch **Postman** Chrome Application as mentioned in pre-requisites.

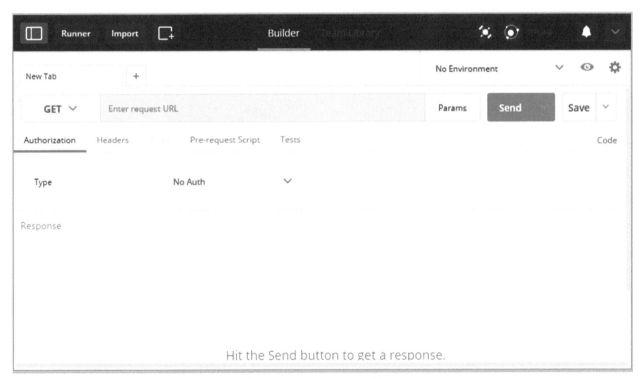

Figure 25.21: Postman Home

2. Test this API.
   a. Select **POST** Method which has to be tested from the dropdown.
   b. Provide URL (localhost:8081+ /fileupload) localhost:8081/fileupload.

c. Select **Body** then select **form-data radio** button.

d. Select **file** from the dropdown.

e. Provide **key** as **file** and choose any file i.e. final.txt to upload as shown below:

Figure 25.22: File Upload Request in Postman

3. Click **Send** to invoke the API to upload the file and read it.

4. Click **Raw** and the response will be shown as below:

```
File Uploaded Successfully...
```

Figure 25.23: File Upload Response in Postman

5. The uploaded file will be saved at the given location with the same file format.

Anticipated Issues

NA

References

1. https://blogs.mulesoft.com/dev/mule-dev/soap-rest-attachments/
2. https://blogs.mulesoft.com/dev/anypoint-studio-dev/handling-file-attachments-handling-multipart-requests-in-mule/

RECIPE 26

Mule Message Encryption and Decryption

The Encryption and Decryption of APIs allow to store information or to communicate with other parties while preventing uninvolved parties from understanding the stored information or understanding the communication.

The Encrypt Data API protects data privacy by scrambling clear data into an unintelligible form. To recover clear data from the encrypted data, use the Decrypt Data which will restore encrypted data to a clear (intelligible) form. Both processes involve a mathematical formula (algorithm) and secret data (key).

This recipe would boost your confidence level on MuleSoft Anypoint Platform for how easy and quick it is to encrypt and decrypt data. It can be achieved in many ways. This recipe uses Java Cryptology Extension (JCE), as part of the Java Cryptography Architecture (JCA) which encodes a message payload, or part of a payload.

GitHub location of this recipe:
https://github.com/WHISHWORKS/mule-api-recipes/tree/publish_v1.0/api-encryption

Pre-requisites
1. MuleSoft Anypoint Studio 6.1 or above (https://www.mulesoft.com/lp/dl/studio) installed
2. MuleSoft CloudHub Account (https://anypoint.mulesoft.com)
3. Application api-encryption is available on GitHub location of this recipe provided above

Process

High Level Steps:
A. Installing Anypoint Enterprise Security
B. Implementation of the API
C. Testing

A. Installing Anypoint Enterprise Security
1. Launch Anypoint Studio.

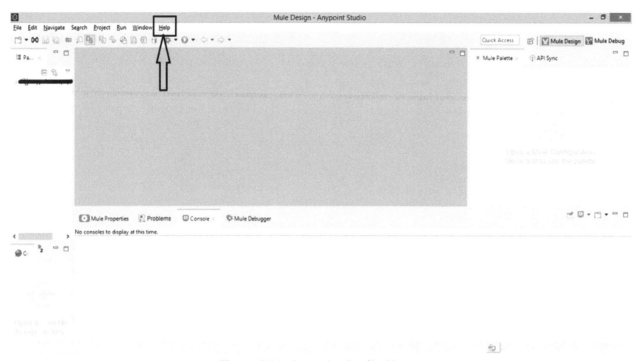

Figure 26.1: Anypoint Studio Home

2. Under the **Help** menu, select **Install New Software** as shown below:

Figure 26.2: Anypoint Studio Help

3.   Install wizard opens. Click the **Add** button next to the **Work with** field.

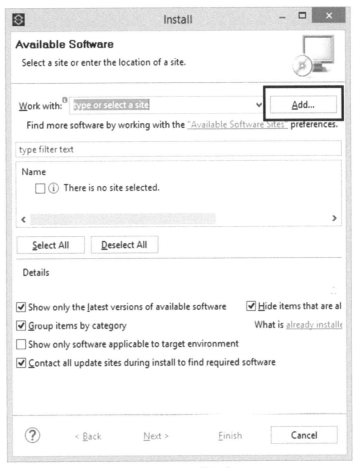

Figure 26.3: Install Software

4.   In **Add Repository** panel, provide a **Name** for the repository as Anypoint Enterprise Security, and provide the link in the **Location** field as http://security-update-site-1.6.s3.amazonaws.com. Click **OK** as shown below:

Figure 26.4: Add Repository

5. In the table, check the box to select **Premium**. Click **Next** as shown below:

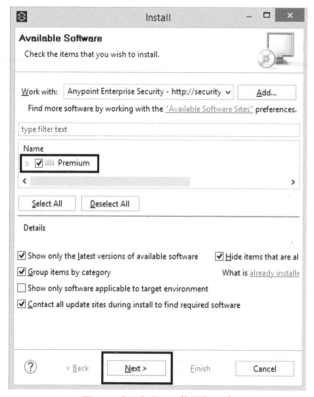

Figure 26.5: Install Wizard

6. Click **Next** in the next wizard pane.
7. Use the radio button to accept the terms of the license agreement, then click **Finish**.
8. Anypoint Studio installs **Anypoint Enterprise Security,** and asks to restart the application.
9. After Anypoint Studio Application's relaunch, Studio displays a new palette group called Security which contains six new message processors as shown below:

Figure 26.6: Palette - Security

B. Implementation of the API

1. Launch Mule Anypoint Studio and create a new **Mule Project** as shown below:
    File > New > Mule Project
2. In the **New Mule Project** dialogue that comes up, provide the **Project Name** as api-encryption. Click **Finish**.

Figure 26.7: New Mule Project

3. This will create a blank project (as shown below) where Mule Flow will be implemented.

Figure 26.8: Project Structure

4. Click on **Global Elements** as shown above.
5. HTTP Connector should be added as a global element.
    a. Click on **Create** button.

Figure 26.9: Global Elements Blank

b. **Choose Global Type** dialogue appears. Search for **http** in **Filter** field for HTTP Listener configuration connector.

Figure 26.10: Choose Global Type

c. Select **HTTP Listener Configuration** that appears under Connector Configuration as shown below and click **OK.**

Figure 26.11: Global Element – HTTP Connector

d. **Global Element Properties** dialogue would be displayed. Click **OK**.

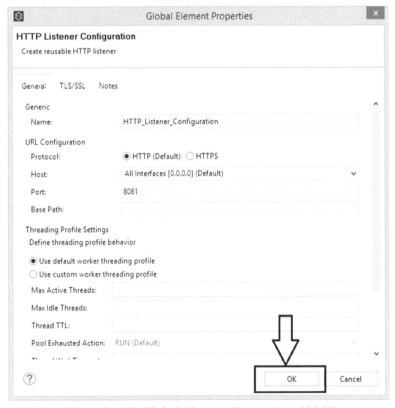

Figure 26.12: Global Element Properties - HTTP

e. The Global Element will be updated in **Global Element** tab as shown below:

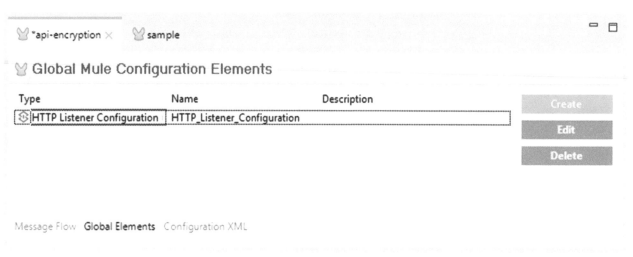

Figure 26.13: Global Elements - HTTP

6. Now, Encryption connector as a global element is also required for this project.
    a. Click on **Create** button
    b. **Choose Global Type** dialogue appears. Search for **encryption** in **Filter** field for Encryption connector.
    c. Select **Encryption** that appears under Connector Configuration as shown below and click **OK.**

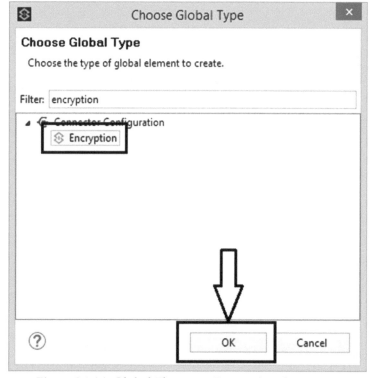

Figure 26.14: Global Element – Encryption Connector

338

d. **Global Element Properties** dialogue would be displayed.

Figure 26.15: Global Element Properties - Encrypter

e. Leave Default Encrypter as **JCE_ENCRYPTER(Default)**. Click Jce Encrypter as shown above.
   i. Select **Define attributes** radio button:
   ii. Provide 16 bytes key i.e. kishankrsoni2512
   iii. Leave other fields as default
   iv. Click OK

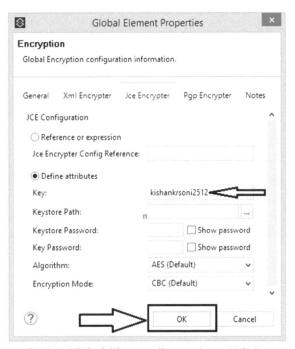

Figure 26.16: Global Element Properties – JCE Encrypter

f.   The Global element will be updated in **Global Element** tab as shown below:

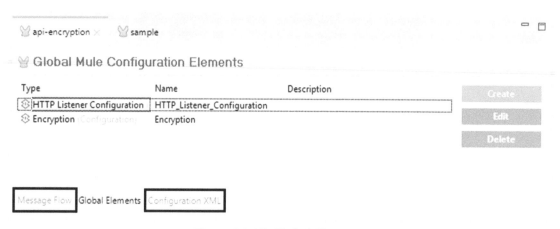

Figure 26.17: Global Elements

7.   Go to **Package Explorer** and open **mule-app.properties** under this application **api-encryption** as shown below:

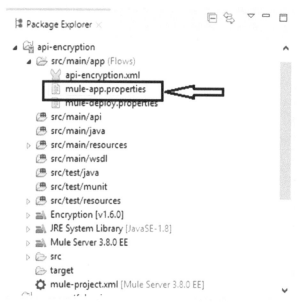

Figure 26.18: Application – Path Update

8.   Provide the path for **path.encryptedFileLocation** and **path.output** as shown below:

Figure 26.19: Mule-app.properties

9. Navigate to **Message Flow** tab.
   a. Drag **HTTP connector** from Mule Palette and drop it in Message Flow as shown below:

Figure 26.20: Message Flow - HTTP

b. Click on the **Configuration XML** tab and search with the flow name i.e. *api-encryptionFlow flow*. The corresponding Mule Flow XML content should look like:

```
<flow name="api-encryptionFlow">
  <http:listener config-ref="HTTP_Listener_Configuration" path="/" doc:name="HTTP"/>
</flow>
```

10. Implement the HTTP method in *api-encryptionFlow* flow.
    a. In this Mule Flow replace the XML with the following XML content:

```
<flow name="api-encryptionFlow">
    <http:listener config-ref="HTTP_Listener_Configuration" path="/jceEncryptor"
doc:name="HTTP"/>
        <set-payload value="kishan" doc:name="Input"/>
          <encryption:encrypt  config-ref="Encryption" using="JCE_ENCRYPTER"
doc:name="JCE Encrypter">
            <encryption:jce-encrypter key="kishankrsoni2512"/>
        </encryption:encrypt>
                <file:outbound-endpoint  path="${path.encryptedFileLocation}"
outputPattern="sample.txt" responseTimeout="10000" doc:name="Writing into Text
File"/>
        <logger level="INFO" doc:name="Encrypted data Value"  message="#[payload]"/>
</flow>
```

In the code above, the request data is received and encrypted through JCE Encrypter and write into text file named as **sample.txt** at the given path provided in **mule-app.properties** as **path.encryptedFileLocation**.

 b. **Save** the file and click on **Mule Flow** tab. The corresponding Mule Flow should now look like:

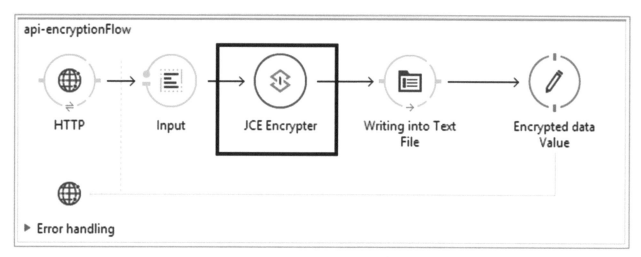

Figure 26.21: Encryption Flow

11. Now, it's time to develop a flow to decrypt encrypted text file and implement it.
12. Again, navigate to **Message Flow** tab.
  a. Drag **HTTP connector** from **Mule Palette** and drop it in the Message Flow as shown below:

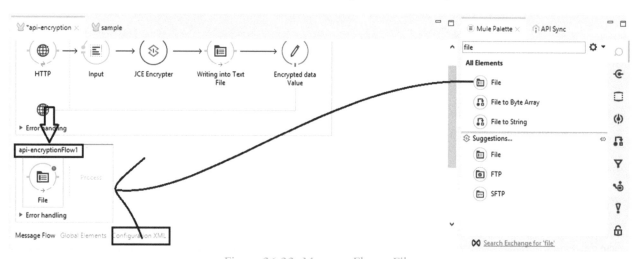

Figure 26.22: Message Flow - File

 b. Change the flow name **api-encryptionFlow1** to **decryptionFlow** by clicking on **Flow name** as shown in above image.

 c. Click on the **Configuration XML** tab and search with the flow name i.e. decryptionFlow flow. The corresponding Mule Flow XML content should look like:

```
<flow name="DecryptionFlow">
        <file:inbound-endpoint responseTimeout="10000" doc:name="File"/>
</flow>
```

13. Implement the HTTP method in *decryptionFlow* flow.
   a. In this Mule Flow, replace the XML with the following XML content:

```
<flow name="DecryptionFlow">
      <file:inbound-endpoint                       path="${path.encryptedFileLocation}"
responseTimeout="10000" doc:name="Read data from text file">
            <file:filename-regex-filter pattern="sample.txt" caseSensitive="false"/>
      </file:inbound-endpoint>
      <file:file-to-string-transformer doc:name="File to String"/>
      <encryption:decrypt config-ref="Encryption" doc:name="Decryption">
            <encryption:jce-encrypter key="kishankrsoni2512"/>
      </encryption:decrypt>
      <set-payload value="#[payload] is a good boy" doc:name="Implementation of
decypted data"/>
      <file:outbound-endpoint   path="${path.output}"   outputPattern="final.txt"
responseTimeout="10000" doc:name="Write into file"/>
</flow>
```

   b. In the code above, the encrypted data will be read from the text file and decrypted through JCE decrypter and written into the text file named as **final.txt** at the given path provided in **mule-app.properties** as **path.output.**
   c. **Save** the file and click on **Mule Flow** tab. The corresponding Mule Flow should now look like:

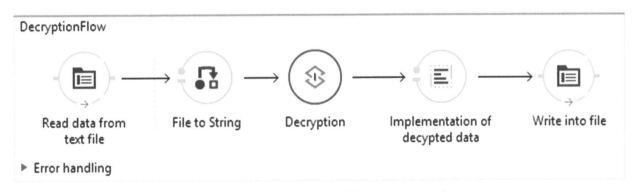

Figure 26.23: Decryption of encrypted data and its implementation

14. Right click on project name and select **Run As > Mule Application** to run this application.

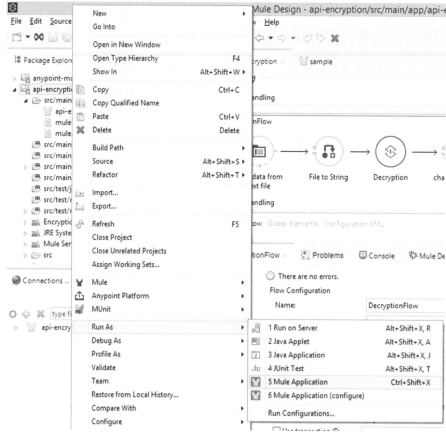

Figure 26.24: Run Application

15. After some time, Application will be started as shown below:

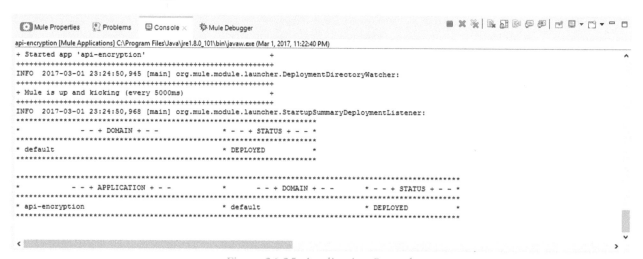

Figure 26.25: Application Started

16. Now, Application is deployed at the local server with URL http://localhost:8081/jceEncryptor.

C. Testing

1. Open the browser and hit the deployed API http://localhost:8081/jceEncryptor. Here, Input is provided as 'kishan'.

+hLzfbyON/TJqt7m41dUIg==

Figure 26.26: Encrypted Result

2. The first flow will encrypt the input 'kishan' to '+hLzfbyON/TJqt7m41dUIg==' and print it into sample.txt file at the path provided.
3. The 2nd flow will come into action once the file is saved in a test folder because the File connector is used as an inbound endpoint.
4. It will decrypt the input to 'kishan' because same key is provided in jce encrypter configuration.
5. After decryption, decrypted data gets implemented and printed to final.txt file at the path provided.
6. Check E:\backup\original path. A file named as final.txt should be available as shown below. Here, the file is opened in Notepad++. However, it can be opened in Notepad or Textpad, etc.

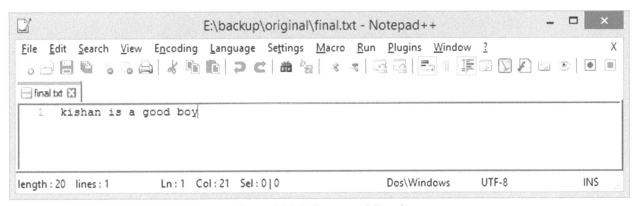

Figure 26.27: Decrypted Result

Anticipated Issues

1. Installation of security provider is required to get Encryption connector in Mule Palette.
2. Folder should be created which is mentioned in pre-requisites.
3. Key should be the same for both encryption and decryption.

References

1. https://docs.mulesoft.com/mule-user-guide/v/3.7/installing-anypoint-enterprise-security
2. http://blog.avenuecode.com/mule-jce-encryption
3. https://docs.mulesoft.com/mule-user-guide/v/3.7/mule-message-encryption-processor

RECIPE 27

Implementing Routing Rule on API Proxy

Anypoint Platform provides the capability to separate the API consumers and providers through the proxy layer. The proxy application exposes the experience layer (the API definition) to the external world so that end users can build the logic of integrating with APIs. For example, the APIs can be exposed to mobile, web, cloud or IoT applications. By doing so, the business logic becomes transparent to changes in the Process and System APIs.

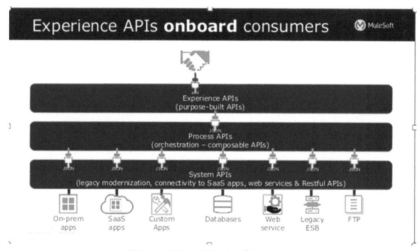

Figure 27.1: API Architecture

The proxy, acting as a gateway to backend services also becomes the governance layer. The objective of this recipe is to implement a Routing Rule at the proxy layer. This may be useful in situations where the control is to be implemented from within the proxy. For example, if the request header or the payload has to be intercepted and based on the payload type, SOAP or JSON, the corresponding service has to be called; this can be implemented with the proxy.

In this recipe, a loan approval proxy API is used to accept loan amount as input. Based on the amount, the proxy decides to process the loan.

GitHub location of this recipe:
https://github.com/WHISHWORKS/mule-api-recipes/tree/publish_v1.0/api-routing-rule/routing-rule/

Pre requisites

1. MuleSoft Anypoint Studio installed **https://www.mulesoft.com/lp/dl/studio/**
2. Access to a backend app routing-rule-app to receive loan request in JSON format is already deployed in CloudHub. **http://routing-rule-app.eu.cloudhub.io/console/**

Process

High Level Steps:

A. Create an API in CloudHub, Deploy & Download Proxy
B. Add Router to Proxy Application
C. Deploy Updated Proxy
D. Testing Proxy Application

A. Create an API in CloudHub, Deploy & Download Proxy

1. Sign in to **CloudHub** account https://anypoint.mulesoft.com/login/#/signin/.

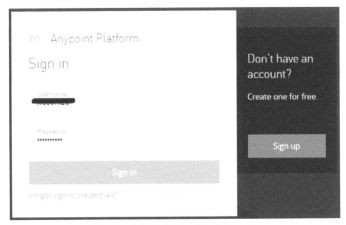

Figure 27.2: CloudHub Login

2. After login, click **API Manager** -> **Open.**

Figure 27.3: API Manager

3.   Create a new API. Click on **Add new API** as shown below:

Figure 27.4: Create New API

4.   Give following details in the dialog box as shown:
      a. **API Name: routing-rule-api**
      b. **Version Name: 1.0**
      c. **API endpoint** & **Description** can be left blank
      d. Click on **Add**

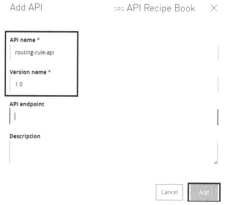

Figure 27.5: Add API

5.   A new API will be created, click on **Define API** in API designer as shown:

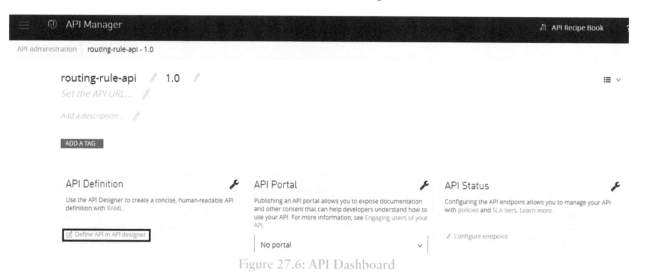

Figure 27.6: API Dashboard

6. Copy & paste the following RAML inside the API Designer view after version 1.0 as shown below:
RAML:

```
baseUri: http://routing-rule-app.eu.cloudhub.io/api/
/loan_approval:
  displayName: Loan Approval Flow
  post:
    description: Trigger different flow based on loan amount
    body:
      application/json:
    responses:
      201:
        body:
          application/json:
      400:
        body:
          application/json:
```

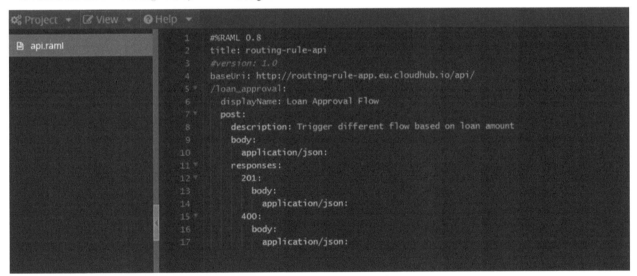

Figure 27.7: RAML Code

7. Save the file by clicking on **Project** -> **Save** as shown below:

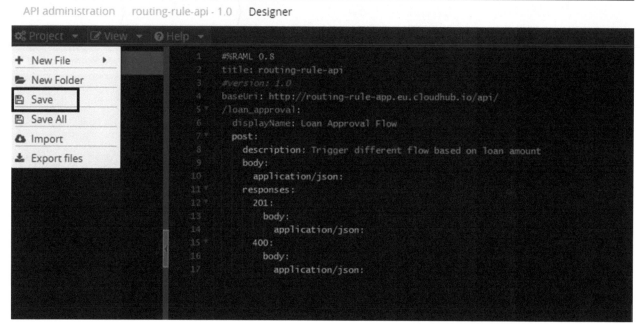

Figure 27.8: Save RAML

8. Go back to previous page by clicking **back** button in the browser window.
9. Click on **Configure endpoint** to deploy proxy for this API in CloudHub.

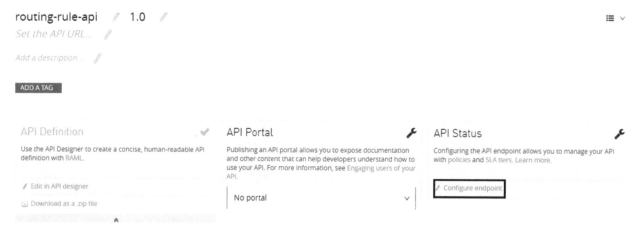

Figure 27.9: Configure Endpoint

10. Provide the following details in the configure endpoint dialogue as shown below:
    a. Click **Get from RAML** and make sure that implementation URL comes into the box as given in RAML file.
    b. Check **Configure Proxy for CloudHub.**
    c. Click **Save** & **Deploy** to deploy the proxy.

Figure 27.10: Configure Proxy

11. Give the CloudHub application name as **routing-rule-api** & select CloudHub environment as **Sandbox** then click **Deploy proxy** as shown below:

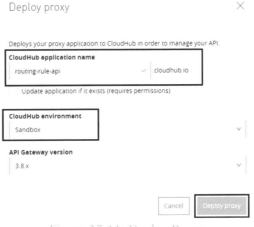

Figure 27.11: Deploy Proxy

12. Once the deployment is successfully completed API Status will be green as shown:

Figure 27.12: API Status

13. Now, download proxy (for latest gateway version 3.8.x) as shown below:

Figure 27.13: Download Proxy

B. Add Router to Proxy Application
1. Open Anypoint Studio and click on **File -> Import.**

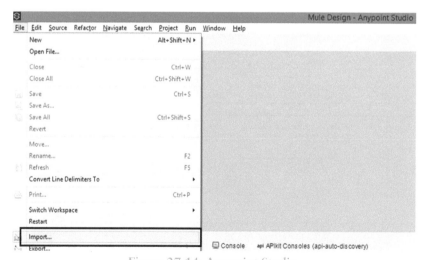

Figure 27.14: Anypoint Studio

2. Select **Anypoint Studio generated Deployable Archive (.zip)**, and click **Next**.

Figure 27.15: Import Project

3. Locate the zip file, give project name as **routing-rule-api-proxy** and click **Finish**.

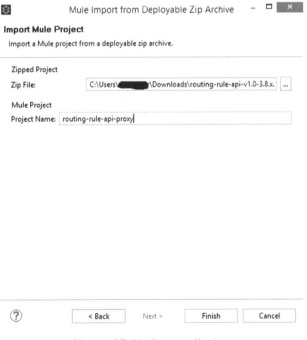

Figure 27.16: Import Project

WHISHWORKS™

4. Initial flow of the proxy would look as shown below:

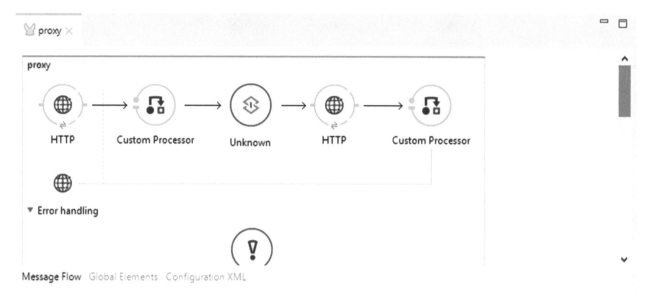

Figure 27.17: Initial Flow

5. The corresponding code for the above flow would be:

```xml
<flow name="proxy" doc:name="HTTP Proxy">
        <http:listener config-ref="http-lc-0.0.0.0-8081" path="![p['proxy.
path']]" parseRequest="false" />
                <custom-processor class="com.mulesoft.gateway.extension.
ProxyRequestHeadersProcessor" />
        <proxy:raml config-ref="proxy-config"/>
            <http:request config-ref="http-request-config" method="#[message.
inboundProperties['http.method']]" path="#[message.inboundProperties['http.
request.path'].substring(message.inboundProperties['http.listener.path'].
length()-2)]" parseResponse="false">
            <http:request-builder>
             <http:query-params expression="#[message.inboundProperties['http.
query.params']]"/>
            </http:request-builder>
            <http:success-status-code-validator values="0..599" />
        </http:request>
                <custom-processor class="com.mulesoft.gateway.extension.
ProxyResponseHeadersProcessor" />
        <exception-strategy ref="defaultExceptionStrategy"/>
    </flow>
```

6. Drag and drop **JSON to Object** component from Mule Palette into the proxy flow as shown below:

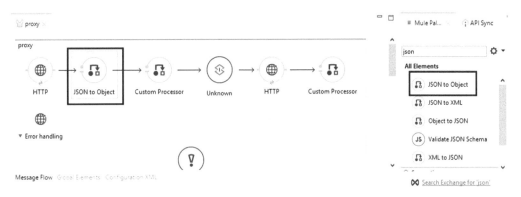

Figure 27.18: Mule Flow

7. Click on **JSON to Object** component and in the **General** settings tab give **Return Class** as **java.util. HashMap** as shown below:

Figure 27.19: JSON to Object Settings

8. Drag and drop **Sub Flow** from Mule Palette into the configuration file.
9. A sub flow, **proxySub_Flow** will be created as shown below:

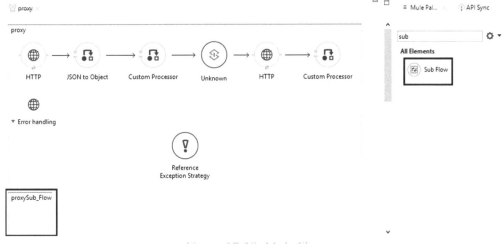

Figure 27.20: Mule Flow

10. Repeat previous step 9 to create another sub flow **proxySub_Flow1**. The resultant Mule configuration would be like:

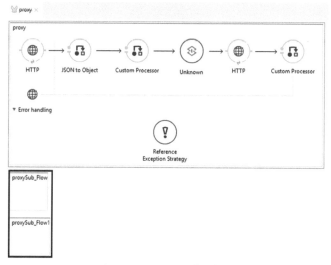

Figure 27.21: Mule Flow

11. Rename the first sub-flow as **"loan_amt>$5000"** & the second as **"loan_amt<$5000"**, respectively.

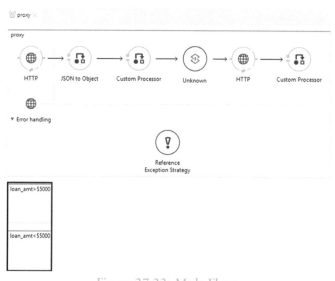

Figure 27.22: Mule Flow

12. Drag and drop **Set Payload** from Mule Palette into the two sub-flows just created.
13. Click on **set-payload** of **loan_amt<$5000** sub-flow and put this into the value.

```
{
"ReferenceID": "1234567",
"Status": "Approved"
}
```

Figure 27.23: Set Payload config

14. Click on **set-payload** of **loan_amt>$5000** sub-flow and put this into the value.

```
{
  "ReferenceID": "23456565",
  "Status": "Require some clarification"
  }
```

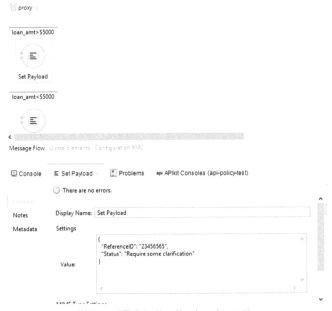

Figure 27.24: Set Payload config

357

15. Drag and drop a **Choice** router from the Mule Palette in the proxy flow after **JSON to Object** transformer.

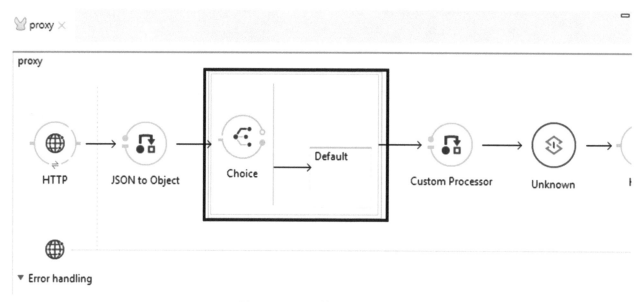

Figure 27.25: Choice Router

16. Drag **Flow Reference** from Mule Palette in to the choice router element and drop it inside the default section as shown:

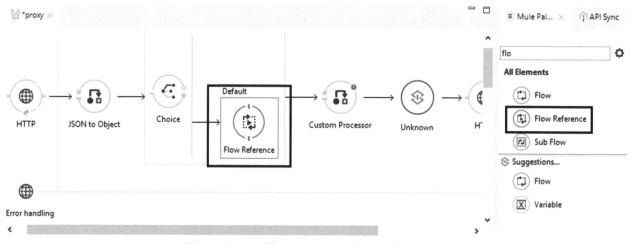

Figure 27.26: Choice Router Flow Reference 1

17. Click on **Flow Reference,** in the Display Name give **loan_amt<$5000,** also click on the drop down for Flow name and select **loan_amt<$5000** as shown:

Figure 27.27: Flow Reference 1 configuration

18. Drag another **Flow Reference** from Mule Palette in to the choice router element and drop it as shown:

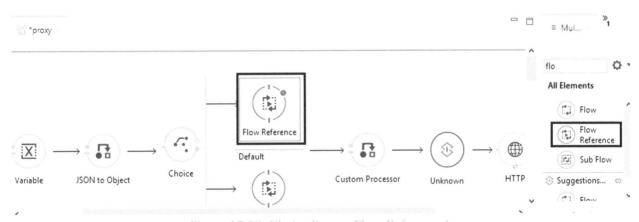

Figure 27.28: Choice Router Flow Reference 1

359

19. Click on **Flow Reference,** in the Display Name give **loan_amt>$5000,** also click on the drop down for Flow name and select **loan_amt>$5000** as shown:

Figure 27.29: Flow Reference 2 configuration

20. Click on **Choice** element and in the **When** configuration for **loan_amt>$5000** sub flow give following Mule expression:

```
#[payload.amount >= 5000]
```

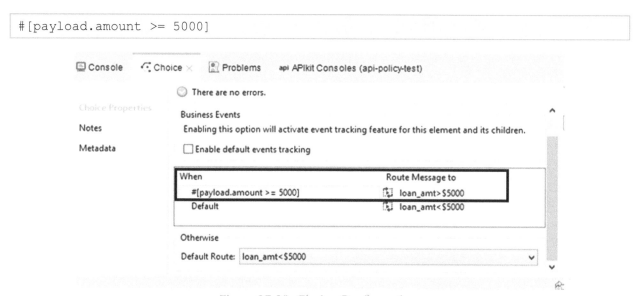

Figure 27.30: Choice Configuration

21. Notice that **Default** condition is set to the other flow reference i.e. **loan_amt<$5000.**
22. Complete **flow** looks as shown:

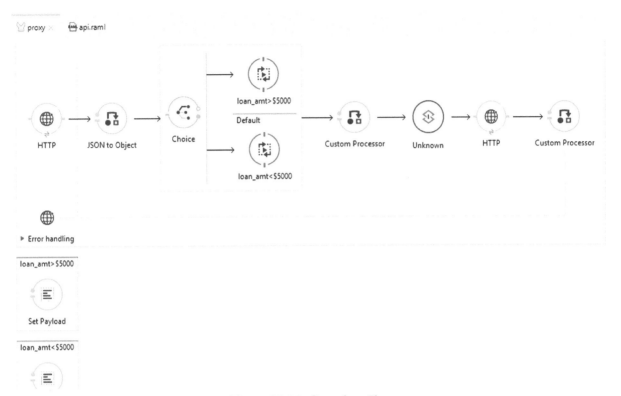

23. Corresponding code for the above flow and logic is:

```
<flow name="proxy" >
        <http:listener  config-ref="http-lc-0.0.0.0-8081"  path="![p['proxy.
path']]" parseRequest="false" doc:name="HTTP"/>
        <json:json-to-object-transformer  returnClass="java.util.HashMap  "
doc:name="JSON to Object"/>
    <choice doc:name="Choice">
        <when expression="#[payload.amount &gt;= 5000]">
            <flow-ref name="loan_amt&gt;$5000" doc:name="loan_amt&gt;$5000"/>
        </when>
        <otherwise>
            <flow-ref name="loan_amt&lt;$5000" doc:name="loan_amt&lt;$5000"/>
        </otherwise>
    </choice>
                <custom-processor  class="com.mulesoft.gateway.extension.
ProxyRequestHeadersProcessor" doc:name="Custom Processor"/>
        <proxy:raml config-ref="proxy-config"/>
        <http:request  config-ref="http-request-config"  method="#[message.
inboundProperties['http.method']]"    path="#[message.inboundProperties['http.
request.path'].substring(message.inboundProperties['http.listener.path'].
length()-2)]" parseResponse="false" doc:name="HTTP">
```

```
        <http:request-builder>
         <http:query-params expression="#[message.inboundProperties['http.
query.params']]"/>
        </http:request-builder>
        <http:success-status-code-validator values="0..599" />
    </http:request>
                <custom-processor    class="com.mulesoft.gateway.extension.
ProxyResponseHeadersProcessor" doc:name="Custom Processor"/>
        <exception-strategy ref="defaultExceptionStrategy" doc:name="Reference
Exception Strategy"/>
    </flow>
    <sub-flow name="loan_amt&gt;$5000">
        <set-payload value="{
 &quot;ReferenceID&quot;: &quot;23456565&quot;,
 &quot;Status&quot;: &quot;Require some clarification&quot;
  }
" doc:name="Set Payload"/>
    </sub-flow>
    <sub-flow name="loan_amt&lt;$5000">
        <set-payload value="{
 &quot;ReferenceID&quot;: &quot;1234567&quot;,
 &quot;Status&quot;: &quot;Approved&quot;
}
" doc:name="Set Payload"/>
    </sub-flow>
```

C. Deploy Updated Proxy

1. Deploy the proxy application from **Anypoint Studio** to **CloudHub.**

Figure 27.32: Anypoint Studio

2. Provide the **Deploying Application** name as **routing-rule-api,** check **Overwrite Existing Application,** select **Worker size** as **0.1vCores** and then click on **Deploy Application.**

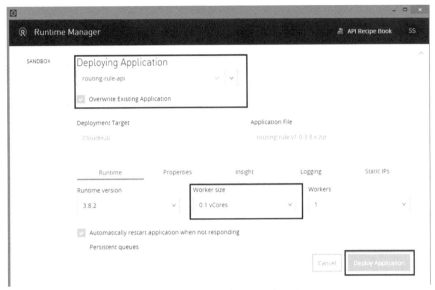

Figure 27.33: Deploy Application

3. Following window appears while the application is deploying:

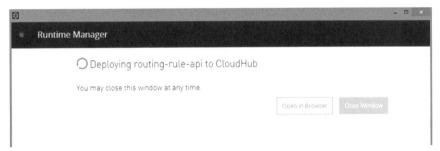

Figure 27.34: Runtime Manager

4. And after successful deployment following window comes up:

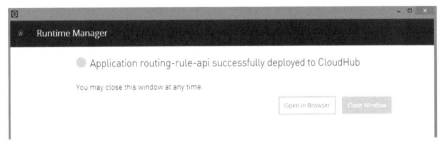

Figure 27.35: Runtime Manager

5. Now the application is deployed and ready to be tested.

D. Testing Proxy

1. Open http://routing-rule-api.eu.cloudhub.io/console/ in a browser, and click on POST (The URL may vary depending on the CloudHub environment).

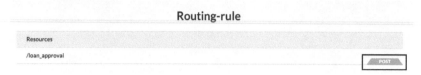

Figure 27.36: Browser window

2. Give input as following and click on POST as shown:

```
{
  "Name": "john",
  "amount": "5000"
}
```

Figure 27.37: Browser window

3. Response from the API is:

Figure 27.38: Response

4. Output as expected:

```
{
  "ReferenceID": "23456565",
  "Status": "Require some clarification"
}
```

5. Give input as following and click on POST as shown:

```
{
  "Name": "john",
  "amount": "4000"
}
```

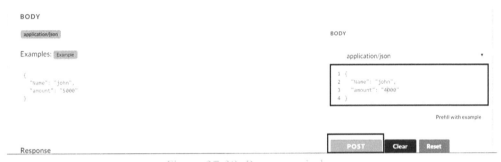

Figure 27.39: Browser window

6. Response from the API is:

Figure 27.40: Response

7.   Output as expected:

```
{
  "ReferenceID": "1234567",
  "Status": "Approved"
}
```

Anticipated Issue

1.   In the recipe, the API service is available from http://routing-rule-api.eu.cloudhub.io/console/. This may change based on the CloudHub region and environment.

Alternates

1.   The routing function could be achieved through a custom policy as well.
2.   To keep the recipe simple and focussed on the concept, flow references are implemented. The code can be extended to complex logic, such as to route to multiple external services or to detect and modify the request and response headers in the gateway.

References

1. https://docs.mulesoft.com/api-manager/setting-up-an-api-proxy
2. https://www.mulesoft.com/infographics/api/mobile-api-led-connectivity

RECIPE 28

Implementing Custom Policy on an API

A policy is a mechanism to enforce filters on traffic. These filters generally control authentication, access, allotted consumption, and service level access (SLA). API Manager offers a number of pre-built policies, listed in Available Policies; custom policies too can be built and applied to an API in Anypoint Platform.

The objective of this recipe is to develop and apply a Custom Policy on an API. Anypoint Studio 6.1 (and newer versions as available) gives the ability to create a policy project, under which custom API policy can be created and applied to the local Anypoint Studio deployments. To make a custom policy available to users, add the policy to Anypoint Platform in API Manager. Users can then see and apply the custom policy listed on the Policies tab of the API version details page of an API.

GitHub location of this recipe:
https://github.com/WHISHWORKS/mule-api-recipes/tree/publish_v1.0/api-custom-policy

Pre requisites

1. **MuleSoft Anypoint Platform** Account with admin privileges
   https://anypoint.mulesoft.com/
2. **Mule 3.8** or later unified runtime
3. **MuleSoft Anypoint Studio** 6.1 or later installed
   https://www.mulesoft.com/lp/dl/studio
4. Access to **Sensitive Data** API deployed on CloudHub
   http://sensitive-data.eu.cloudhub.io/console/
5. GitHub location for the implementation app for Sensitive Data API
   <GitHub location of this recipe>/api-sensitive-data-app/

Process

High Level Steps:

A. Creating Custom Policy
B. Adding Custom Policy in Anypoint Platform
C. Applying Custom Policy to an API
D. Testing the API

A. Creating Custom Policy

Use Case 1: Certain API implementations require masking of sensitive information. For such requirements, a policy should be applied on the API which will do the task.

Use Case 2: There may be a requirement to log request and response payload for an API, a custom policy can be created for this case.

Also policy order preference can be set so that sensitive information can be masked before it gets logged and misused.

A custom policy requires the following files:

Policy Definition: YAML file that describes the policy and its configurable parameters. In order to understand the policy settings, the YAML file is the starting point.

Policy Configuration: XML file with the backend processes that implement the policy. This will hold the logic pertaining to the YAML definition.

1. Open Anypoint Studio and create a new API Custom Policy Project (Beta).

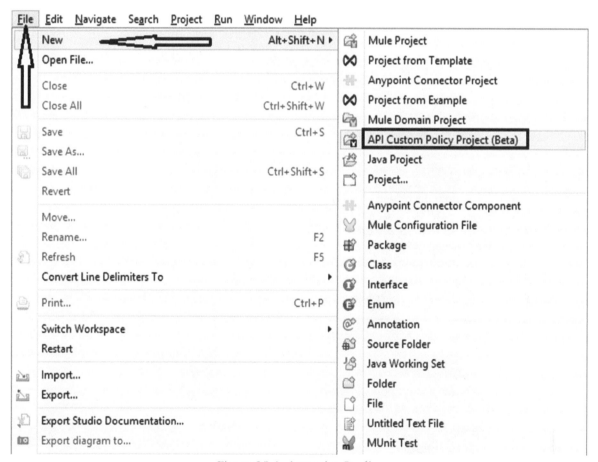

Figure 28.1: Anypoint Studio

2. Provide **name** to the project as api-masking-policy.

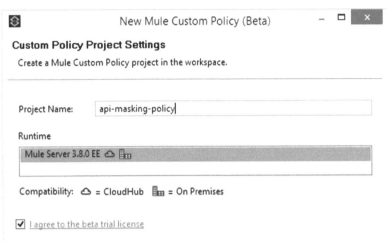

Figure 28.2: New Mule Custom Policy (Beta)

3. Click Next -> Next -> Finish as shown below:

Figure 28.3: Custom Policy Project Settings

4. Notice that the api-masking-policy.xml and api-masking-policy.yaml are created by default in the project.

Figure 28.4: Anypoint Studio

5. Replace the content of the XML file with the code for Masking Policy, it is available in <GitHub location of this recipe>/api-masking-policy/src/main/policy/api-masking-policy.xml/.

6. Following code snippet is a part of the complete code which is used to mask sensitive data from payload:

```
<mule:expression-component>
        <![CDATA[
        import org.json.simple.JSONObject;
        import org.json.simple.parser.JSONParser;
        JSONParser parser = new JSONParser();
        JSONObject obj = parser.parse(flowVars['payloadValue']);
        obj.put("CC", "XXXX-XXXX-XXXX-XXXX");
        flowVars['payloadValue'] = obj.toJSONString();
        ]]>
</mule:expression-component>
```

7. Replace the content of the YAML file with the following for Masking Policy. The code is also available in <GitHub location of this recipe>/api-masking-policy/src/main/policy/api-masking-policy.yaml/.

```
id: mask-sensitive-data
name: Masking Sensitive Data
description: Protects Sensitive Data details by Masking
category: Security
type: custom
standalone: true
requiresConnectivity: false
providedCharacteristics: [Masking]
requiredCharacteristics: []
configuration:
  - propertyName: mask
    name: Mask sensitive data
    description: Allows Masking of sensitive data
    type: boolean
    defaultValue: true
    sensitive: false
```

8.   Similarly, create another Custom Policy Project named api-log-payload-policy with the api-log-payload-policy.xml and api-log-payload-policy.yaml files as shown:

Figure 28.5: Anypoint Studio

9.   Replace the content of the XML file with the code for log-payload Policy, it is available in <GitHub location of this recipe>/api-log-payload-policy/src/main/policy/api-log-payload-policy.xml/.

10.   Following code snippet is a part of the complete code which is used to log request payload:

```
<mule:set-payload value="#[flowVars['payloadValue']]"/>
<mule:set-variable variableName="newLine" value="#[System.getProperty('line.
separator')]" />
<mule:logger message="Request Payload #['[' + message.getId() + ']:' + flowVars.'newLine'
+ flowVars.'payloadValue']" level="INFO" />
```

Replace the content of the YAML file with the following for log-payload Policy. The code is also available in <GitHub location of this recipe>/api-log-payload-policy/src/main/policy/api-log-payload-policy.yaml/.

```
id: log-payload
name: Log Payload
description: Enables logging messages
category: Logging
type: custom
standalone: true
requiresConnectivity: false
providedCharacteristics: [Message Logging]
requiredCharacteristics: []
configuration:
  - propertyName: log-payload
    name: Log Payload
    description: Allows logging a message payload
    type: boolean
    defaultValue: true
    sensitive: false
```

B. Adding Custom Policy in Anypoint Platform

    1.   Sign in to CloudHub account https://anypoint.mulesoft.com

Figure 28.6: CloudHub Login

    2.   After login, click **API Manager -> Open.**

Figure 28.7: API Manager

3. From the menu on the right, click **Custom Policies.**

Figure 28.8: Custom Policies

4. Click **Add custom policy.**

Figure 28.9: Add Custom Policy

5. **Add custom policy** dialogue appears. Give the new policy a name, for example **Masking Sensitive Data** as per the above example.

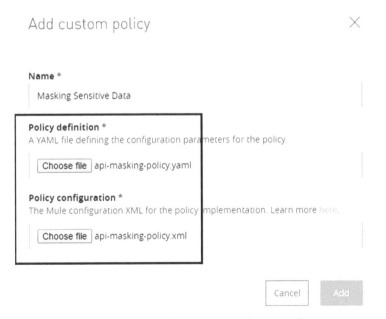

Figure 28.10: Add Custom Policy Details

6. Browse to and select the YAML and XML files created in the studio and upload them from computer's file system.

7. The policy **Masking Sensitive Data** should be displayed on the list as below:

Custom policies

Create custom policies that will be available to all APIs in your organization.

Add custom policy

Name	Files	Fulfills	Requires	
Masking Sensitive Data	YAML ⬇ XML ⬇	Masking		Delete

Figure 28.11: Custom Policies

8. Notice that the policy's XML and YAML files can be downloaded to computer and edited for further enhancement.

Custom policies

Create custom policies that will be available to all APIs in your organization.

Add custom policy

Name	Files	Fulfills	Requires	
Masking Sensitive Data	YAML ⬇ XML ⬇	Masking		Delete

Figure 28.12: Custom Policies Edit

9. Repeat step 1-6 with name of the policy being "log-payload". The policy **log-payload** should be displayed on the list as below:

Custom policies

Create custom policies that will be available to all APIs in your organization.

Add custom policy

Name	Files	Fulfills	Requires	
Masking Sensitive Data	YAML ⬇ XML ⬇	Masking		Delete
log-payload	YAML ⬇ XML ⬇	Message Logging		Delete

Figure 28.13: Custom Policies

C. Applying Custom Policy in Anypoint Platform

1. Sign in to CloudHub account https://anypoint.mulesoft.com.

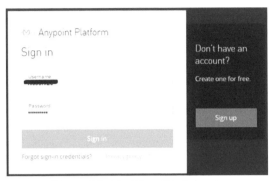

Figure 28.14: CloudHub Login

2. After login, click **API Manager -> Open.**

Figure 28.15: API Manager

3. From the API Manager search for Sensitive Data, click on **Sensitive Data 1.0** API.

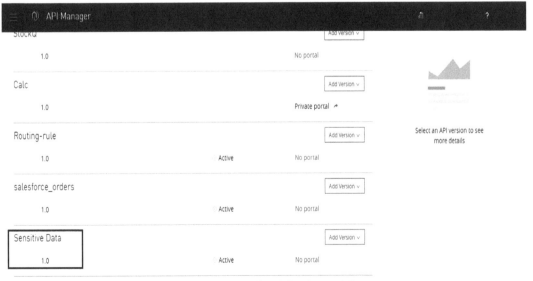

Figure 28.16: Sensitive Data 1.0

4. Click on the **Polices** tab.

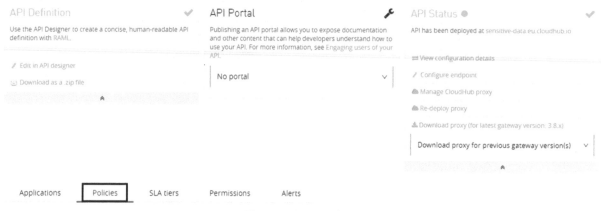

Figure 28.17: Policies

5. Apply the **Masking Sensitive Data** policy.

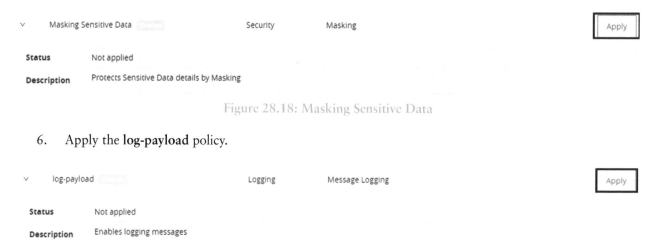

Figure 28.18: Masking Sensitive Data

6. Apply the **log-payload** policy.

Figure 28.19: log-payload

7. More than one policy can also be applied with order preference by clicking **Edit policy order** as shown below:

Figure 28.20: Edit policy order

D. Testing the API
1. Open in a browser http://sensitive-data.eu.cloudhub.io/console/.
2. Click on **Post** request.

Figure 28.21: Post Request

3. This will mask the sensitive data as well as log the request and response payload. This is because of the two policies applied on the API.
4. Open the console logs of the API, in the API administration page click on **Manage CloudHub Proxy** as shown below:

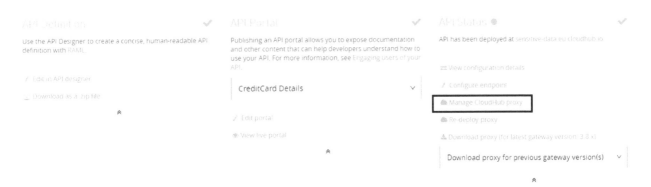

Figure 28.22: Manage CloudHub Proxy

5. A new window opens then click on **Logs.**

Figure 28.23: Runtime Manager Application logs

6. Following screen shows the logs of the request with sensitive data masked as shown:

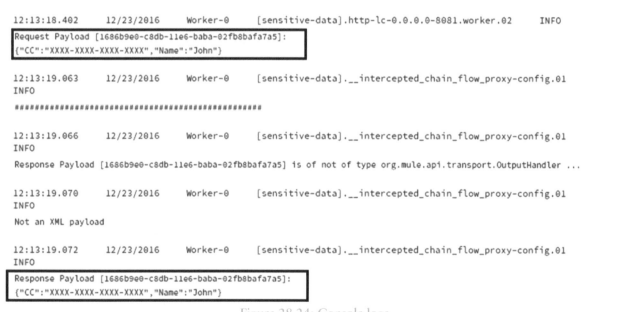

Figure 28.24: Console logs

7. Since the order of policies is to first mask the sensitive data and then log the payload, sensitive data will be masked first before logging.

Anticipated Issues

1. If the policy is not applied correctly, check the CloudHub logs to troubleshoot.
2. Key in the payload for sensitive data should be "CC" (case sensitive), please recheck.

References

1. https://docs.mulesoft.com/api-manager/creating-a-policy-walkthrough#creating-a-new-policy.
3. https://docs.mulesoft.com/api-manager/custom-policy-reference#policy-configuration-xml-file
4. https://github.com/mulesoft/api-policies
5. https://docs.mulesoft.com/anypoint-studio/v/6/studio-policy-editor#applying-the-custom-policy-in-your-local-deployment

RECIPE 29

Functional Testing of APIs using MUnit

Functional testing is performed using the functional specifications provided by the customer and verify the system against the functional requirements. MUnit is a Mule Application testing framework that allows you to easily build automated tests for your integrations and APIs.

Application used in this recipe implements HTTP operations GET, POST, and DELETE for Salesforce Order.

GitHub location of this recipe:
https://github.com/WHISHWORKS/mule-api-recipes/tree/publish_v1.0/salesforce-order/

Pre requisites:
1. **Anypoint Studio** installed
   https://www.mulesoft.com/lp/dl/studio/
2. **Salesforce** Developer Account and credentials
3. **MUnit** plugin should be installed in Anypoint Studio
   https://docs.mulesoft.com/munit/v/1.1.1/using-munit-in-anypoint-studio/

Process

High Level Steps:
A. Creating MUnit Test Cases in Anypoint Studio
B. Running the Test cases

A. Creating MUnit Test Cases in Anypoint Studio
1. Download source code from GitHub location provided above and import application **salesforce-order** in Anypoint
2. After successful import, 6 flows should be available, including **GET, POST** and **DELETE.**

⊠ api ×

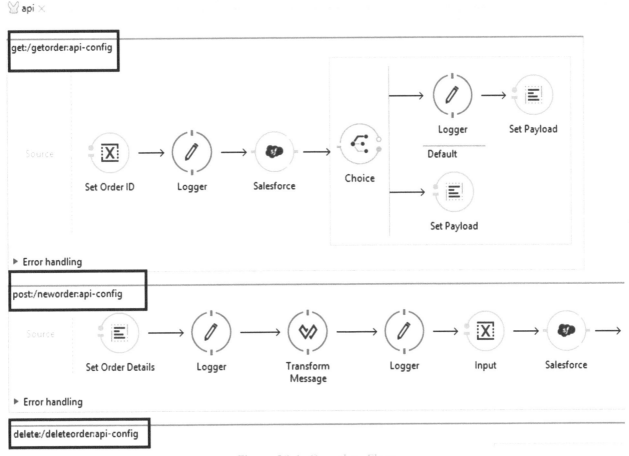

Figure 29.1: Complete Flow

3. Open **mule-app.properties** file and provide the Salesforce account credentials.
4. Right click on **GET** flow and select **MUnit -> Create new api.xml suite** as shown in the figure below:

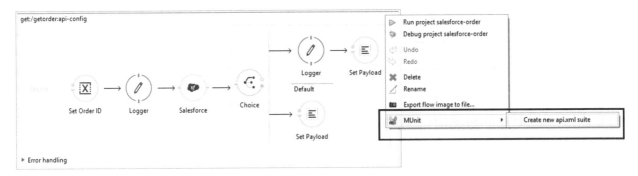

Figure 29.2: Creating MUnit for GET

5.   A new tab will open with the flow as shown in the figure below:

Figure 29.3: MUnit api-test-suite and GET Flow

6.   Click on **Configuration XML** tab and add the following code in between **<munit:test> </munit:test>** tags as shown below:

```
<munit:set payload="801280000010Em2AAE" doc:name="Set Message"/>
      <http:request config-ref="HTTP_Request_Configuration" path="/api/getorder"
method="GET" doc:name="HTTP">
            <http:request-builder>
                <http:query-param paramName="id" value="#[payload]"/>
            </http:request-builder>
        </http:request>
        <munit:assert-true message="Status Code dosen't match" condition="#[me
ssageInboundProperty('http.status').is(eq(200))]" doc:name="Assert True"/>
```

NOTE: The payload should contain a valid order ID from Salesforce

7. Click on **Message Flow** tab, select **HTTP component** and click on add icon to **add new Connector Configuration** as shown below:

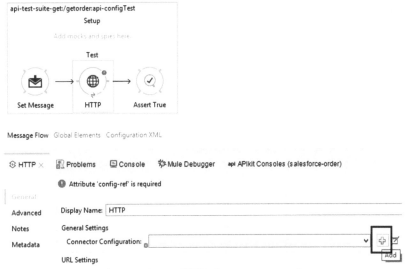

Figure 29.4: HTTP Connector config

8. Give connection details as shown below:
    Host: localhost
    Port: **8081**

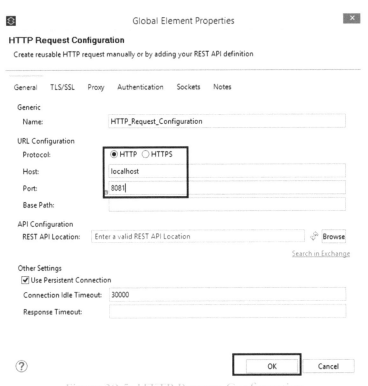

Figure 29.5: HTTP Request Configuration

9. Similarly right click **POST** flow and select **MUnit -> Add test to suite -> Add test to api-test-suite suite** as shown in the figure:

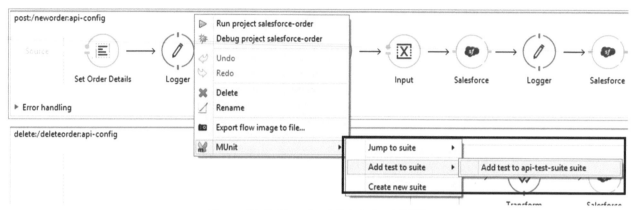

Figure 29.6: Creating MUnit for POST

10. A new flow will be created in **MUnit** tab as shown in the figure below:

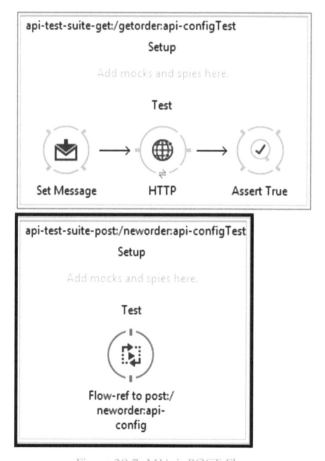

Figure 29.7: MUnit POST Flow

11. Click on **Configuration XML** tab and add the following code in between **<munit:test> </munit:test>** tags as shown below:

```
<set-payload value="{&quot;EffectiveDate&quot;: &quot;2017-03-01
&quot;,       &quot;Status&quot;: &quot;Draft&quot;,
&quot;BillingCity&quot;: &quot;New York&quot;,
&quot;AccountId&quot;: &quot;0012800001Bo16l&quot;,
&quot;ContractId&quot;: &quot;80028000000dtZV&quot;}"
mimeType="application/json" doc:name="Set Payload"/>
 <http:request config-ref="HTTP_Request_Configuration"
path="/api/neworder" method="POST" doc:name="HTTP"/>

        <munit:assert-true message="Status Code dosen't match" condition="#[me
ssageInboundProperty('http.status').is(eq(201))]" doc:name="Assert True"/>
```

12. Similarly, right click **DELETE** flow and select **MUnit -> Add test to suite -> Add test to api-test-suite suite** as shown in the figure below:

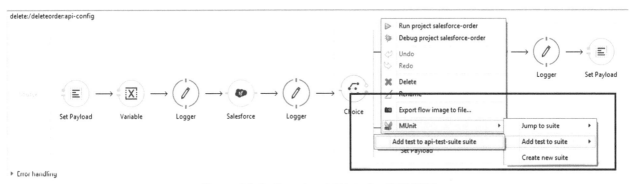

Figure 29.8: Creating MUnit for DELETE

13. A new flow will be created in **MUnit** tab as shown below:

Figure 29.9: MUnit DELETE Flow

14. Click on **Configuration XML** tab and add the following code in between **<munit:test> </munit:test>** flags as shown below:

```
<munit:set payload="801280000010DTCAA2" doc:name="Set Message"/>

        <http:request config-ref="HTTP_Request_Configuration" path="/api/
deleteorder" method="DELETE" doc:name="HTTP">

      <http:request-builder>

          <http:query-param paramName="id" value="#[payload]"/>
      </http:request-builder>

    </http:request>

    <munit:assert-true message="Status Code dosen't match" condition="#[me
ssageInboundProperty('http.status').is(eq(200))]" doc:name="Assert True"/>
```

15. Complete **MUnit Flows** looks as shown below:

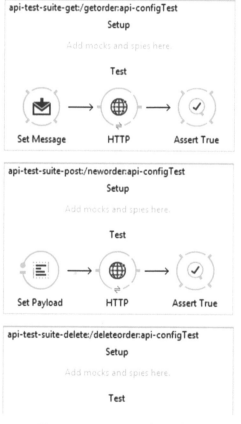

Figure 29.10: Complete Flow

16. Complete MUnit Test Suite XML (api-test-suite.xml) code is available at <GitHub location of this recipe>/src/test/munit/api-test-suite.xml

B. Running MUnit Test Cases

1. Go to **Global Elements** tab.

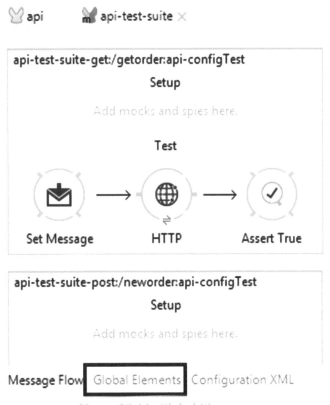

Figure 29.11: Global Elements

2. Double click on **MUnit Configuration** and uncheck **Mock Mule transport connectors** and **Mock Inbound endpoints** and click **OK** as shown below:

☺ Global Mule Configuration Elements

Type	Name
▯ MUnit configuration (Configuration)	munit
☺ Import (Configuration)	Import
☺ HTTP Request Configuration (Configuration)	HTTP_Request_Configuration

Figure 29.12: MUnit Configuration

Figure 29.13: MUnit Basic Settings

3. Right click on empty space in the message flow of the test suite and select **Run MUnit Suite** as shown below:

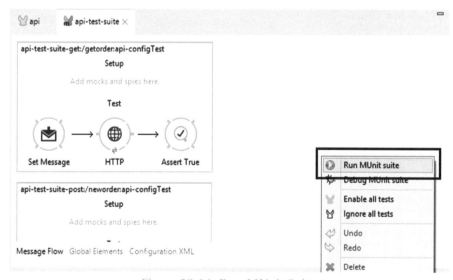

Figure 29.14: Run MUnit Suite

4. If the test cases run successfully, following tab will appear:

Figure 29.15: Test Run Successful

Anticipated Issues

1. For GET and DELETE test cases, order id should exist in Salesforce.
2. If B.1 and B.2 is not configured accordingly then test case run will throw an error.

References

1. https://docs.mulesoft.com/munit/v/1.1.1/
2. https://docs.mulesoft.com/munit/v/1.1.1/using-munit-in-anypoint-studio
3. https://docs.mulesoft.com/munit/v/1.1.1/example-testing-apikit

RECIPE 30

Functional Testing of APIs using SOAP UI

Functional testing is performed using the functional specification provided by the client and verifies the system against the functional requirements. Soap UI is universally used to ensure quality while developing APIs and Web Services.

GitHub location of this recipe:
https://github.com/WHISHWORKS/mule-api-recipes/tree/publish_v1.0/salesforce-order/

Pre requisites:
1. **Salesforce** Developer Account.
2. Access to salesforce-order-app deployed in CloudHub
   http://salesforce-order-app.eu.cloudhub.io/console/
3. Soap UI Open Source
   https://www.soapui.org/downloads/soapui.html

Process

High Level Steps:
  A. Creating Test Cases in Soap UI
  B. Running the Test cases

A. **Creating Test Cases in Soap UI**
  1. Start **Soap UI** & following screen comes up:

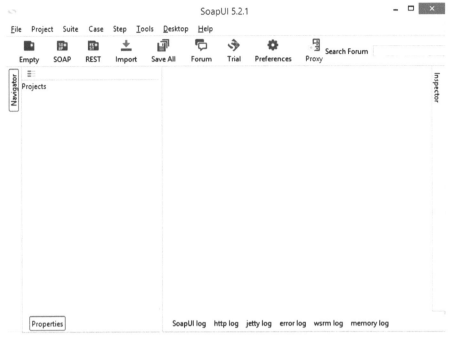

Figure 30.1: Soap UI

2. Create a new REST project by clicking on **REST** and give the following URL in the dialogue http://salesforce-order-app.eu.cloudhub.io/api and click on Ok as shown below:

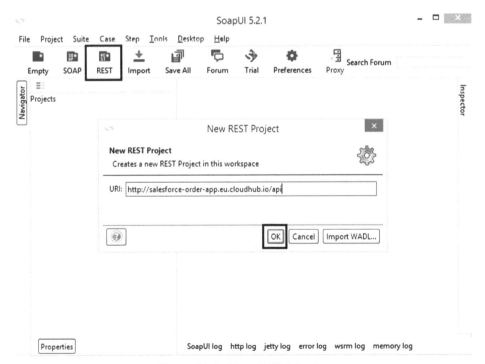

Figure 30.2: New REST Project

3. Right click on **Request 1** inside the SOAP UI and rename it to **POST Request** and click **OK** as shown below:

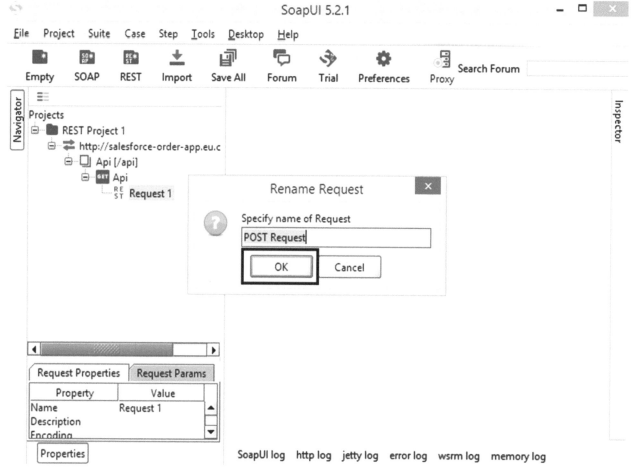

Figure 30.3: New POST Request

4. Double click on **POST Request** and select as shown in the figure below:
   i. Method as **POST**
   ii. Resource as **/api/neworder**
   iii. Application/json body as

```
{
  "EffectiveDate": "2017-03-01",
  "Status": "Draft",
  "BillingCity": "New York",
  "AccountId": "0012800001Bo16l",
  "ContractId": "80028000000dtZV"
}
```

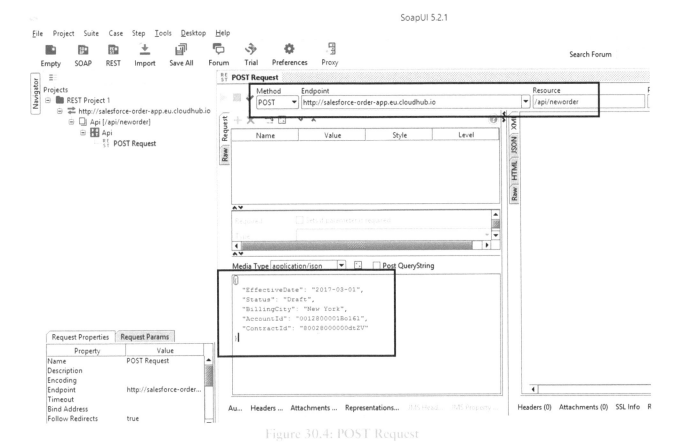

Figure 30.4: POST Request

5. Then click on **Add this REST Request to a TestCase** icon, provide **CURD Operations** as TestSuite Project name when prompted as shown below:

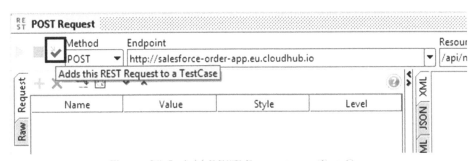

Figure 30.5: Add REST Request to a Test Case

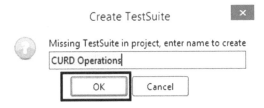

Figure 30.6: Test Suite: CURD Operations

6. Specify the TestCase name as **POST** and click on **OK** as shown below:

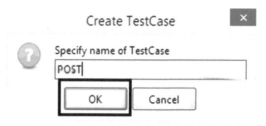

Figure 30.7: Test Case: POST

7. Click on **OK** on **Add Request to Test Case** dialogue as shown below:

Figure 30.8: Add Request to TestCase

8. Add an assertion to this request by clicking on the **plus** sign as shown below:

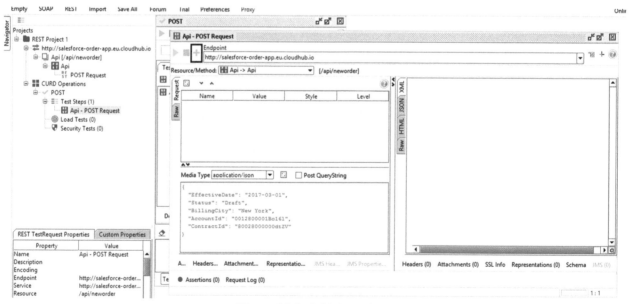

Figure 30.9: Add Assertion

9.   Select **Property Content** -> **Contains** -> **Add** as shown below:

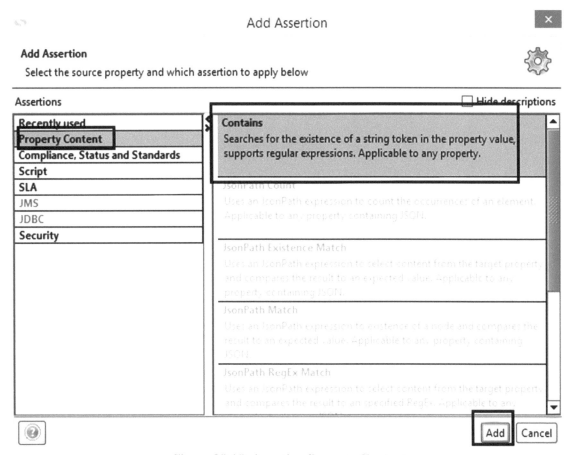

Figure 30.10: Assertion Property Content

10. In the content dialogue provide **Order Created Successfully** and click **OK** as shown below:

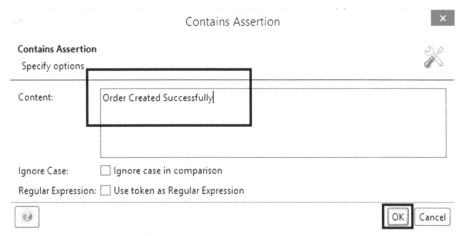

Figure 30.11 Contains Assertion

11. Right click on Method name **Api** and rename it to **POST** as shown below:

Figure 30.12: Rename Method

12. Also right click on resource name **Api** and rename it to **New Order** as shown below:

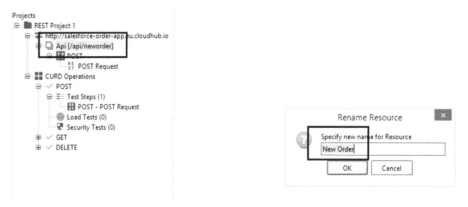

Figure 30.13: Rename Resource

13. Add a new resource **Get Order** as shown below:

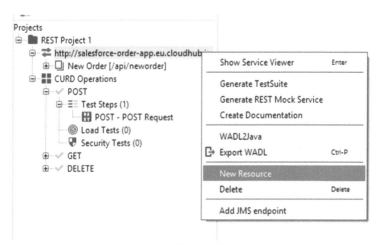

Figure 30.14: New Resource

14. Give the new resource the path as **/api/getorder** and click **OK.**

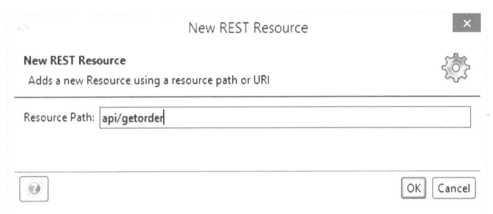

Figure 30.15: New REST Resource

15. Right click on **Method 1** and rename it to **GET** and click **OK** as shown below:

Figure 30.16: Rename Method

16. Right click on **Request 1** and rename it to **GET Request** as shown below:

Figure 30.17: Rename Request

17. Double click on **GET Request** and select as shown in the figure:
    i.   Method as **GET**
    ii. Resource as **/api/getorder**
    iii. Parameters as **?id= 801280000010DTRAA2**
    NOTE: value of **id** should be available in Salesforce order, otherwise the test case will fail.

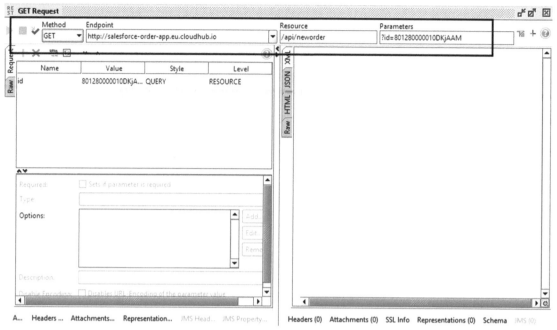

Figure 30.18: GET Request

18. Now click on **Add this Request to TestCase** icon and select **CURD Operations -> Create New Test Case** option as shown below:

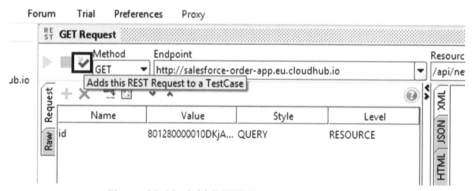

Figure 30.19: Add REST Request to Test Case

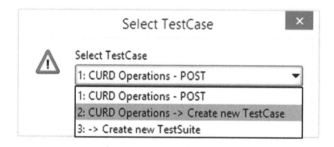

Figure 30.20: Select TestCase

19. Specify the new test case name as **GET** as shown below:

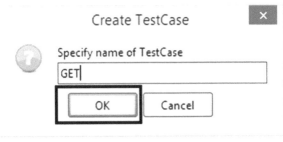

Figure 30.21: Create TestCase

20. Click on **OK** on **Add Request to Test Case** dialogue as shown below:

Figure 30.22: Add Request to TestCase

21. Add an assertion to this request by clicking on the **plus** sign as shown below:

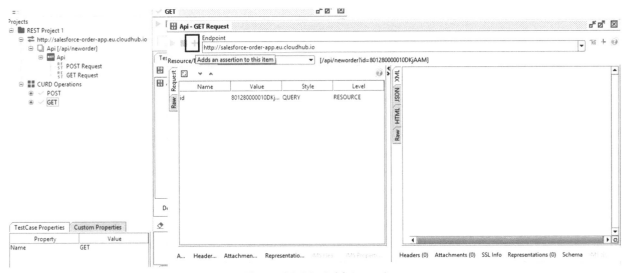

Figure 30.23: Add Assertion

22. Select **Property Content** -> **Contains** -> **Add** as shown below:

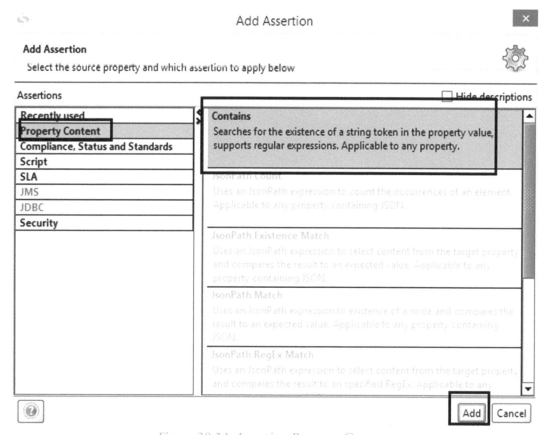

Figure 30.24: Assertion Property Content

23. In the content dialogue provide **"Status": "Draft"** and click **OK** as shown below:

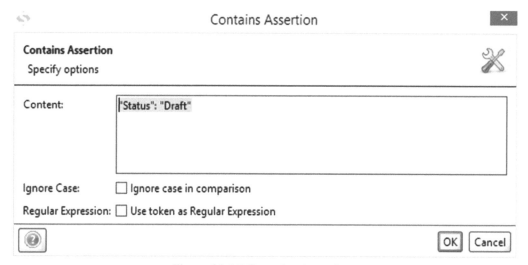

Figure 30.25 Contains Assertion

24. Add a new resource **Delete Order** as shown below:

25. Give the new resource the path as **/api/deleteorder** and click **OK.**

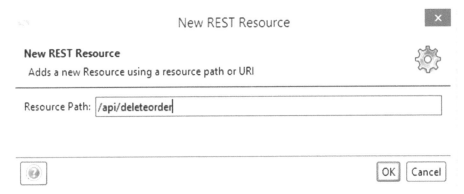

Figure 30.27: New REST Resource

26. Right click on **Method 1** and rename it to **DELETE** and click **OK** as shown below:

Figure 30.28: Rename Method

27. Right click on **Request 1** and rename it to DELETE **Request** as shown below:

Figure 30.29: Rename Request

28. Double click on **DELETE Request** and select as shown in the figure:
     i.   Method as **DELETE**
     ii.   Resource as **/api/deleteorder**
     iii. Parameters as **?id=801280000010DTRAA2**
     NOTE: value of **id** should be available in Salesforce order, otherwise the test case will fail.

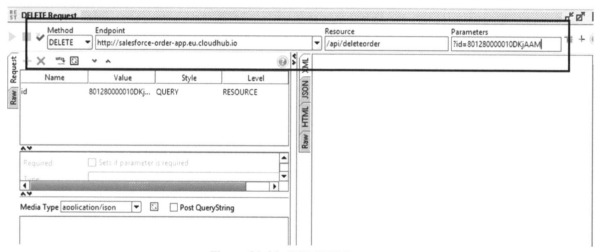

Figure 30.30: DELETE Request

29. Now click on **Add this Request to TestCase** icon and select **CURD Operations -> Create New Test Case** option as shown below:

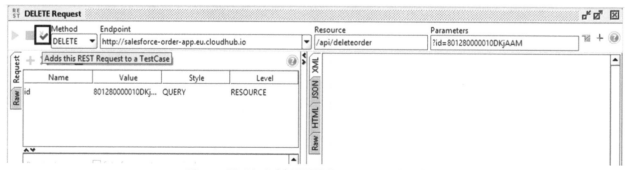

Figure 30.31: Add REST Request to Test Case

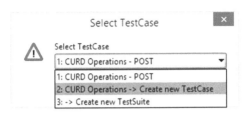

Figure 30.32: Select TestCase

30. Specify the new test case name as **DELETE** as shown below:

Figure 30.33: Create TestCase

31. Click on **OK** on **Add Request to Test Case** dialogue as shown below:

Figure 30.34: Add Request to TestCase

32. Add an assertion to this request by clicking on the **plus** sign as shown below:

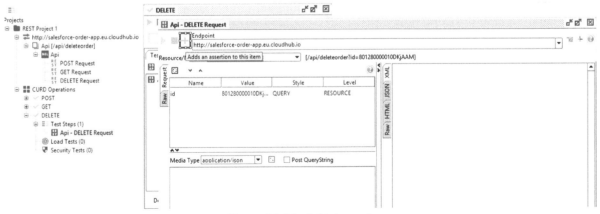

Figure 30.35: Add Assertion

33. Select **Property Content** -> **Contains** -> **Add** as shown below:

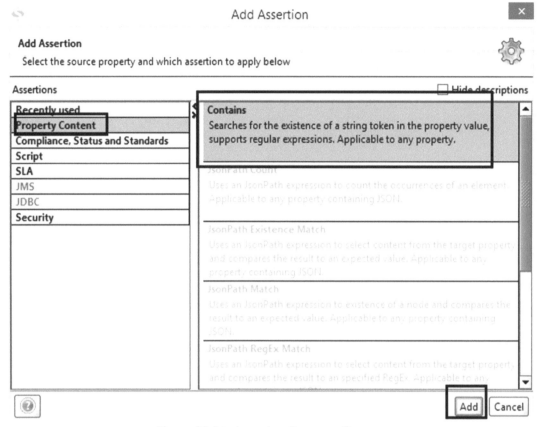

Figure 30.36: Assertion Property Content

34. In the content dialogue, provide **Deleted ID:** and click **OK** as shown below:

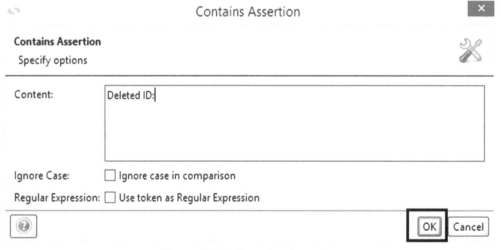

Figure 30.37 Contains Assertion

35. Save the project by right clicking on **project** -> **Save Project** as shown below:

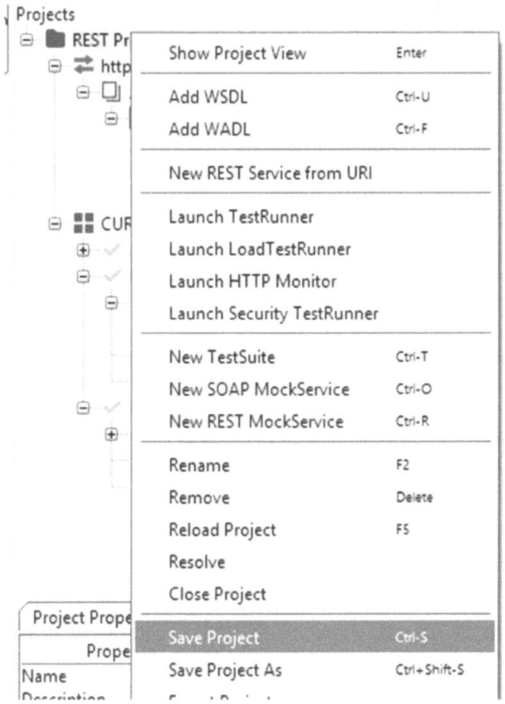

Figure 30.38: Save Project

B. **Running the Test cases**
   1. Right click on **CURD Operations** and click on **Show Test Suite Editor**, click play as shown below:

Figure 30.39: Test Suite Editor

2.   When the test cases are running, the following will appear:

Figure 30.40: Test Cases Running

3.   After successful completion of the test cases, the following result will be displayed:

Figure 30.41: Test Cases Completed Successfully

Anticipated Issues

1.   For GET and DELETE test cases order id should exist in salesforce.

References

1. https://www.soapui.org/downloads/soapui.html
2. https://www.soapui.org/functional-testing/getting-started.html

RECIPE 31

Performance Testing of APIs

To create a reliable API, performance of an API should be tested. Though the User interface of an API may be outstanding, but it is the performance of the API that matters the most. The process to test performance of an API includes load testing i.e. the memory bottleneck and data limitations. The memory bottleneck situation occurs when the server is not able to handle multiple requests at a time. And data limitations occur when the request posts different data from what the API expects. This recipe uses Apache JMeter tool which is open source, to test the API.

This recipe focuses on how to create a test plan with HTTP Request and run it successfully. Also, with this recipe, the API user will get an idea on how to test memory bottlenecks and data limitations for a given API.

GitHub location of this recipe:
https://github.com/WHISHWORKS/mule-api-recipes/tree/publish_v1.0/customer-service-api

1. Access to customer-service-api deployed in CloudHub.
2. Apache JMeter Open Source (http://jmeter.apache.org/download_jmeter.cgi)

Process

High Level Steps:
A. Setting Up HTTP Request in Apache JMeter
B. Testing the API
C. Test for memory bottleneck and data limitations

A. Setting Up HttpRequest in Apache JMeter
1. Open Apache JMeter.

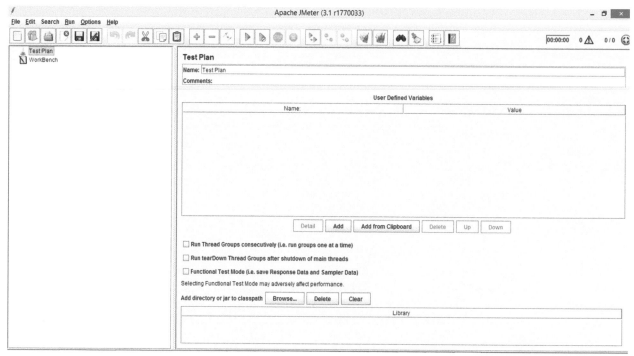

Figure 31.1: Apache JMeter

2. Click on **Test plan** and change the name to **customer-service-api** as shown in the figure and click **WorkBench** on the Apache JMeter tool to save the changes.

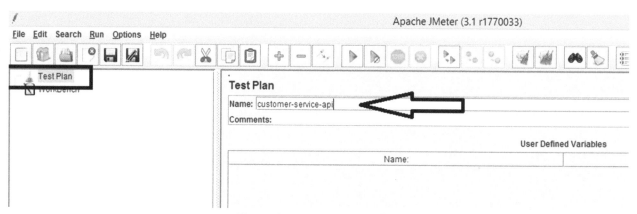

Figure 31.2: Create Test Plan

3. Right click on **customer-service-api** and then click on **Add,** thereby choosing **Threads (Users)** and creating a **Thread Group.**

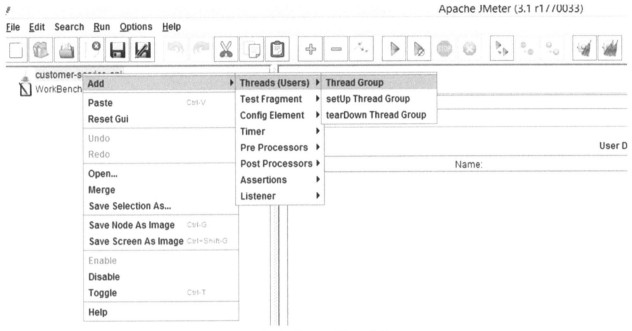

Figure 31.3: Create Thread Group

4. Edit the **Name** of the Thread Group as **"Customer-post-service".**

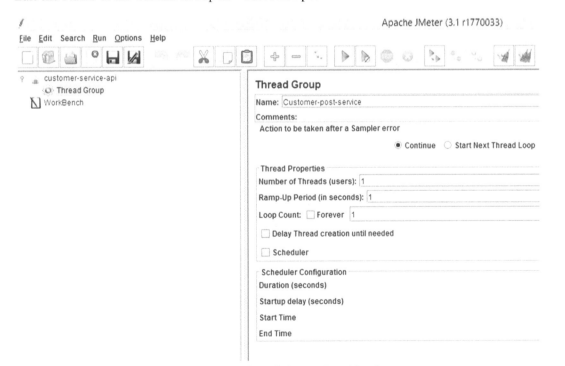

Figure 31.4: Thread Group Specification

5. Add **HTTP Request** by right clicking on **Customer-post-service** and click on **Add -> Sample -> HTTP Request**.

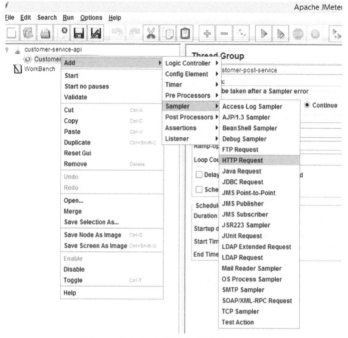

Figure 31.5: Add HTTP Request

6. HTTP Request form will appear.

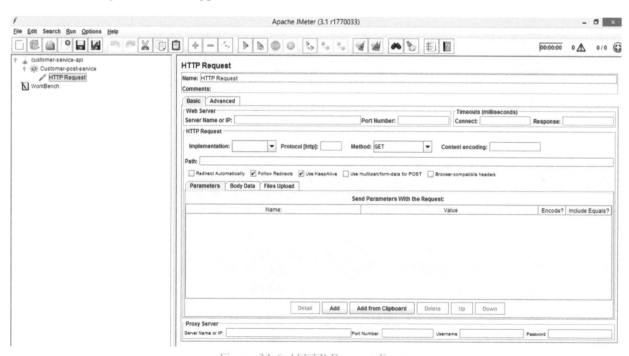

Figure 31.6: HTTP Request Form

7. Specify the **Server Name or IP** and **Protocol [HTTP]**.

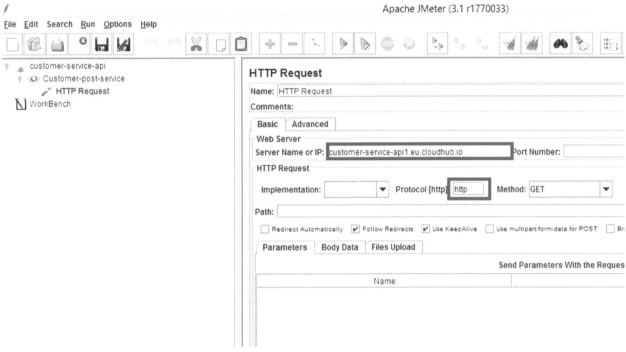

Figure 31.7: Http Request Details

8. Specify the HTTP Request **Method** selection and **Path** for the request.

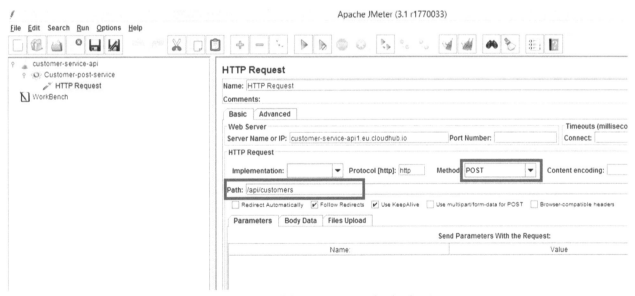

Figure 31.8: HTTP Request method selection

9. Click on **Body Data** and add the request data which has to POST.

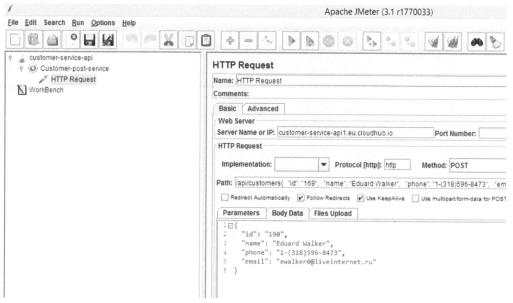

Figure 31.9: POST Request Data

10. Sample request data for this project is as below :

```
{
  "id": "169",
  "name": "Eduard Walker",
  "phone": "1-(318)596-8473",
  "email": "ewalker0@liveinternet.ru"
        }
```

11. Click on **Save** icon as shown in the figure below:

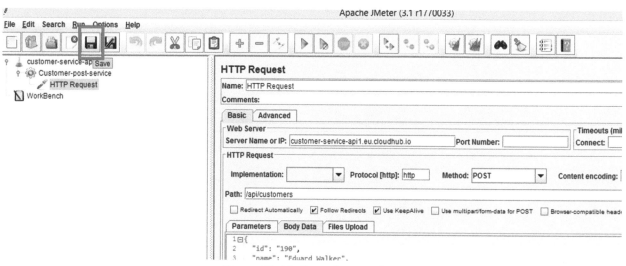

Figure 31.10: Save the test plan

12. Save form will appear, user can select name and path as per requirement.

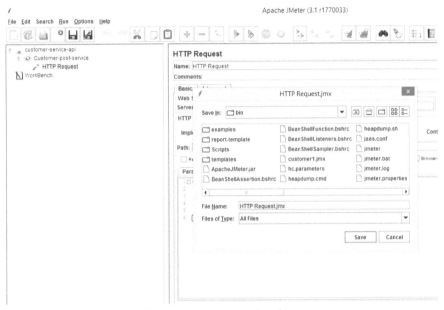

Figure 31.11: save plan form

13. Add **View Results Tree** by right clicking on **Customer-post-service** and click on **Add** -> **Listener** -> **View Results Tree.**

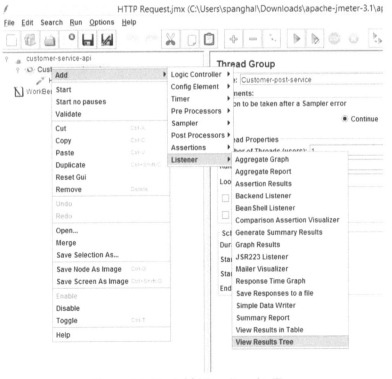

Figure 31.12: Add View Results Tree

14. Add **View Results in Table** by right clicking on **Customer-post-service** and click on **Add -> Listener -> View Results in Table.**

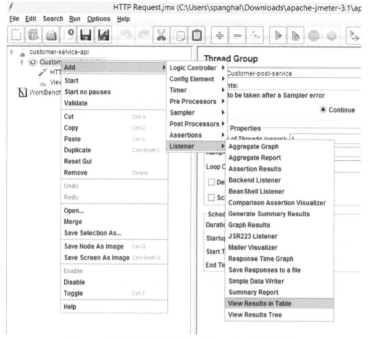

Figure 31.13: Add View Results in Table

15. Add **Summary Report** by right clicking on **Customer-post-service** and click on **Add -> Listener -> Summary Report.**

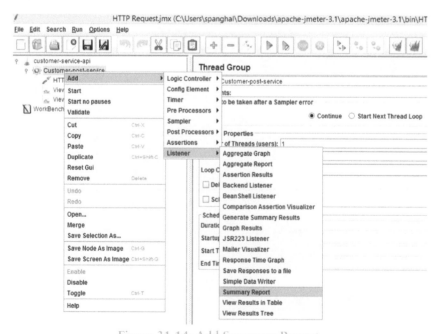

Figure 31.14: Add Summary Report

16. Add **Aggregate Report** by right clicking on **Customer-post-service** and click on **Add -> Listener -> Aggregate Report.**

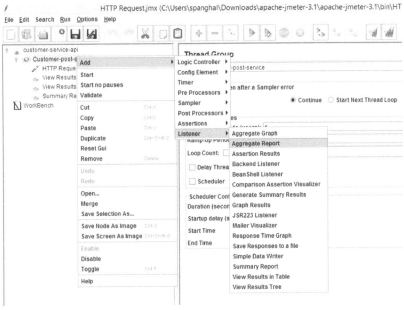

Figure 31.15: Add Aggregate Report

17. Add **HTTP Header Manager** by right clicking on **HTTP Request** and click on **Add -> Config Element -> HTTP Header Manager.**

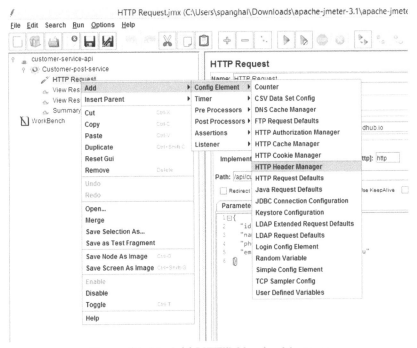

Figure 31.16: Add HTTP Header Manager

18. Click on **Add button** as highlighted in the image below to add a new header.

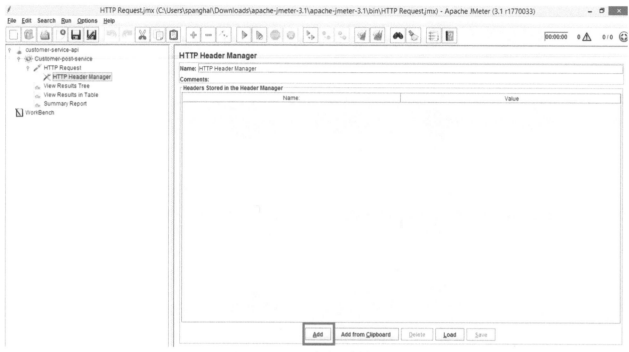

Figure 31.17: Click Add button

19. Add the header **"Content-Type"** with value **"application/json"**.

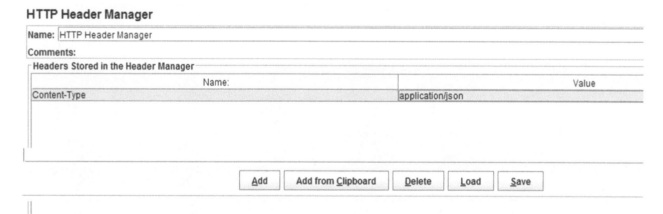

Figure 31.18: Add HTTP Header

20. Save the test case.

B. Testing of API

1. Click on the highlighted green button to run the saved test case.

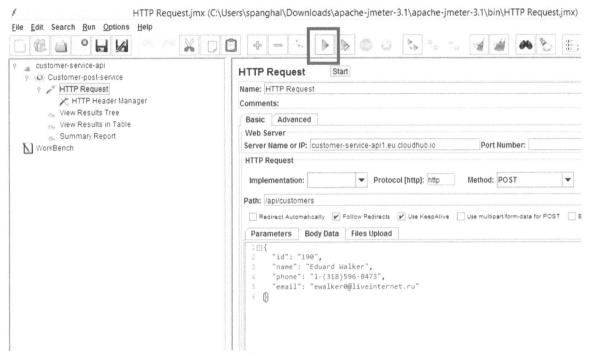

Figure 31.19: Run the test case

2. Click on **View Results Tree** to verify whether the test case was successfully run or not.

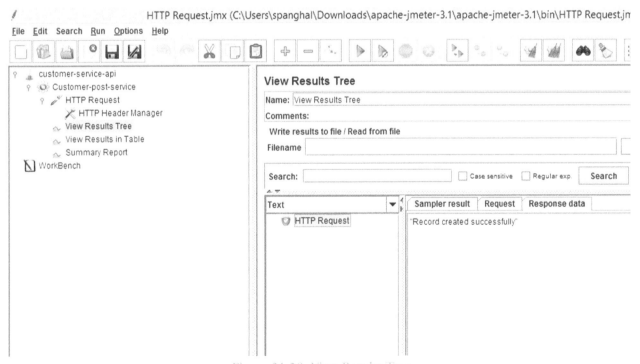

Figure 31.20: View Results Tree

3. Click on **View Results in Table** to see the performance in table form.

Figure 31.21: View Results in Table

4. Click on **View Summary Report** of the performance.

Figure 31.22: View Summary Report

5. One can see that in Thread Group, Number of Threads i.e. users are set to be 1. Change the value of Number of Threads to send multiple request in one go.

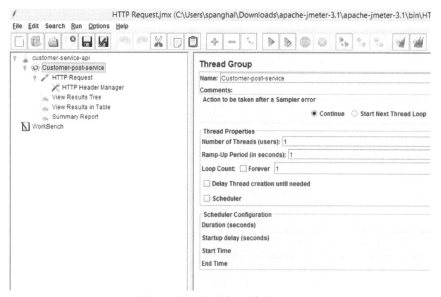

Figure 31.23: Thread Group

6. Change the value of Number of Threads to 50. The value of Loop Count means that the above provided number of threads will run for the Loop Count number of times. This must be changed to 300.

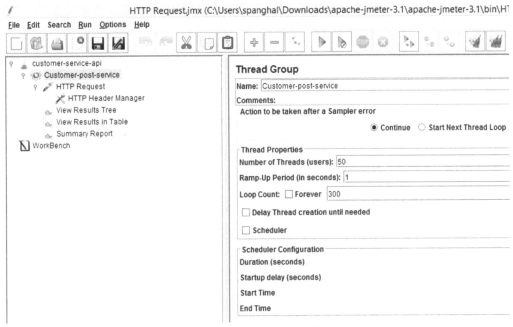

Figure 31.24: Edited Thread Group

7. Click on **View Results Tree** to see the performance of multi requests. All the requests failed because of the duplicate primary key error, as we were trying to POST all the requests with the same data (i.e. same customer id).

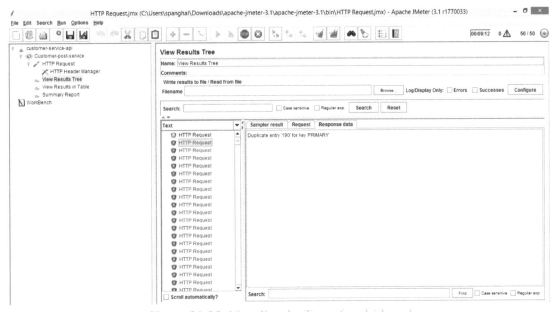

Figure 31.25: View Results Tree of multithread

8. Click on **View Results in Table** to see the performance in table form.

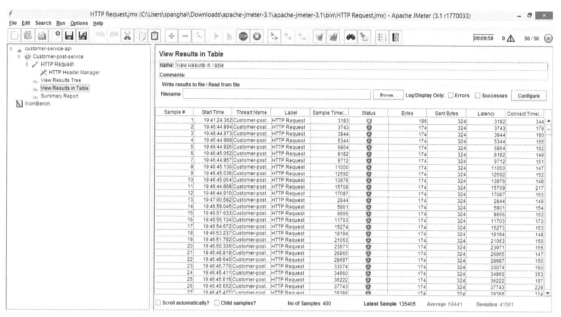

Figure 31.26: View Results in Table for multithread

9. Click on **Summary Report** to see the performance.

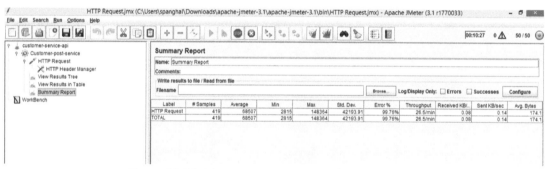

Figure 31.27: View Summary Report for multithread

C. Test for memory bottleneck and data limitations

1. Create an Excel sheet with around 250 different records for customer service (column A should be unique as customer id is the primary key in the database). Save the Excel sheet in CSV format.

Figure 31.28: Excel Sheet for multiple records

2. Now create a **CSV Data Set Config** by right clicking on **Customer-post-service -> Add -> Config Element -> CSV Data Set Config**.

Figure 31.29: Add CSV Data Set Config

3. Specify the file path in the Filename fields and variable names in comma separated format.

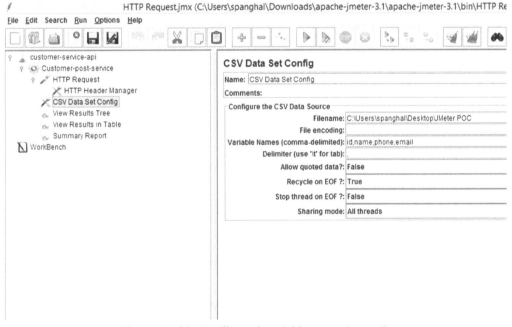

Figure 31.30: Set file and variable name in config

4.   4. Change the Body Data in the HTTP Request as shown in the figure below:

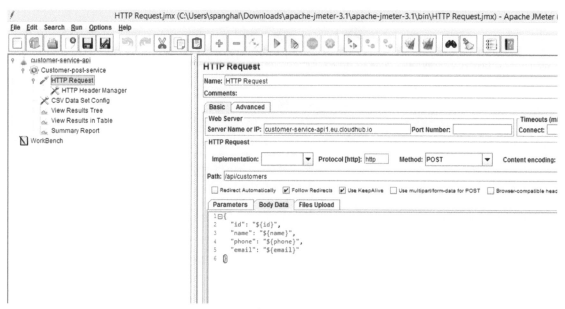

Figure 31.31: Body Data in HTTP Request

5.   Change the number of threads in customer-post-service with the number of records that is created in CSV file.

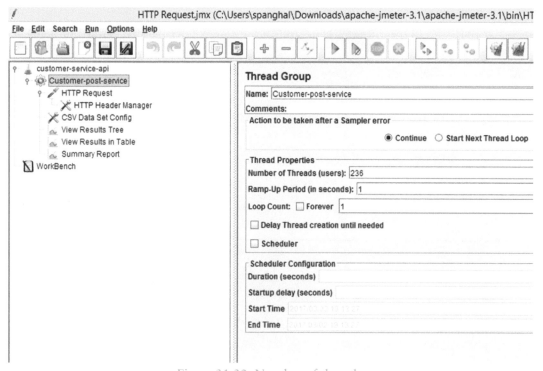

Figure 31.32: Number of threads

6. Run the test case and check the summary report. Error % is 23.31.

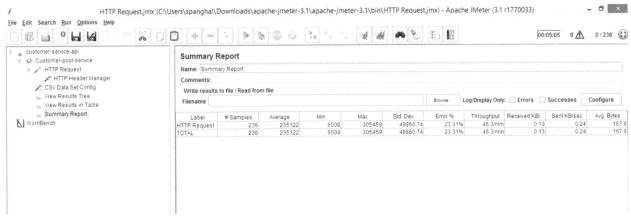

Figure 31.33: Summary Report

7. Analyse the performance in **View Results in Table.**

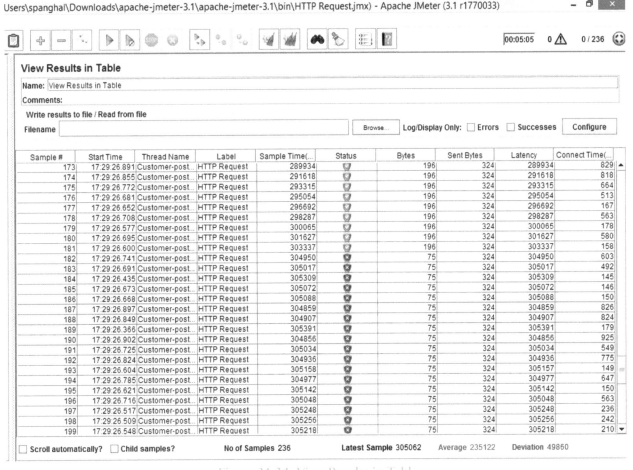

Figure 31.34: View Results in Table

8. Check the **View Results Tree.** By clicking on the **HTTP Request,** the reason behind the failure of few requests will be known. It is due to the timeout error i.e the memory bottleneck. The server could not take more than 181 requests at a time from our system. The value 181 depends on various circumstances like CPU RAM, server memory, etc.

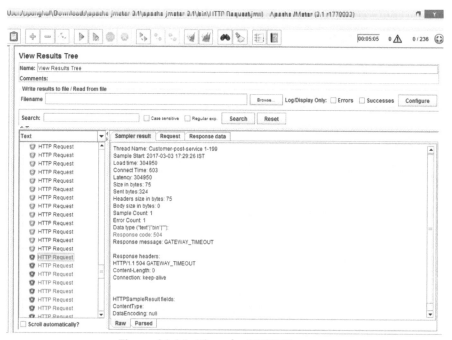

Figure 31.35: View the HTTPRequest

9. If the user changes the Body Data in HTTP Request and specifies the field name as 12, an integer, where the customer service expects the name in string format, then the API shows an error. And this error is due to data limitation.

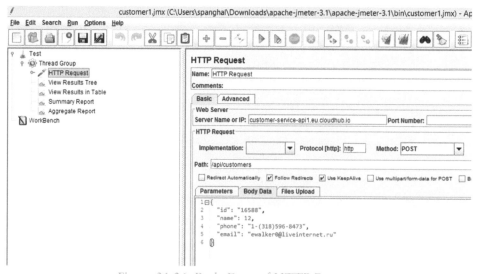

Figure 31.36: Body Data of HTTP Request

10. One can see the error by clicking on **HTTP Request** that "instance type (integer) does not match any allowed primitive type (allowed: ["string"])".

Figure 31.37: Error due to data limitations

Anticipated Issues

1. Make sure to put all the headers in place for HTTP Request.
2. Save the Excel sheet containing test cases as .csv format.

References

1. https://www.3pillarglobal.com/insights/performance-testing-of-a-restful-api-using-jmeter

Appendices

1. Implementing a Simple API and Deploying to CloudHub
   a. https://docs.mulesoft.com/apikit/apikit-tutorial
   b. https://docs.mulesoft.com/mule-user-guide/v/3.7/publishing-and-consuming-apis-with-mule
   c. https://docs.mulesoft.com/mule-management-console/v/3.7/rest-api-reference
   d. https://dzone.com/articles/design-raml-based-rest-api-using-mulesoft-anypoint
   e. https://docs.mulesoft.com/getting-started/deploy-to-cloudhub

2. Securing an API with OAuth2
   a. http://www.whishworks.com/blog/uncategorized/oauth-a-great-way-to-keep-your-apis-secure/
   b. https://dzone.com/articles/oauth-20-mule

3. Implementing custom policy on an API
   a. https://blogs.mulesoft.com/dev/howto/howto-custom-api-policy-with-anypoint-platform/
   b. https://docs.mulesoft.com/api-manager/custom-policy-reference

4. Exposing legacy SOAP based Web Service as RESTful API
   a. https://dzone.com/articles/how-to-expose-a-wsdl-service-soap-as-rest-api
   b. https://docs.mulesoft.com/mule-user-guide/v/3.8/publishing-a-soap-api

5. Setting up CloudHub environment
   a. https://docs.mulesoft.com/access-management/environments
   b. https://docs.mulesoft.com/runtime-manager/managing-cloudhub-specific-settings\

6. Managing API through API console
   a. https://docs.mulesoft.com/mule-management-console/v/3.7/using-the-management-console-api
   b. https://docs.mulesoft.com/api-manager/manage-api-reference

7. Adding JSON Schema as Reference in RAML
   a. https://github.com/raml-org/raml-spec/blob/master/versions/raml-08/raml-08.md

8. Designing your API with Swagger in Anypoint API Designer
   a. https://apigee.com/about/blog/developer/design-first-approach-building-apis-swagger

9. Implementing Cross Origin Resource Sharing (CORS) on an API
   a. https://blogs.mulesoft.com/dev/anypoint-platform-dev/cross-domain-rest-calls-using-cors/
   b. http://ryandcarter.blogspot.in/2013/02/cross-origin-resource-sharing-with-mule.html

10. Setup Email Alerts in Applications in CloudHub
    a. https://docs.mulesoft.com/api-manager/using-api-alerts
    b. https://docs.mulesoft.com/runtime-manager/custom-application-alerts

11. Performance Testing of API
    a. https://blogs.mulesoft.com/dev/mule-dev/measuring-the-performance-of-your-mule-esb-application/
    b. https://blogs.mulesoft.com/tag/performance/

12. RAML Editor for API Implementation
    a. https://docs.mulesoft.com/api-manager/designing-your-api
    b. http://raml.org/

13. Implementing Routing Rule on API Proxy
    a. http://docs.apigee.com/api-services/content/understanding-routes

14. API Auto Discovery
    a. https://docs.mulesoft.com/api-manager/api-auto-discovery-reference

15. Manage Anypoint MQ with its APIs
    a. https://docs.mulesoft.com/anypoint-mq/mq-understanding
    b. https://blogs.mulesoft.com/dev/anypoint-platform-dev/setting-up-queues-and-exchanges-with-anypoint-mq/
    c. https://docs.mulesoft.com/anypoint-mq/mq-apis

16. Handle Salesforce Streaming Content with API
    a. http://www.whishworks.com/blog/soa/salesforce-streaming-api-integration-using-mule-esb/
    b. https://blogs.mulesoft.com/dev/anypoint-studio-dev/durable-streaming-api-with-mulesoft-salesforce-connector/
    c. http://www.mstsolutions.com/blog/content/integrating-salesforce-mule-using-streaming-api

17. Mule Message Encryption and Decryption
    a. http://blog.avenuecode.com/mule-jce-encryption

18. Enabling Custom Business Events to Track Incoming Requests on API
    a. http://www.whishworks.com/blog/soa/anypoint-platform-custom-business-events-2/
    b. https://docs.mulesoft.com/mule-management-console/v/3.7/tracking-and-querying-business-events
    c. https://docs.mulesoft.com/mule-user-guide/v/3.6/business-events

19. Functional Testing of API using SOAP UI
    a. https://www.soapui.org/test-automation/running-functional-tests.html
    b. https://dzone.com/articles/some-thoughts-integrating

20. Sharing API with Developers and Partners
    a. https://docs.mulesoft.com/api-manager/tutorial-use-a-portal-as-an-app-developer

21. Implementing Caching Strategy on a Mule Flow
    a. https://dzone.com/articles/mule-caching-strategy-with-redis-cache
    b. https://www.appnovation.com/blog/improving-performance-cache-mulesoft
    c. https://www.ricston.com/blog/mule-33-caching/

22. Functional Testing of API using MUnit
    a. https://docs.mulesoft.com/mule-user-guide/v/3.6/functional-testing
    b. https://docs.mulesoft.com/mule-user-guide/v/3.7/introduction-to-testing-mule

23. Deploy a Proxy on CloudHub
    a. https://docs.mulesoft.com/api-manager/tutorial-set-up-and-deploy-an-api proxy
    b. https://docs.mulesoft.com/api-manager/proxy-depl-cloudhub

24. API Traffic Management using SLA and Throttling polies
    a. https://docs.mulesoft.com/api-manager/rate-limiting-and-throttling-sla-based-policies
    b. https://docs.mulesoft.com/api-manager/rate-limiting-and-throttling
    c. https://docs.mulesoft.com/api-manager/tutorial-manage-an-api

25. JSON & XML Threat Protection of API
    a. https://dzone.com/articles/importance-threat-protection

26. Implementing Asynchronous RESTful API
    a. https://docs.mulesoft.com/mule-user-guide/v/3.7/activemq-integration
    b. https://blogs.mulesoft.com/dev/newbie/mule-school-jms-tutorial/

27. Implementing Custom OAuth Provider
    a. https://dzone.com/articles/soap-rest-attachments-mule'

28. Implementation of new API through API-led Connectivity
    a. https://www.ricston.com/blog/what-is-api-led-connectivity/
    b. https://blogs.mulesoft.com/dev/api-dev/apis-great-architecture/

CPSIA information can be obtained
at www.ICGtesting.com
Printed in the USA
BVHW021322130220
572292BV00004B/151